The Dictionary of Shrubs in colour

The Dictionary of
Shrubs
in colour

S. Millar Gault

Photographs supplied by Ernest Crowson

Foreword by C. D. Brickell

Published in collaboration with The Royal Horticultural Society

Ebury Press and Michael Joseph Limited, London

First published in Great Britain by
Ebury Press
Chestergate House, Vauxhall Bridge Road,
London SW1V 1HF and
Michael Joseph Limited
52 Bedford Square, London WC1
1976

This book was designed and produced by
The Rainbird Publishing Group Limited,
Marble Arch House, 44 Edgware Road,
London W2, England.

ISBN: 0 7181 1406 X

Designer: Jonathan Gill-Skelton

Printed by Jolly & Barber Limited,
Rugby, England.
Bound in Great Britain

Contents

Foreword

Few gardeners today can claim such a wide-ranging knowledge of plants as Millar Gault, a distinguished horticulturist whose thorough and practical approach to gardening may readily be appreciated in this most useful and informative book.

As joint author with Patrick Synge of *The Dictionary of Roses in colour*, an indispensable reference work for rose enthusiasts since its publication in 1971, he has already dispensed some of his long experience and understanding of gardening and those who read this book may be assured that the information provided is based on his sound, personal knowledge and is not one of the plagiaristic distillations of horticultural fact and fiction which are far too frequently offered nowadays.

As a result of plant exploration, particularly in the early part of this century, an enormous diversity of shrubs has been introduced into cultivation and a wide range of excellent shrubs, together with numerous hybrids, is now available for use by gardeners.

The upsurge in the popularity of shrubs has been one of the main developments in gardening during the last three decades and the use of shrubs to form the main framework of the garden is proving to many a most satisfying and effective means of achieving their aim of producing beauty and colour throughout the year. One of the problems which faces both experienced and inexperienced gardeners is how to choose the most suitable shrubs for his or her purpose and, as one might expect, there is no shortage of modern books on shrubs which provide a bewildering mass of information. Gardeners are given instructions on how to plant, feed, prune, mulch and propagate their shrubs and are given detailed descriptions of the plants concerned to whet their appetites. Even the most accurate of descriptions, however, gives only a limited idea of the beauty of a particular shrub and cannot compete with a description accompanied by a good coloured illustration in assisting with that most difficult of gardening problems – how to choose a particular plant for a particular site.

The Dictionary of Shrubs in colour has been prepared mainly with this problem in mind and should fulfil admirably its author's intention of bringing a very wide range of attractive and beautiful shrubs to the attention of the gardening public.

As may be expected the format closely resembles that of its successful predecessors *The Dictionary of Garden Plants in colour* and *The Dictionary of Roses in colour*. In addition to the concise descriptions of shrubs with brief details of cultivation and propagation there are over 500 admirable coloured photographs by Ernest Crowson who contributed largely to *The Dictionary of Garden Plants in colour* and took all the photographs for the companion volume on roses.

A high standard of production, fine quality coloured photographs and a sound practical text are blended to make this a book which may be commended to all who love gardens and gardening.

C. D. Brickell

Director
The Royal Horticultural Society's Garden

Introduction

Part of the purpose of this book is to show in colour some trees suitable for the smaller garden and also to show, not only the beauty but the great diversity of shrubs which can be grown in all types of garden. Large gardens are a minority group when compared with the ever increasing number of small gardens.

In America visiting gardens has not become the very popular pastime it has in Britain, but often 'benefit' tours with chartered buses hired for the occasion, are arranged to visit one or several public or private gardens of high merit. In the U.S. the gardens at restored colonial Williamsburg and at George Washington's Mount Vernon are outstandingly popular with tourists. Many of the finest gardens in Britain are opened at some time or other during the year to visitors. Some are open over many days in summer, others on special occasions only. There is a great diversity of these gardens, from the very large to the small. Visitors to gardens frequently see plants which they like and admire. Perhaps a picture in this book will remind them of the name and give them an idea as to whether they can grow it or not. No garden is really complete without a tree or a shrub. Trees can provide a background or a framework or a focal point in the garden. If you like a little privacy in your garden, trees can, given a little time, provide that also, especially when combined with shrubs, really the backbone of any garden. In addition to privacy, functional buildings which may not appeal can be hidden, or even utilized for siting shrubs and thus do much to enhance the appearance of the garden. Roses or clematis scrambling over old sheds charm with their beauty in spring and summer, and evergreens are of great value during the winter months. On a hot summer day you appreciate shade, shrubs and trees can provide it as they provide beauty. Beauty of leaf, beauty of flower, not to mention the even greater beauty in many cases before leaf fall. Trees are desirable, but they must be in the right scale and in the right place. How often have you seen a Weeping Willow so lovely in spring in the full glory of its weeping branches and its young leaves, possibly the most beautiful of moisture-hungry weeping trees but presenting such a problem when it outgrows a small garden. Not only does it become much too large for its environment, but its moisture hungry roots block up all the drains as well. It is important then to choose trees in particular, which are in scale with your garden and will give you pleasure without presenting problems some years later.

In view of this, it may be thought that to include *Eucalyptus gunnii*, in warmer regions one of our fastest growing trees when established, is to say the least unwise. My reason is simply that by annual pruning every spring you reduce this tree to shrub-like dimensions, retaining the juvenile foliage, thus providing an unsurpassed effect for the greater part of the year and also useful if you require a few twigs for indoor decoration. Likewise *Robinia pseudo-acacia* 'Frisia' may grow too large for your rather small garden, but again pruned in spring every year, you will have a glorious golden sunshine effect until autumn.

The majority of the pictures depict shrubs, old ones, new ones, loved ones and a few neglected ones. I hope you will be agreeably surprised with the wide diversity of shrubs which are to be seen and your appetite whetted to try some of them in your garden. They vary from plants only inches high to many at home in the larger garden. Some are deciduous, others evergreen, some have beautiful flowers, even in mid-winter where climate permits and others are beautiful in fruit. Several are scented in addition.

A large number of plants you will notice have the letters A.G.M. with the year added. These are plants in Britain which have been given the Award of Garden Merit in that particular year by the Royal Horticultural Society. This is an award given to plants of good constitution and which have proved to be excellent for ordinary garden decoration. Only plants which are well known are recommended for this award. Their availability, and being superb plants, make the way simple for the plant lover toward improved garden decoration. The letters F.C.C. after the description of a shrub or tree indicate that it has been awarded a First Class Certificate by the Council of the Royal Horticultural Society as a plant of great excellence. The additional letter 'T' in some instances indicates that the award has been made after trial at the Society's Garden at Wisley, Surrey, England. In the U.S. no awards are given for shrubs, trees or vines (climbers) except in the category of roses where A.A.R.S. stands for All-American Rose

Selections, but awards of other countries are recognized in addition to certain Medals and Gold Medals of American bodies.

Shrubs are, in the main, easily grown woody plants, and can be planted in natural settings or formal layouts and being perennial are unlikely to require replacement. Some can be grown in the smallest gardens, even in tubs or troughs. Eventual size depends on soil, district and situation and can be influenced by pruning. Indications of height given are of plants well situated and will, I hope, serve as a guide to wise placing in your own garden. You may find some shrubs you have never seen or heard of! I hope so, I am always delighted when I find a plant which is different but worth growing, and I will be equally delighted if readers also share in this, one of the many joys of gardening.

The photographs have, in the main, been taken of growing plants in the garden, the few exceptions are of particularly good plants exhibited at the Royal Horticultural Society shows at Westminster.

PROPAGATION

One of the most satisfying aspects of gardening is to produce a new plant whether for your own enjoyment or to pass on to a friend. Nature's method in the main is by sowing seed but where a particular plant is required this is usually done by vegetative production, mainly by cuttings or where only a few plants are required by layering. Other ways of giving a plant a separate existence is by division or by joining part of the desired plant to the root system of another. That is by budding or grafting. The pride which many gardeners and householders take in plants from home raised seedlings, apples, oranges, peaches frequently and others with little apparent merit to an outsider, causes one to realize that this is often a basic desire in those who love plants.

Air-layering

Air-layering has become popular in recent years, or at least publicized, but has been used for many years in glasshouses for some subjects, often to get larger plants and with foliage to the base, than is possible with cuttings. For shrubs and trees it is a useful method of obtaining young plants of very choice subjects which are difficult to propagate by other means or where such equipment as a mist unit, a propagating frame or a greenhouse are not available. The operation is comparatively simple

and should generally be carried out in April when growth has become active. It is similar to the method long employed for border carnations in that a cut is made at a node into the centre of the growth, which should be a year old. The cut is extended towards the tip for a couple of inches forming a tongue. This cut surface is then dusted with hormone rooting powder, the tongue kept open with a match stick or some moss which prevents it growing together again. The whole is surrounded by moist sphagnum moss, chopped fine and covered with polythene (polyethylene) and sealed with adhesive tape. Sealing must be done to exclude air and retain moisture and the whole enclosure should be tied to a stake or another branch to ensure support for the prospective young plant. In due course, if all goes well, the young roots can be seen through the polythene and the shoot can be cut away from the parent plant. The polythene and moss carefully removed, the young plant should be potted and kept closed in a frame until established. This can be verified by careful inspection, or if roots appear at the drainage holes then the plant can be hardened off in a cold frame where it should be kept for the first winter, potting on if necessary to prevent the roots becoming pot bound.

Budding

Budding is a form of propagation practised on a large scale by rose growers, professional and amateur, and also for flowering cherries, crabs etc. It is in reality grafting but with a single bud, instead of a piece of twig with two or three buds. Budding is usually done in July and August, when the bark parts freely from the wood. The bud of the desired variety is cut with a shield of bark an inch long on either side, roughly boat shaped and a thin sliver of wood behind the bud which has to be carefully removed without damage to the bud. A 'T' shaped incision is made in the bark of the stock, and the bud held by the leaf stock is pushed under the flaps of the bark which have been lifted by the budding knife handle (specially designed for this purpose) keeping the bud facing outwards and pushing it down as far as it will go. The end of the shield is then cut off level with the top of the flaps. Tying in, leaving the bud exposed, used to be done with moist raffia but this has been replaced, so far as professional growers are concerned, with rubber or plastic ties which fasten with a clip. Books on propagation deal with these methods in greater detail than is possible in a general book and should be consulted where more information is desired.

Some plants, such as the common grape vine, have for long been propagated by buds or 'eyes' as they are usually called, cut out from young growth of the previous year in spring before growth commences, much as described for roses. These buds are inserted in pots, leaving the tip exposed and placed in heat. A similar method has been used to propagate camellias and mahonias, but in this the bud is cut out with a leaf attached and inserted in a mixture of sand and peat in a propagating frame. This method has proved of considerable value in the increase of cultivars of *Mahonia* × *media* forms.

Cuttings

The increase of plants by cuttings is of great importance to the amateur gardener. It is by this means generally that particularly good forms of shrubs or trees may be propagated for oneself or made available to others. These good forms may arise from seedlings when one plant may be superior or different in colour and habit from all the others, or it may occur as a sport or mutation in a particular clone. It is important also to the nurseryman as there is usually a demand for the better forms of plants by interested gardeners, so every care should be taken to perpetuate such plants. Many shrubs and some trees can be increased by 'hard wood' cuttings taken in late autumn or winter and placed in shallow trenches in open ground or a sheltered border where they will root and can be

Hardwood or ripened cuttings inserted in outside border on a base of sharp sand.

Leaf cuttings
1 Camellia leaf cuttings prepared, note the basal buds which must be retained. 2 After the first year. 3 Potted on, showing flowers in second year

moved the following autumn and given more room for growing on. Such cuttings can usefully be made in wet weather, tied in bundles and plunged in damp sand until conditions improve. In heavy soils a layer of sharp sand appears to improve the 'take'. These cuttings are usually about a foot (30 cm.) cut just below a node with a sharp knife. Most of the plants referred to in this book are usually increased from cuttings taken in the period from mid July until early September when growth has become somewhat firm, generally termed 'semi-ripe' or 'semi-hardwood'. Placed in a propagating frame inside a greenhouse, and kept close and shaded in hot weather, a good proportion will eventually root. This process has been speeded up considerably in recent years not only by the use of special hormone preparations but also by mist propagation. The latter method has rendered closed frames and shading unnecessary at least for many subjects. Good propagators usually have their own particular methods for difficult plants and fortunately not many are secretive about them. Small propagating cases are obtainable from garden shops and centres, some cases include an electric heating element in which the temperature can be controlled by an adjustable thermostat. Some are successful with a simple arrangement of a box covered with a sheet of plastic or glass.

Mist units are operated electrically so that the time honoured methods of spraying or damping to keep cuttings fresh and prevent drying out is now performed automatically. In the system which I have used spraying is controlled day and night by a device known as an 'artificial leaf'. This is placed amidst the cuttings, where on becoming dry a valve opens and the mist spray is turned on. When sufficiently damp the spray is automatically cut off.

Good drainage is essential when a 'mist unit' is employed and a bed of sharp sand with a little peat is usually used although other materials such as vermiculite and perlite are also favoured. Spray nozzles must be kept cleaned regularly and it is important to have a clean water supply. Hard water can cause trouble particularly for ericaceous subjects, covering the leaves with a calcareous deposit which prevents them functioning normally. Cuttings can be rooted much more quickly by this method, but it is important to have a weaning unit in which the young plants, after transfer, can be gradually inured to dryer, cooler more normal conditions. Generally speaking, all plants rooted under these conditions cannot be transferred to outdoors until the following year. Reference is made in the text regarding the normal method of propagation of individual subjects.

Saddle Grafting
1 *Rhododendron ponticum*, **established in a pot for one season for use as stock. 2 Same stock cut back to receive scion. 3 Scion prepared for saddle graft and binding tape. 4 Scion fitted to stock by saddle graft and binding started**

Division

Division is a very simple method of propagation, but not one employed much for shrubs as few make the required type of growth. Some of the dwarf spiraeas, *Euonymus fortunei* and its forms, and *Mahonia aquifolium*, all of which make fresh basal growths with attached roots, are suitable for treating in this way. Where plants are well rooted this division can take place in autumn or spring, in the latter case just as growth commences. Plants not well rooted or which are scarce and valuable will benefit from potting and a sojourn in a greenhouse or frame until established.

Grafting

Grafting is an operation which requires a considerable degree of skill and much practice and is in the main confined to nurserymen, who use it very largely for some of the best forms of ornamental trees and some shrubs. These are grafted upon a stock of a common type, but which are either of the same or a closely related species. There are several methods of grafting employed by skilled propagators, but in all, the same common principle prevails. That is, the inner bark or cambium, of the scion (the desired plant) and that of stock must be placed in contact. Then, and only then, can union take place. The most successful grafting takes place

when the scion and the stock are equal in growth, then the greatest amount of cambium of each is brought into contact with each other.

Many plants are grafted under glass in spring, the stocks grown in pots so that they can be started into growth before the scions, which are usually heeled in the soil until required. Scions are usually only a few inches long and when joined by 'whip grafting' the most simple method in which similar slanting cuts are made and the two bound together with raffia and sealed with grafting wax to keep the parts airtight. Special tapes are now available for this purpose.

Inarching

This is a method of grafting by approach used frequently for grape vines, but owing to the decline in this branch of horticulture, now seldom seen. In this case the stock is usually growing in a pot and is placed near the plant it is desired to propagate. The union is made by slicing a piece of one and a corresponding slice of the other. The two are tied together, cambium to cambium at least on one side

Side Grafting
1 Rhododendron stock. 2 Side grafting of rhododen-dron. 3 *left*, plant prepared with scion also prepared; *right*, plant grafted and bound with grafting tape. 4 Scion being inserted before binding

of the cut, but again preferably on the two and sealed with grafting wax, pitch or commercial tree-sealing compound. When union takes place and growth is being made, ties may have to be loosened to prevent strangulation. Or a new tie should be given until the union becomes strong; then the new plant can be separated and allowed to grow on its new root system.

Layering

Layering is a most useful method of increasing shrubs or trees where branches are close enough to the ground to permit the operation; indeed it often happens naturally where branches reach the ground and produce roots. This operation can be carried out at any time of the year when it is most convenient, but spring is really the best. Since in nature, many plants will emit roots if they are brought into contact with or are covered by soil – it is really a very simple operation basically. It becomes a little more complicated when the subject does not emit roots so readily and the flow of sap has to be checked to hasten the process. This is

Layering a rhododendron
1 Bark scraped underneath, peg ready to hold layer down. 2 Covered with compost. 3 Rhododendron layer lifted with peg pulled out

done by scraping the bark, cutting notches or a slit not too far from the end of the shoot when it is about one or two years old. This part should be pegged into the ground, and a compost of leaf mould and sand placed around the part, and keeping it well moistened will be helpful. One season is generally sufficient for many plants to form enough roots for severance and removal, but in some cases two may be required. In some nurseries stool beds are established in order to produce young growths for layering, but some plants such as ericas can often be increased by placing some compost into the plant and keeping the growths in place with stones. The potential layers must be kept in a fixed position and not allowed to dry out in summer.

Root cuttings

Root cuttings can be used to increase certain subjects such as *Aralia elata, Rhus, Prunus tenella, Romneya* etc. The roots are best if taken from relatively young plants during winter or early spring 8 to 13 cm. in length and laid in a box of peat and sharp sand in equal parts. The young plants should be established in pots before being planted in a nursery or their permanent quarters.

Seed

For an amateur gardener who only requires a limited number of plants, seeds generally are better sown in pots or pans than in the open ground. Soil mixtures for seed sowing are nowadays procurable ready for use. Good drainage is essential, in the past generally provided by crocks which are still good if available. Gravel or small stones can be used instead and this should be covered by some fibrous material, peat fibre or half rotted leaves to prevent the compost filtering through. Those fortunate enough to live in the country may have access to their own compost and can use sifted loam and leaf mould in equal parts with half the quantity of sharp sand or as old gardeners were wont to do, roadside grit from a country lane. Where ericaceous subjects such as rhododendrons are to be sown, the loam can be left out, peat can of course, be substituted for leaf mould where this is unprocurable. Seeds should not be sown too deeply, very fine seeds are better on the surface with just a pepper dusting of fine sand. Large seeds are covered to their own depth, an age-old practice which still holds good. Moisture is essential and in general, especially for very fine seeds, the compost should be moist before sowing, and if placed in a close frame and shaded, germination may take place before any further watering is required. When this is so, standing the pot in a tray of water and allowing moisture to rise by capillary attraction is a sensible method for choice seeds. A modern capillary irrigation bench can also be utilized where available. Where a greenhouse with some heat is available this is of considerable help especially for spring sowing, but good results have been obtained by many gardeners in cold frames, even under what are known as cloches in Europe and PMG's (Portable Miniature Greenhouses) in the U.S. Sometimes a pane of glass over a box will be of assistance. Newly harvested seeds frequently germinate more readily, but as is usual, this is in autumn, and the difficulty of getting tiny seedlings through the winter months has to be taken into account. This is why spring sowing is generally favoured, the seeds being stored preferably in cool conditions. Much research has been done on this subject which can be followed up, but this is hardly the place for it.

PREPARING THE GROUND AND PLANTING

Shrubs and trees, especially the latter, are likely to be permanent residents after planting so that to ensure satisfactory results it is generally necessary to prepare the site well previously. Unless the planting is on a considerable scale and the preparatory work can be done mechanically, it will be necessary to get busy with a spade. Only the fortunate few can choose a site where the soil will be all that is desired, and most of us have to accept the garden as it exists and to try to improve the soil sufficiently to grow the plants we desire. If fortunately, the soil is neutral or on the acid side you will be able to grow most plants with some success. If however, you inherit a garden with a highly alkaline soil, there are lots of plants you can grow but the large group of plants classified as Ericaceae, which includes *Rhododendron*, will be barred to you. Barred is possibly too strong a word, it may be possible but only after a great deal of soil preparation. If, however, you are determined to grow rhododendrons, the chlorosis which arises from the presence of lime or chalk, and shows up very quickly by the sickly yellow appearance of the leaves, can be overcome by repeated watering with Sequestrene. Heavy dressings of peat will also help as will an adequate supply of moisture in summer. Where a supply of leaf mould is available, regular top dressing will also make a considerable difference in the health of the plants. If you want to specialize you will probably enjoy the challenge, but it is really better at least when starting off, to grow plants which will be reasonably happy in your soil conditions.

Digging is hard work as well as good exercise, and is really necessary in order to prepare the soil properly. Double digging is better, but of course harder work, so that most people settle for digging one spit deep, that is one depth of the spade. To ensure there is no hard pan below, the next spits depth should be broken up with a digging fork and some well rotted compost mixed in as the work proceeds. It is important to add organic matter of some kind, leaf mould, compost, moist peat, even straw or farmyard manure. The latter is almost impossible for town gardens, where peat is much more likely to be obtainable. This should never be applied dry, but always moistened and some should be retained for mixing around the roots of your plants. This will help them to make a good start. Perennial weeds should, of course, be removed when digging. Annual weeds can be buried as can most grasses if you are breaking up new ground. Skim the turfs off, chop it up and put it in the bottom of the trench. The ground should be allowed a few weeks to settle down before planting begins. When planting trees or shrubs a hole large enough to take the roots when well spread out should be dug, and it should be of sufficient depth to allow the new plant to be planted to the same depth as it had been in the nursery. Trees generally require a stake and this should be driven in before planting. The stake should be long enough to support the stem but not so tall as to interfere with the branches. The tree should be placed in the hole to the leeward side of the stake and the soil filled in gradually, shaking the tree as the work proceeds and firming so as to prevent air pockets being formed. Proprietary tree-ties are available for securing them to the stake and two will be required for standards with a 6 ft (1·85 m.) stem. Container grown trees are more popular these days and can be planted out in the same way. They can, of course, be planted at any time when the soil conditions are suitable, always using care to see that the roots are moist before planting. Bare root trees should be soaked if dry. These are usually planted between October and March. Any covering, such as sacking, should be removed before planting as should the container, of course. Where trees are being moved to a fresh site in the same garden, it is usual to try and do so with a 'ball' of earth attached, thus ensuring as little disturbance as possible. It is usually necessary to fix the ball with some covering, hessian or strong sheet plastic in the case of small trees, to prevent it breaking up. Shrubs can be moved in a similar manner to trees, but in general do not require staking unless the site is a windy one. Stakes should always be placed to the windward side if required.

Many newcomers to gardening find container grown plants more suitable than the older method of planting when trees and shrubs are almost dormant. It certainly has the advantage that the planting can generally be carried out when weather conditions are more congenial. Care should always be taken that the plant is well established in the container. Thus when lifted by the stem, container and soil should lift as well. Plants recently placed in containers should be allowed time to get well established before planting.

Trees and shrubs purchased from a nursery may arrive at an inconvenient time for planting. Good nurseries usually give instructions regarding treatment in such cases. The first requirement is to ensure the roots are moist, if not they should be stood in a tank of water for a few hours, then heeled in. This consists of placing them in a trench and covering the roots with moist soil, as dryness is always detrimental and should be avoided or losses will occur. If arrival takes place in bad weather, with ground frozen, place the trees or shrubs in a shed which is free from frost and protect the roots with straw, bracken or any material readily available. Planting should of course, be carried out at the first opportunity. Evergreens in the main should be transplanted in late September or early October when their roots are still active and they have time to become re-established before winter sets in. If inconvenient at that time, late April and early May when new growth is recommencing is another suitable time. Rhododendrons which have a dense mass of fibrous roots and can be lifted with a large ball of soil, can be treated with more latitude. All newly planted shrubs require great care in their first season if a dry spring sets in. Take care to see the roots do not dry out and an overhead spray on occasion will help them over a difficult period.

New shrubs should be planted at the same depth as they were growing, the bamboo shows planting level

Where shrubs or trees are planted in lawns or areas of grass it benefits them greatly, especially in the early years, if an area around the plant is kept clear of grass. Three feet (90 cm.) should be allowed from the plant to the edge, this not only allows full benefit from natural rainfall or irrigation, but should ensure that damage from mowers does not occur. Stems of standard trees such as *Prunus* are particularly subject to damage from grass-boxes and may take years to recover. Tree ties should be inspected regularly and even label ties can choke a branch or even the main stem if allowed to become too tight. A top dressing of old rotten manure, leaf-mould or compost will also greatly benefit most shrubs especially if applied in early spring.

PRUNING

Before planting shrubs or trees in small gardens, consideration should be given to their ultimate size so as to avoid a lot of pruning to keep them in bounds. It is important to allow them to develop their natural habit in general, especially if grown as specimens where good shape is appreciated. In some cases to achieve this, the leading shoot should be encouraged, especially if the plant is naturally of a weeping habit. Then by tying a leading shoot when young to a stake, a much more effective specimen can, in due course, be produced.

Generally all branches which cross or rub each other or seem likely to should be removed to ensure that the balance is not disturbed. Plants propagated

A hydrangea being pruned in spring, old flower heads removed and old growths also to allow room for young basal growths

by budding or grafting frequently produce suckers from the base or on the stem, these should be removed cleanly with a sharp knife. Secateurs, or trimming shears, usually leave a snag which produces another crop. Sometimes basal suckers can be removed by a sharp tug, resulting in no further trouble.

Shrubs which were originally sports occasionally produce growths which have reverted, thus a variegated plant may have a branch with green leaves. Removal should take place as soon as possible. Any large cuts should be trimmed off with a sharp knife and painted with a bituminous compound, or grafting paint, such as 'Arbrex' though this is more likely to be needed with trees than shrubs.

Some of the small flowering trees mentioned in this book form a dense crown, especially when grown on stems as standards. To overcome this thinning out a branch here and there without spoiling the shape of the tree is the method which should be employed. Lopping branches, a method all too frequently seen, should not be done, this only results in a general chaos of young growths. Branches should be cut in sections and then removed cleanly at the base or close to another branch, taking care not to leave any snags.

Many gardeners still prefer to prune in the winter months, the traditional time, but in general, most shrubs and trees are better pruned in August when the cuts heal more quickly. *Prunus* should be pruned even earlier to prevent the incidence of fungal diseases. Conifers should preferably be kept

to a single leader, especially where specimens of upright habit are required. Many grow naturally in this fashion such as *Chaemaecyparis lawsoniana* 'Columnaris' but *C. lawsoniana* 'Fletcheri' one of the most popular cultivars, however behaves rather differently so that basal growths should be removed where it is desired to keep to the single leader, an asset where snow causes problems in winter.

Pruning of shrubs has generally been dealt with in the descriptions so that only general principles need be mentioned here. Thus shrubs like *Buddleia davidii*, *Fuchsia* and *Potentilla* which flower on growths produced during the current year will respond to hard pruning in March or April. Spring flowering shrubs flower mainly on growths of the previous year, so *Forsythia*, *Ribes*, *Deutzia* and *Philadelphus* should have the old flowering growths removed back to where young growths are breaking on the branches.

Evergreen shrubs do not, as a rule, require pruning except to keep them within the limits of space available. Generally speaking, pruning should be carried out where necessary after flowering is over. If an evergreen such as *Rhododendron* has outgrown its quarters it should be cut back hard, preferably in spring just before growth begins. This may result in the loss of the flowers of a very late cultivar but will benefit the plant by producing young basal growths more quickly.

Many shrubs which tend to grow into a mass of twiggy growths will benefit from the removal of odd branches at times, especially if weak and straggly.

DISEASES

The emphasis on good cultivation made in this book will, if observed, in conjunction with good garden hygiene, help to control, or better still, prevent disease on shrubs or trees in the garden. As a further aid the following basic points are worth attention.

1. Always buy good plants, cheap lots on offer at a local market all too frequently are starved, diseased plants, usually inferior varieties unsold in the nursery. The same applies to plants which have been in stores under unfavourable conditions, often for some weeks. On occasion you may be lucky, but generally such plants are a bad buy and bring disappointment. Good plants are an investment, growing in value and giving much greater pleasure.

2. Always plant carefully in soil which has been

well prepared and allowed to settle. Make sure roots are well spread out and not planted too deeply. Never allow plants to be around with roots exposed, be sure they are not dry when planting.

3. Feed if necessary, foliar feeding can help plants become established. Always be sure newly planted shrubs do not suffer from lack of moisture.

4. Observe good garden hygiene by removing all dead, damaged or diseased growths or leaves. Burn, do not put diseased material on the compost heap. Clean up any wounds with a sharp knife or chisel and treat with a paint dressing or preferably bituminous, asphalt compound.

5. If, in spite of these precautions, trouble still occurs try to identify it, or ask for advice from someone of repute who can recognize the most common diseases. Nurserymen usually have a member of their staff competent to do this or can advise regarding horticultural institutes and societies where help can be relied upon. On positive identification, spray with a suitable fungicide, keeping in mind most are protectants rather than eradicants. Always follow the instructions, never try a little extra 'for luck'.

There are several different fungicides which can be used for the control of diseases. Some are more effective than others depending to some extent on the particular environmental conditions. It may therefore be necessary for the gardener to experiment to find which fungicide gives the best control of any disease which affects his plants. Whenever possible those approved by an independent authority should be used, and if found to be successful, without being over expensive, should not be changed. If, however, after a few seasons success becomes limited or failure occurs, then another must be tried.

Acer Scorch

This is a disorder, not a disease caused by a parasite, but is very common amongst these very ornamental foliage plants. Turning brown around the margins, curling and shrivelling and a generally scorched appearance are the symptoms sometimes followed by premature leaf fall and the production of another crop of leaves in the same season. The primary cause may be frost or cold winds when growth is still soft, as the symptoms usually appear early in the season. Once it has appeared, little can be done during that season, but if it is a regular occurrence it may be necessary to move the plant to a more sheltered site.

Much can be done by good cultivation, by seeing the soil is well prepared and well laced with leaf mould or peat and mulched with these same materials. Reasonable moist soil without water-logging is also necessary. Where the trees are fairly old a spring feed with a complete fertilizer at 2–3 oz. per square yard or old well-rotted farmyard manure will be of benefit. In severe cases, where a valuable specimen has become partially defoliated, the modern technique of applying a foliar feed will help more quickly to restore vigour, which in its turn will help to encourage a more vigorous root action.

Clematis Wilt

Only affects young plants of the large flowered hybrids. The whole plant suddenly droops from the top downwards. Cut the wilted portion back to the base and spray with a copper or dithiocarba-mate fungicide at two week intervals during early growth. Benlate is also recommended by some authorities.

Coral Spot

This is a fungus *Lectria cinnabarina*, often seen growing on dead twigs of shrubs, especially under damp conditions, but may at times enter living tissue becoming quite destructive. Easily recognized when it appears on the bark as numerous pink or red cushion like pustules. Any shrub or tree which has branches showing these pustules should have them removed and the cuts painted over. It should hardly be necessary to say that all dead wood should be removed in any case, thereby reducing any chance of infection.

Fire Blight

A disease caused by the bacterium *Erwinia amyl-ovora*. It is a disease which affects *Cotoneaster*, *Pyracantha* and *Sorbus* in addition to 'Laxton's Superb' pear and Hawthorn or May (*Craetaegus oxyacantha*) and in the U.K. must be reported to the authorities. Apparently less virulent in recent years because of the vagaries of the British climate this disease might well be called the hot weather disease as it is more virulent if high temperature, 60°F or more, prevail during the period the shrubs or trees are in flower.

This disease only attacks during the active growing period of the plants, when the bacteria enters the nectaries in the flowers, which when infected turn black. Infection spreads rapidly down lateral twigs invading main branches so that leaves on affected areas lose their natural shine and turn black inwards from the margin. The bark of the affected branch loses its normal healthy colour and if scraped off the tissues underneath are a foxy brown colour. As the disease progresses the tissues become drier and the leaves turn brown, giving the scorched appearance which provides the name of the disease. Where the disease has taken possession removal and burning of the whole plant should be carried out. Where only small branches are affected these should be removed right back to where the tissues under the bark are green and healthy, scraping with a knife will ascertain this. Cuts should be treated with a bituminous or asphalt tree compound paint. No control has as yet been found effective in the British Isles, so compulsory destruction is necessary and prudent. In the U.S. however properly spraying with the antibiotic Agri-Strep gives fine control of the blossoming blight phase, but should not be used on *Crataegus mollis*. A zineb spray at mid-blossoming also furnishes control. 'Laxton's Superb' pear trees have been eliminated from commercial orchards because of this disease and although not largely planted in private gardens, would be better grubbed out and destroyed in these also.

Heather Wilt

Where heathers are grown they sometimes die out in patches from this disease. The plants should be dug up and burned. Soil should be changed or sterilized with formalin before replanting.

Honey Fungus *Armillariella* (syn. *Armillaria*) *mellea*

One of the worst troubles encountered by growers of trees and shrubs in gardens and which frequently causes losses before it is discovered. In some seasons toadstools are produced in late summer or autumn which may emerge around old tree stumps or even in the grass growing over old dead roots. Produced in dense clumps, variable in size and colour, but at some stage the stalk or cap is honey coloured, hence the name. It has been called by other names descriptive of some stage of the fungus, of these Bootlace Fungus is probably best known. So called from the long black or brown root like cords called rhizomorphs which may be found on examination of the dead or dying plant when these growths will be found growing from the softened, blackened bark. These bootlace like growths grow to several feet in length if still attached to a food source and on contact with living plants are able to penetrate and grow through to the inner bark. The white mats of fungal growth, which when fresh have a strong smell of mushrooms, then form and become parasitic on the plant tissues and eventually death of the plant results.

Fortunately, this fungus is infrequently found in small gardens, unless in wooded areas where trees have been felled. It often reveals its presence progressing through a privet hedge and resulting in a few more dead plants each season. Indiscriminate in its choice of plants it can cause havoc where there are old or weak trees, but perfectly healthy plants can also be infected and succumb more quickly if growing in adverse conditions such as badly drained or very poor dry soil. Once it has occurred in a garden the fungus it may prove impossible to eliminate completely, but the following suggestions should help at least to reduce losses.

Dead shrubs should be examined and cause of demise ascertained by an expert if necessary. If, Honey Fungus is confirmed dig up all dead and dying plants and burn. Look for and burn rhizomorphs working about a yard outside the apparently infected area. In a small area it may be feasible to sterilize. Vegetables are rarely long enough in the soil to become infested. All tree stumps infected or otherwise should be removed and burned. In shallow soils a trench dug around the infected area may help to prevent the fungus from spreading, but this is hardly worth while on deep or light soils where it may pass underneath. The fungus is likely to die out through lack of food if the sources, stumps and roots, have been removed, especially if left fallow or sown down with grass.

Good cultivation is always worthwhile, with attention to drainage and nutrition so that vigorous growth will help to ward off an attack. Annual mulching, feeding and attention to watering where feasible in dry weather will all help. All dead wood should be pruned back to clean live tissue and wounds protected. Arbex or Arborite is useful in this respect. In recent years a phenolic emulsion, a proprietary product called Armillatox has been found to kill the fungus in laboratory tests. There is some evidence that the use of this material will in certain circumstances save shrubs or trees which are infected. It may well be worthwhile to try it, the sooner treatment is carried out, the greater the chance of affecting a cure. The distributors also suggest using it for soaking trenches and treating stumps which cannot be removed. The use of a stump chipper on tree stumps left after felling has been recommended. The chips produced by this means are too small for the fungus to live on. This type of work is usually carried out by tree surgeons of repute.

In a small area free of plants a thorough soaking of the newly forked soil with 2% Formalin solution may be worth a trial. This will kill living plants so a barrier of thick polythene/polyethylene should be made in order to avoid contact with the roots of live plants. The area treated should be covered with polythene or sacks for twenty-four hours, and should not be planted for at least three weeks in light soils or six weeks if heavy.

Plants known to be susceptible to infection from Honey Fungus include *Cotoneaster, Forsythia, Hydrangea, Ligustrum* (Privet), *Malus, Prunus, Rhododendron, Rosa* species and cultivars, *Salix, Syringa* (Lilac) and *Viburnum*.

Leaf Spots

There are several leaf-spotting fungi, most being specific to certain host plants. Possibly the best known is Rose Black Spot which does not affect any other host. The roundish brown or black spots are easily seen, have fringed edges and in severe attacks may coalesce and cause premature leaf fall. Most leaf-spotting fungi overwinter on fallen leaves so these should be burnt.

Maneb, Benlate, Captan are all recommended fungicides for control. Some growers prefer to prune early after a severe attack, in December or January, burning the debris and following on with Bordeaux mixture sprayed over the roses and the soil surface. This has not been found effective in some areas. Spraying with one of the recommended fungicides should be undertaken as soon as the leaves unfold and throughout the summer as necessary. Some varieties are more susceptible than others.

Lichens and Moss

Shrubs and trees eventually develop on their bark some of the simpler forms of plant life, algae, fungi, lichens and moss especially in areas where humidity is high. Thus, in warm moist areas where many choice subjects are so much at home such growths are common, particularly on plants which are in poor health or have become neglected. Lichens and mosses can be killed on most deciduous shrubs and trees by the treatment generally meted out to fruit trees of spraying while dormant, December, January, with a 5% tar oil wash.

This treatment however, is not recommended for deciduous azaleas or pyracanthas and is undesirable on trees with a light coloured surface, such as Silver Birch because of discoloration. Lime-sulphur applied at one pint to two gallons of water in the dormant period is an alternative, which can be used in these cases. Whichever treatment is applied it should only be necessary once in four years to keep these superficial growths in check. Unfortunately these sprays are not safe to use on affected evergreens although it has been suggested the fungicide Captan may give some control. It might be worthwhile to try this out for one season at fortnightly intervals in order to see what result is obtained. Good cultivation of evergreens as recommended already in this book, is probably the best specific in order to keep the plants full of vigour.

Pyracantha Scab

Similar to the scab disease which sometimes attacks apples and pears. Captan or Benlate can be used as sprays.

Powdery Mildew

Probably the easiest disease to identify is powdery mildew. This produces a white powdery coating on many plants, among these being roses and members of the apple genus, *Malus*. Powdery Mildew also affects Bay Laurel, Laurel and *Euonymus*, especially where used as hedges. The young growths which appear after clipping appear to be particularly susceptible. The fungus causing the disease is specific to the host, so the fungus causing mildew on roses does not affect *Malus* and vice versa. When the plants are very dry at the roots they seem more susceptible, especially if the atmosphere is humid. Sulphur has been found the most effective control. For rose-powdery mildew, Milfaron, Benlate and Dinocap; the latter still effective in some areas but less so in others. For apple mildew – Benlate, Phaltan (Folpet), Dinocap and lime-sulphur except on sulphur shy varieties.

Rhododendron and Azalea Gall

This is caused by a fungus parasite *Exobasidium vaccinii*, which attacks *Rhododendron* and some other allied plants, such as *Andromela, Arelostaphylos* and *Sedum*. Varying in size from a pea to a small plum the galls are irregular in shape and may appear on leaves or flowers. At first reddish becoming white because of the floury bloom which is a coating of spores. These galls should be cut off and burned before they become white and begin to produce spores, though in the U.S. they are eaten by some people and where they are called pinxter-apples. If severe spraying with Bordeaux mixture or liquid copper will prevent germination of any spores already released. Spraying in spring before the new leaves appear will be an additional safeguard. Zineb is also recommended.

Rhododendron Bud Blast

This disease attacks the buds of evergreen rhododendron species, and hybrids. Fortunately, it is not likely to be troublesome on the smaller rhododendrons which comprise the greater number dealt with in this book. It is most likely to cause trouble on the large rhododendrons, and causes a drastic reduction in flower production. The disease organism is a fungus but it is the attack of the rhododendron leaf-hopper which is mainly responsible for spreading the disease.

The first symptoms are seen between October and December, when affected buds turn grey or brown. By spring they are dead and covered with black bristle like growths, which stay on the plants for two or three years. The development of bud blast and its connection with the activities of the leaf-hopper are not established as yet, but it is known to be most prevalent in areas infested and control of the leaf-hopper reduces the severity of the disease.

This is aided by removing and burning affected buds thereby reducing the amount of infection. The adult leaf-hoppers are $\frac{3}{8}$ inch long, and marked with two red longitudinal lines on a green background. They fly if disturbed but soon settle again and are not always easily seen. Some control may be obtained by spraying with Malathion two or three times during August and September, allowing a fortnightly interval between. Alternatively, a systemic insecticide may prove to have some effect.

Rusts

These fungi can be seen on infected leaves generally in the form of brown or orange yellow masses of spores. Rose rust can be a serious disease in some areas, badly infected plants being weakened to such an extent that death may occur. Diseased leaves should be conveyed to a fire for disposal in order to prevent the spores spreading. Formulations of Maneb, Zineb or Thiram are recommended for control and a more recent fungicide, Plantvase has given good results in recent years.

Silver Leaf Disease *Stereum purpureum*

This is usually associated with Plums, in particular the variety 'Victoria', but many ornamental shrubs may also be attacked. *Azara*, Rhododendrons, Roses, *Syringa microphylla*, *Laburnum*, Portugal Laurel are amongst those which have suffered. The first apparent symptom is the silvering of the leaves, but other signs are required for positive identification. If an affected branch is cut or sawn across and shows a brown or black stain in the wood this is confirmatory evidence of the disease.

As infection only takes place through wounds it is important that any branches removed should have the wounds on the tree treated with a protective paint. Where only a branch is affected, this should be cut back until no stain is visible and the paint applied. Trees have been known to recover from this disease, so that young trees should be encouraged by good cultivation and given another season to see if recovery has taken place. Treatment is best carried out during the growing season. The actual fungus does not show except on dead wood when it appears as flattish or bracket like fructifications, purple when damp, dull brown when dry. Spores are released from these which can cause infection of other trees.

Some trees suffer from what is sometimes called False Silver Leaf which may be caused by other conditions, most of which can be called poor cultivation or bad husbandry.

A valuable tree should not be destroyed until seen by an expert.

Verticillum Wilt

Sometimes attacks *Cotinus coggyria*. If an odd branch suffers remove, and burn, treating the wound on the plant with Arbrex or asphalt compound. In a severe attack remove the whole plant and burn.

PESTS

Adalges (*Chermis*)

Frequently attack dwarf pines; spraying with Malathion should keep them under control.

Aphis

Most people with gardens must be familiar with these tiny insects, be they green, brown or black, which has a weakening effect on the plants they attack and may also be instrumental in the transfer of virus diseases from infected to clean plants. A disfiguring by-product in the form of a sooty mould on plant leaves frequently occurs on many plants after an attack.

Control may be obtained in the case of deciduous shrubs such as roses, *Euonymus* and *Prunus* by using a Tar Oil Winter Wash during the dormant period. This can be followed by a systemic insecticide, such as a formulation of formathion or a contact insecticide such as Malathion or nicotine. In the latter case a repeat spraying after a few days interval should be applied to deal with any later arrivals. This follow-up treatment can be applied to evergreen shrubs also.

Azalea White Fly

Not the pest which is usually found in greenhouses, this one attacks azaleas and is specific to them. It can be controlled by contact spraying with Malathion or by a systemic in the U.K. In the U.S. it is recommended to spray in spring, before the adults emerge, with a diluted summer oil emulsion as well as with the contact spray later of Malathion or dimethoate or systemic poison – at weekly intervals if necessary.

Birds

Birds may cause considerable damage to flower buds especially of *Forsythia*. Proprietary products such as Morkit, which is distasteful but not harmful, are effective for a time but require renewal after rain to remain so.

Capsid bugs

In appearance these are something like an enlarged aphis but being very active are often difficult to see. However, the damage done to plants is easily seen and can be recognized by the contorted punctured appearance of the leaves particularly at the young growing tips. A wide range of plants are attacked in some cases flowering is much reduced, especially in the case of *Caryopteris* and *Fuchsia*. The use of a systemic insecticide should reduce the activities of this pest also, so that when used against aphids as in the case of roses, a regular spraying programme at two weekly intervals from end of April to end of July, if necessary, should take care of both pests. Hydrangeas may also be attacked, but are sensitive to systemics and should in consequence be sprayed with Malathion or Diazinon.

Caterpillars

They frequently drop off trees in woodland gardens and damage shrubs underneath. Where numbers are few handpicking will suffice, but if a major infestation spraying with a proprietary preparation should do the job. Birds also help.

Red Spider, Spider Mite

This effects plants in very dry hot situations, particularly some *Prunus*, roses and *Picea glauca albertiana* 'Conica'. Malathion is frequently recommended but does not seem to be effective everywhere; Meta-Systox-R and Kelthane are considered effective in the U.S. Spraying with water in hot weather, in conjunction with good cultivation, is a useful control.

Scale

These can often be found on bay trees and camellias. Use a contact spray such as Malathion towards the end of May or early in June.

Slugs

Usually find shrubs rather tough, but may attack young plants. Pellets with a metaldehyde base are usually effective.

Vine Weevil

The adults do considerable damage to leaves of rhododendrons, growing close to or on the ground. Feeding takes place at night, the leaves have notches taken out. Spraying or dusting with a proprietary preparation, at dusk during the summer months when the damage is seen, should be carried out.

Woolly aphis, Woolly Apple Aphis

So well known as a pest of apple trees, also attacks *Pyracantha* and *Cotoneaster* and should be controlled by the use of a systemic.

PLANT DISORDERS

Chlorosis

Lime-induced chlorosis occurs on plants growing in soils where the pH is high. Typical symptoms are yellowing between the veins, with leaves especially on young growth becoming almost white. These can occur on all types of plants on very alkaline soils, such as Hydrangea and Chaenomeles. Acid loving plants such as Rhododendrons and Camellias require soils with a low pH, otherwise in addition to leaf chlorosis poor growth and curtailed flowering will result. When chlorosis occurs, green colouring can frequently be brought back by applying chelated compounds. This however, is only worthwhile if alkalinity is reduced by digging in heavy dressings of peat, leaf mould and crushed bracken, plus a heavy application of Flowers of Sulphur.

Magnesium deficiency

This is common on light acid soils, especially after heavy rain, and may show up by discoloured leaves, more orange-yellow than the pale yellow of lime-induced chlorosis. Some purpling may also occur, these areas later turning brown. If these symptoms show up early in the season spraying with Epsom salts in solution $\frac{1}{2}$ oz to $2\frac{1}{2}$ gallons of water plus a good spreader either proprietary or soft soap. Two or three applications at fortnightly intervals may be given.

Acknowledgments

The author is greatly indebted to Mr J. Hope Findlay, M.V.O., V.M.H., for his cooperation and help and allowing photographs to be taken in the Savill Gardens, Windsor Great Park, England. Thanks are also due to Mr Tom Wellsted, without whose help this book would not have been written and to Rachel Dunham for deciphering my writing and other help.

The author would also like to thank Mr C. D. Brickell, B.Sc. Director of the Royal Horticultural Society's Garden, Wisley and members of his staff. Mr R. Legge, Superintendent of Regent's Park, London and members of his staff. Mr L.G. Turner, Secretary of the Royal National Rose Society, Chiswell Green Lane, St. Albans, Hertfordshire. Mr S. L. Lord, Superintendent of the Gardens, Shenley Hospital, St Albans, Hertfordshire. Mr A. N. Kinnear, Ridge, St Albans, Hertfordshire. Mr J. R. Hare, M.V.O., N.D.H., Bailiff of the Royal Parks.

Thanks also to Mr Ernest Crowson for the benefit of his skill and the exercise of his patience in securing the photographs.

The Plates

1
Abeliophyllum
distichum

2
Abutilon ×
suntense

3
Abutilon
vitifolium
'Album'

4
Acer palmatum
'Dissectum'

5
Acer palmatum
'Dissectum
atropurpureum'

6
Acer palmatum
'Senkaki'

7
Aesculus ×
mutabilis
'Induta'

8
Amelanchier
confusa,
A. canadensis

9
Aralia elata
'Aureovarie-
gata'

10
Arctostaphylos
uva-ursi

11
Artemisia
arborescens

12
Arundinaria
variegata

13
Atriplex
halimus

14
Berberis
'Barbarossa'

15
Berberis
darwinii

16
Berberis ×
lologensis

17
Berberis ×
ottawensis
'Superba'

18
Berberis
sargentiana

19
Berberis
wilsoniae
subcaulialata

20
Berberis ×
stenophylla

21
**Berberis
thunbergii
'Aurea'**

22
**Buddleia
alternifolia**

23
Buddleia crispa

24
**Buddleia
davidii
'Royal Red'**

25
**Buddleia
davidii 'White
Profusion'**

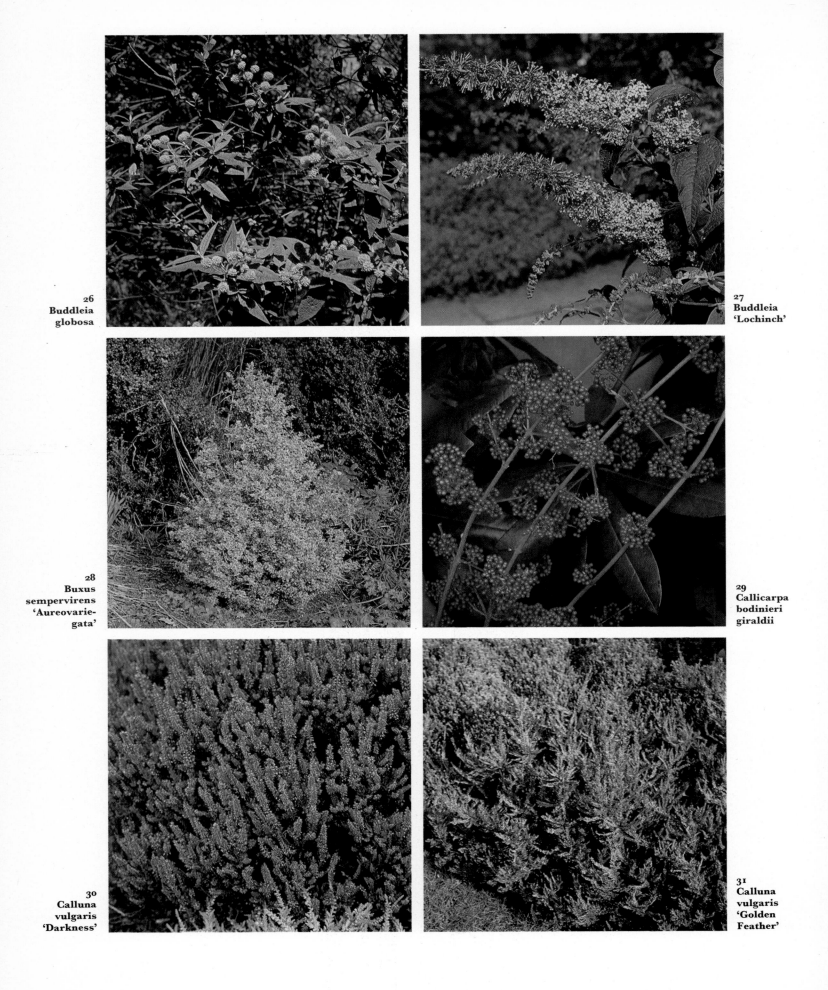

26
Buddleia
globosa

27
Buddleia
'Lochinch'

28
Buxus
sempervirens
'Aureovarie-
gata'

29
Callicarpa
bodinieri
giraldii

30
Calluna
vulgaris
'Darkness'

31
Calluna
vulgaris
'Golden
Feather'

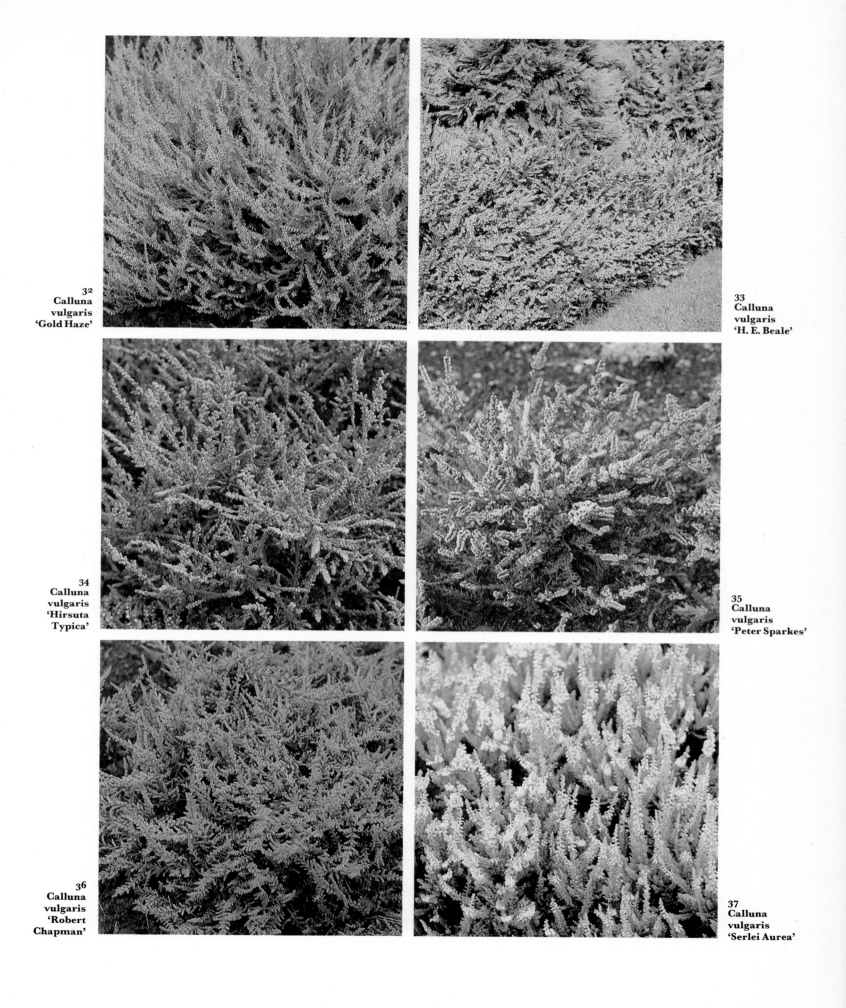

32
Calluna
vulgaris
'Gold Haze'

33
Calluna
vulgaris
'H. E. Beale'

34
Calluna
vulgaris
'Hirsuta
Typica'

35
Calluna
vulgaris
'Peter Sparkes'

36
Calluna
vulgaris
'Robert
Chapman'

37
Calluna
vulgaris
'Serlei Aurea'

38
Calluna
vulgaris 'Tib'

39
Camellia
'Cornish Snow'

40
Camellia
'Inspiration'

41
Camellia
japonica
'Adolphe
Audusson'

42
Camellia
japonica
'Ama-no-kawa'

43
Camellia
japonica
'J. J. Whitfield'

44
Camellia
japonica
'Apollo'

45
Camellia
japonica
'Gloire de
Nantes'

46
Camellia
japonica 'Lady
Clare'

47
Camellia
japonica
'Pink
Perfection'

48
Camellia
japonica
'Tricolor'

49
Camellia ×
williamsii
'Donation'

50
Camellia ×
williamsii
'J. C. Williams'

51
Camellia ×
williamsii
'St Ewe'

52
Carpenteria
californica

53
Caryopteris ×
clandonensis

54
Cassiope
'Muirhead'

55
Ceanothus
'Cascade'

56
Ceanothus
dentatus

57
Ceanothus
'Gloire de
Versailles'

58
Ceanothus
impressus

59
Ceanothus
mendocinensis

60
Ceanothus
thyrsiflorus
repens

61
Ceanothus
'Topaz'

62
Celastrus
orbiculatus

63
Ceratostigma willmottianum

64
Cercis siliquastrum

65
Chaenomeles 'Moerloosii'

66
Chaenomeles 'Crimson and Gold'

67
Chaenomeles 'Pink Lady'

68
Chamaecyparis lawsoniana 'Columnaris'

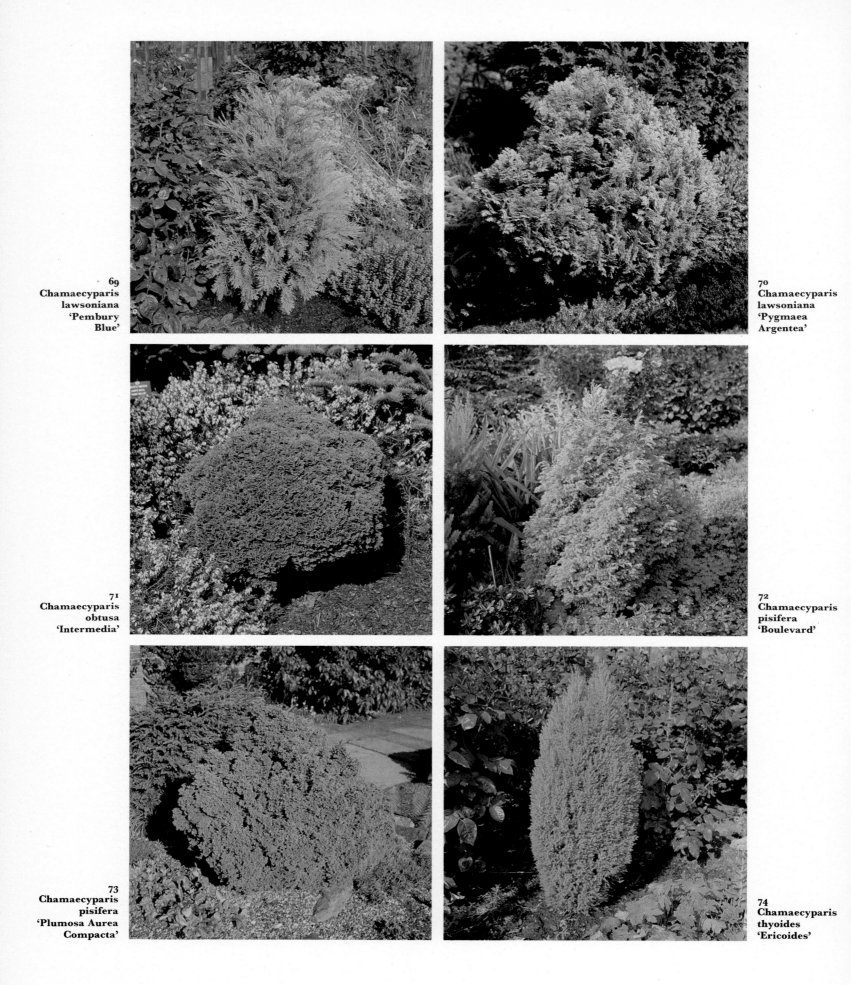

69
Chamaecyparis
lawsoniana
'Pembury
Blue'

70
Chamaecyparis
lawsoniana
'Pygmaea
Argentea'

71
Chamaecyparis
obtusa
'Intermedia'

72
Chamaecyparis
pisifera
'Boulevard'

73
Chamaecyparis
pisifera
'Plumosa Aurea
Compacta'

74
Chamaecyparis
thyoides
'Ericoides'

82
Cistus ×
purpureus

83
Cistus 'Silver
Pink'

84
Clematis ×
eriostemon
'Hendersonii'

85
Clematis ×
jouiniana
'Praecox'

86
Clematis
montana
'Tetrarose'

87
Clematis
orientalis

88
Clematis
rehderana

89
Clematis
tangutica

90
Clematis
texensis
'Etoile Rose'

91
Clematis
viticella
'Abundance'

92
Clematis
viticella
'Kermesina'

93
Clematis
'Barbara
Dibley'

94
Clematis
'Hagley hybrid'

95
Clematis
'Marie
Boisselot'

96
Clematis
'Nelly Moser'

97
Clematis
'Perle d'Azur'

98
Clematis
'Ville de Lyon'

99
Clematis
'William
Kennet'

100
Clerodendron
bungei

101
Colletia armata
'Rosea'

102
Cornus alba
'Variegata'

103
Cornus baileyi

104
Cornus 'Eddie's
White Wonder'

105
Cornus florida

106
Cornus kousa

107
Cornus kousa
chinensis

108
Cornus kousa
chinensis

109
Cornus mas

110
Cornus
stolonifera
(C. sericea)
'Flaviramea'

111
Coronilla
glauca

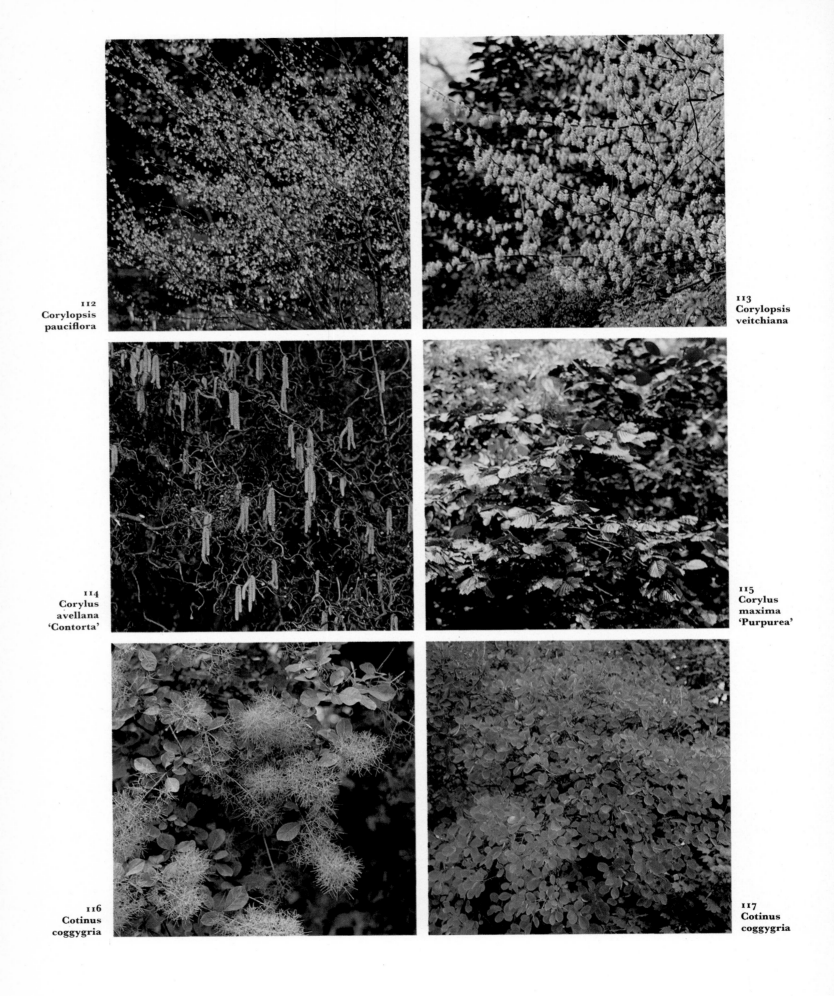

112
Corylopsis
pauciflora

113
Corylopsis
veitchiana

114
Corylus
avellana
'Contorta'

115
Corylus
maxima
'Purpurea'

116
Cotinus
coggygria

117
Cotinus
coggygria

118
Cotinus
coggygria
'Notcutt's
variety'

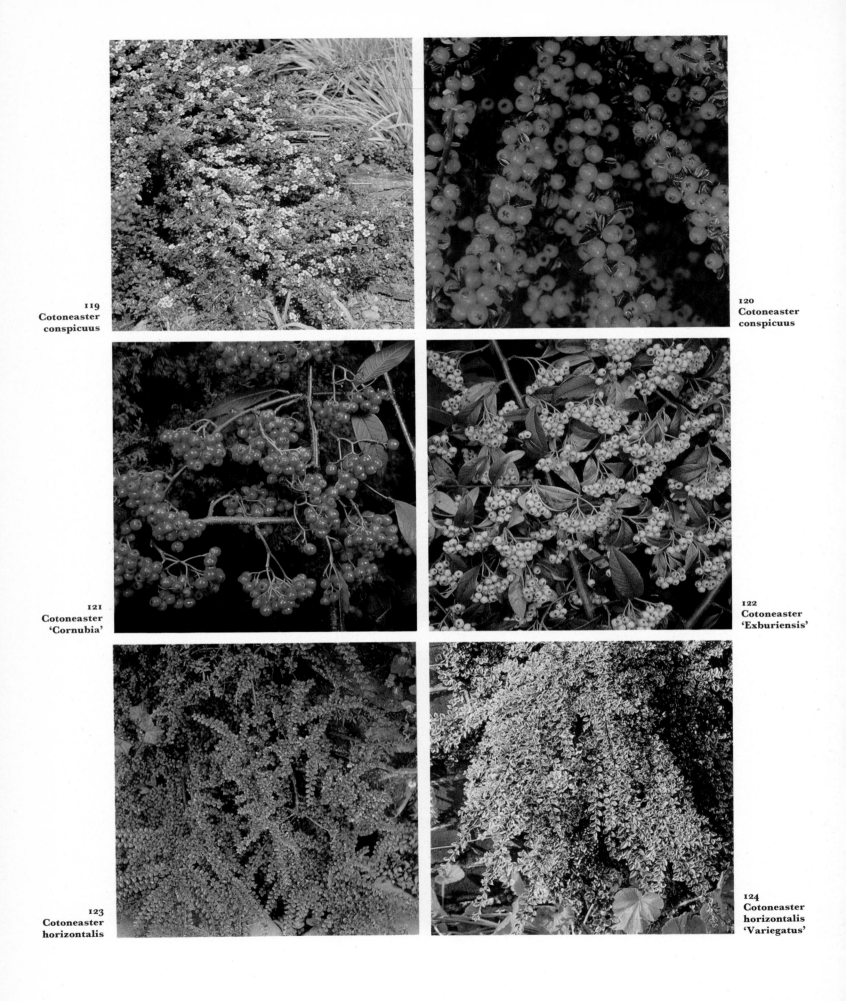

119
Cotoneaster
conspicuus

120
Cotoneaster
conspicuus

121
Cotoneaster
'Cornubia'

122
Cotoneaster
'Exburiensis'

123
Cotoneaster
horizontalis

124
Cotoneaster
horizontalis
'Variegatus'

125
Cotoneaster
'Hybridus
Pendulus'

126
Cotoneaster
'John Waterer'

127
Cotoneaster
lactea

128
Crinodendron
hookeranum

129
Cryptomeria
japonica
'Elegans'

130
Cryptomeria
japonica
'Globosa'

131
Cytisus
battandieri

132
Cytisus ×
beanii

133
Cytisus ×
kewensis

134
Cytisus
'Allgold'

135
Cytisus ×
praecox
'Goldspear'

136
Cytisus
purpureus

137
Cytisus
'Burkwoodii'

138
Cytisus 'Joan
Clark'

139
Cytisus
'Johnson's
Crimson'

140
Cytisus 'Lena'

141
Cytisus 'Luna'

142
Cytisus
scoparius
prostratus

143
Daboecia
cantabrica
'Alba'

144
Daboecia
cantabrica
'Atropurpurea'

145
Daboecia
'William
Buchanan'

146
Daphne ×
burkwoodii
'Somerset'

147
Daphne
mezereum

148
Daphne odora
'Aureo-
marginata'

149
Daphne retusa

150
Daphne
tangutica

151
Decaisnea
fargesii

152
Dendromecon
rigida

153
Deutzia ×
elegantissima

154
Deutzia ×
rosea
'Carminea'

155
Disanthus
cercidifolius

156
Drimys
winteri

157
Edgworthia
papyrifera

158
Eleagnus
pungens
'Frederickii'

159
Elaeagnus
pungens
'Maculata'

160
Embothrium
coccineum
lanceolatum

161
Embothrium
coccineum
lanceolatum
'Flamenco'

162
Enkianthus
campanulatus

163
Enkianthus
perulatus

164
Erica arborea
'Alpina'

165
Erica arborea
'Gold Tips'

166
Erica cinerea
'Atrorubens'

167
Erica cinerea
'Cevennes'

168
Erica cinerea
'Hookstone
White'

169
Erica ×
darleyensis
'Arthur
Johnson'

170
Erica ×
darleyensis
'Darley Dale'

171
Erica ×
darleyensis
'George
Rendall'

172
Erica
erigena

173
Erica herbacea
'December Red'

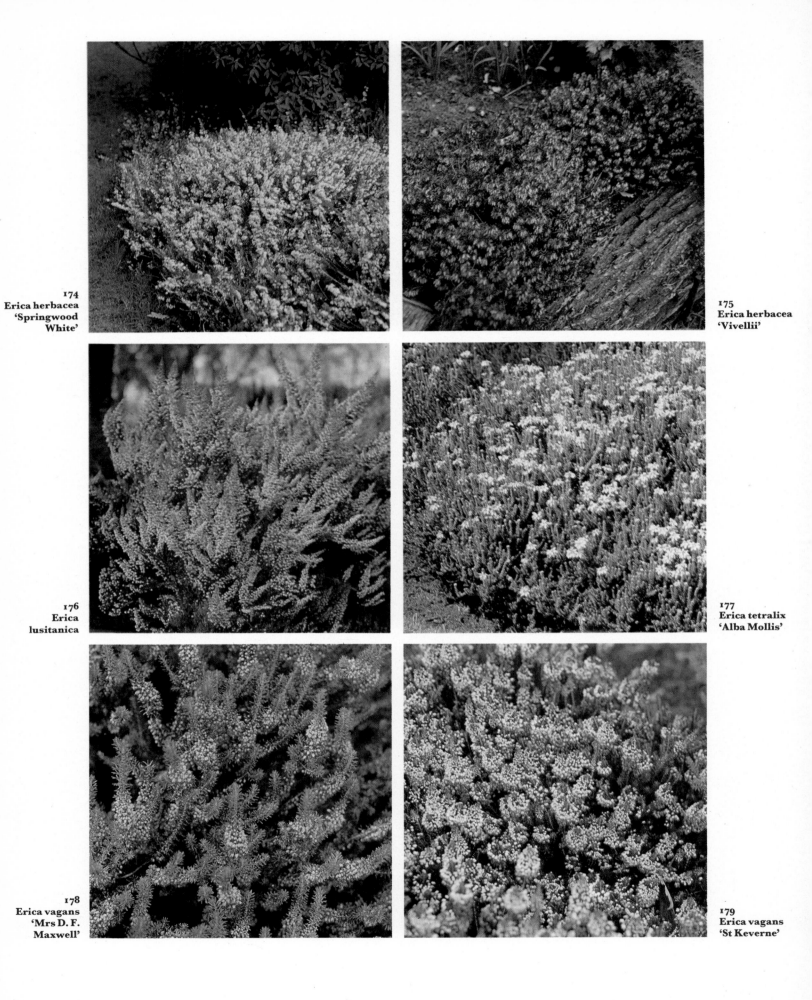

174
Erica herbacea
'Springwood
White'

175
Erica herbacea
'Vivellii'

176
Erica
lusitanica

177
Erica tetralix
'Alba Mollis'

178
Erica vagans
'Mrs D. F.
Maxwell'

179
Erica vagans
'St Keverne'

180
Erica ×
veitchii

181
Erythrina
crista-galli

182
Escallonia
'Sleive Donard'

183
Eucalyptus
gunnii

184
Eucryphia
glutinosa
'Flore Pleno'

185
Eucryphia ×
intermedia
'Rostrevor'

186
Euonymus
europaeus

187
Euonymus
fortunei
'Emerald
Gaiety'

188
Euonymus
fortunei
'Emerald 'n
Gold'

189
Euonymus
fortunei
'Silver Queen'

190
Euonymus
japonicus
'Ovatus
Aureus'

191
Euphorbia
characias

192
Exochorda ×
macrantha
'The Bride'

193
Fabiana
imbricata

194
Fatsia japonica

195
Fatsia japonica
'Variegata'

196
Forsythia
'Beatrix
Farrand'

197
Forsythia ×
intermedia
'Spectabilis'

198
Forsythia
'Lynwood'

199
Forsythia
suspensa
atrocaulis

200
Fothergilla
major

201
Fothergilla
major

202
Fremontoden-
dron
californicum
'Californian
Glory'

203
Fuchsia 'Army
Nurse'

204
Fuchsia
'Drame'

205
Fuchsia
'Enfant
Prodigue'

206
Fuchsia
magellanica
'Versicolor'

207
Fuchsia
'Mrs Popple'

208
Fuchsia
'Phyrne'

209
Garrya
elliptica

210
Genista
aetnensis

211
Genista cinerea

212
Genista
sagittalis

213
Gleditsia
triacanthos
'Sunburst'

214
× Halimiocistus
sahucii

215
× Halimiocistus
wintonensis

216
Hamamelis
× intermedia
'Diane'

217
Hamamelis
mollis
'Goldcrest'

218
Hamamelis
mollis
'Pallida'

219
Hebe albicans

220
Hebe 'Carl
Teschner'

221
Hebe
'Fairfieldii'

222
Hebe
'Alicia
Amherst'

223
Hebe 'Great
Orme'

224
Hebe
'Simon
Delaux'

225
Hedera helix
'Conglomerata'

226
Helianthemum
lunulatum

227
Helianthemum
nummularium
'Afflick'

228
Helianthemum
nummularium
'Wisley Pink'

229
Helianthemum
nummularium
'Wisley
Primrose'

230
Helichrysum
splendidum

231
Hibiscus
syriacus
'Blue Bird'

232
Hibiscus
syriacus
'Diana'

233
Hibiscus
syriacus
'Hamabo'

234
Hibiscus
syriacus
'Red Heart'

235
Hibiscus
syriacus
'William R.
Smith'

236
Hibiscus
syriacus
'Woodbridge'

237
Hydrangea
aspera

238
Hydrangea
heteromalla

239
Hydrangea
macrophylla
'Benelux'

240
Hydrangea
macrophylla
'Generale
Vicomtesse de
Vibraye'

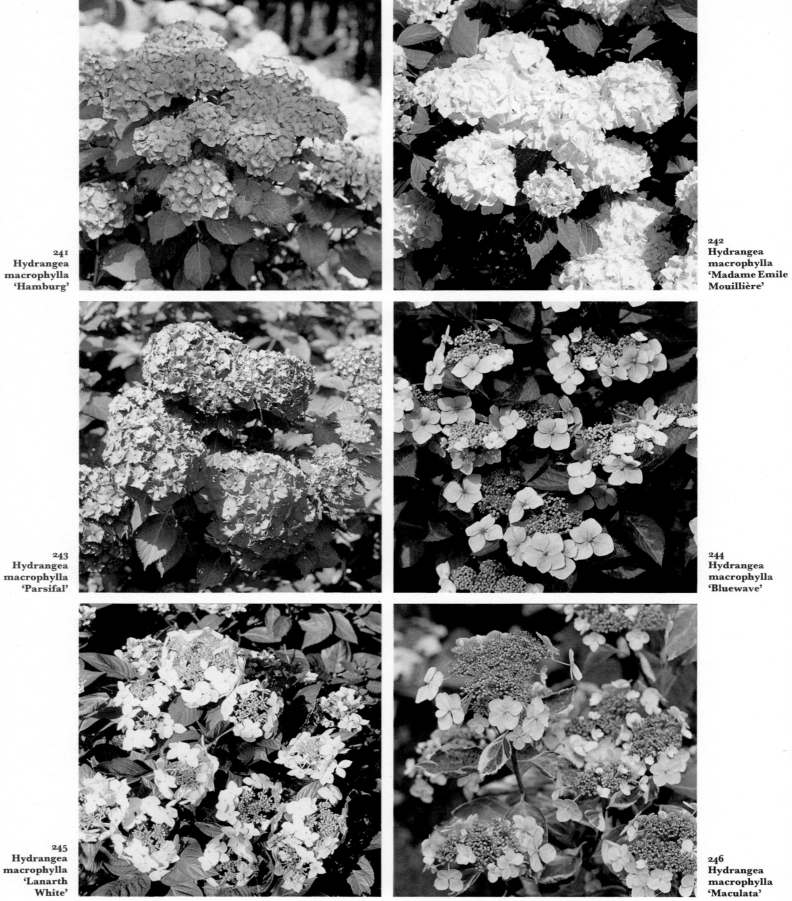

241
Hydrangea
macrophylla
'Hamburg'

242
Hydrangea
macrophylla
'Madame Emile
Mouillière'

243
Hydrangea
macrophylla
'Parsifal'

244
Hydrangea
macrophylla
'Bluewave'

245
Hydrangea
macrophylla
'Lanarth
White'

246
Hydrangea
macrophylla
'Maculata'

247
Hydrangea
serrata
'Bluebird'

248
Hydrangea
serrata
'Grayswood'

249
Hydrangea
serrata
'Grayswood
White'

250
Hydrangea
paniculata
'Grandiflora'

251
Hydrangea
paniculata
'Praecox'

252
Hydrangea
paniculata
'Tardiva'

253
Hypericum ×
inodorum
'Elstead'

254
Hypericum
'Hidcote'

255
Hypericum
moseranum

256
Hypericum
moseranum
'Tricolor'

257
Ilex ×
altaclarensis
'Lawsoniana'

258
Itea
ilicifolia

259
Jasminum
stephanense

260
Juniperus
communis
'Depressa
Aurea'

261
Juniperus
communis
'Repanda'

262
Juniperus
conferta

263
Juniperus
'Grey Owl'

264
Juniperus
horizontalis
'Bar Harbor'

265
Juniperus ×
chinensis 'Hetzii'

266
Kalmia
latifolia

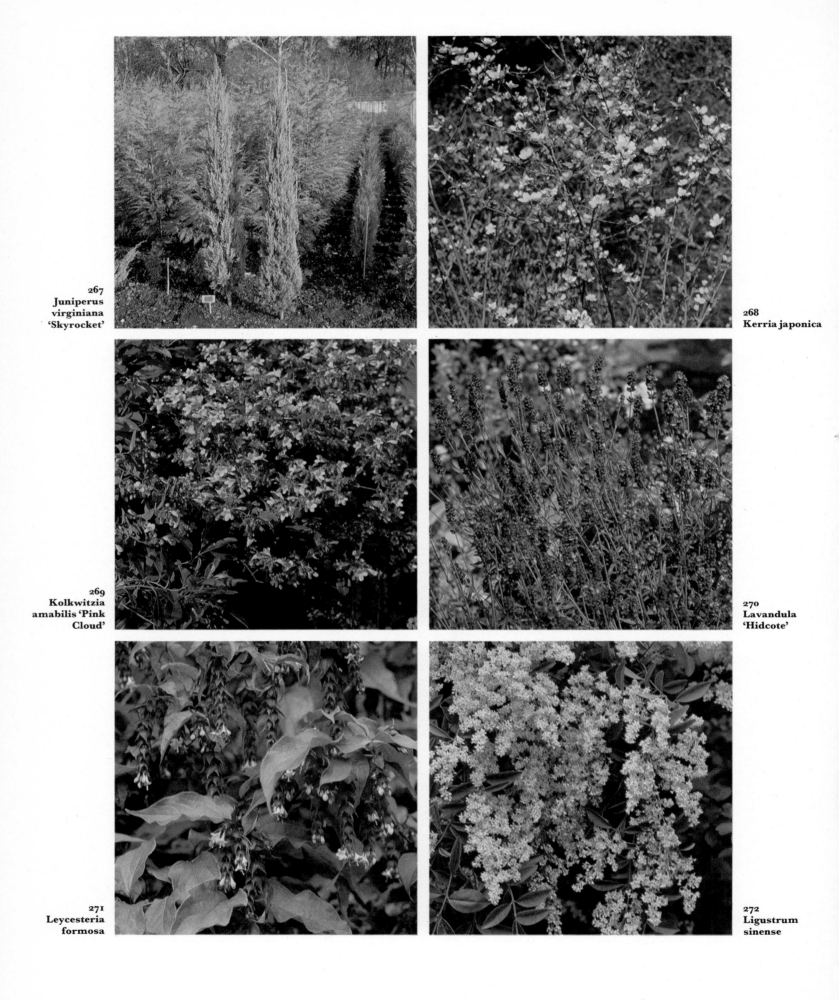

267
Juniperus
virginiana
'Skyrocket'

268
Kerria japonica

269
Kolkwitzia
amabilis 'Pink
Cloud'

270
Lavandula
'Hidcote'

271
Leycesteria
formosa

272
Ligustrum
sinense

273
Lithospermum
diffusum
'Grace Ward'

274
Lonicera ×
americana

275
Lonicera
japonica
'Halliana'

276
Lonicera
maackii

277
Lonicera
maackii

278
Lonicera
periclymenum
'Serotina'

279
Lonicera ×
purpusii

280
Lonicera
sempervirens

281
Lonicera
tragophylla

282
Magnolia
cylindrica

283
Magnolia
liliiflora
'Nigra'

284
Magnolia ×
loebneri
'Leonard
Messel'

285
Magnolia sinensis

286
Magnolia × **soulangiana**

287
Magnolia × **soulangiana 'Lennei'**

288
Magnolia × **soulangiana 'Picture'**

289
Magnolia × **soulangiana 'Rustica Rubra'**

290
Magnolia stellata

291
Magnolia
wilsonii

292
Mahonia
japonica

293
Mahonia
× media
'Charity'

294
Malus 'Golden
Hornet'

295
Malus
sieboldii

296
Menziesia
ciliicalyx

297
Moltkia
suffruticosa

298
Myrtus
communis

299
Olearia mollis

300
Olearia ×
scilloniensis

301
Osmanthus
delavayi

302
Osmanthus
heterophyllus
'Variegatus'

303
Oxydendrum
arboreum

304
Paeonia
delavayi

305
Paeonia ×
lemoinei
'Argosy'

306
Paeonia
suffruticosa
'Godaishu'

307
Pernettya
mucronata

308
Pernettya
mucronata
'Atrococcinea'

309
Pernettya
mucronata
'Pink Pearl'

310
Pernettya
mucronata
'White Pearl'

311
Perovskia
atriplicifolia
'Blue Spire'

312
Philadelphus
coronarius
'Variegatus'

313
Philadelphus
× lemoinei

314
Phillyrea
decora

315
Phlomis
fruticosa

316
Picea abies
'Nidiformis'

317
Picea pungens
'Procumbens'

318
Pieris formosa
forrestii

319
Pieris japonica

320
Pieris japonica
'Blush'

321
Pieris japonica
'Variegata'

322
Pileostegia
viburnoides

323
Pinus
sylvestris
'Watereri'

324
Pittosporum
tenuifolium
'Garnettii'

325
Plagianthus
betulinus

326
Potentilla
arbuscula

327
Potentilla
arbuscula
'Goldfinger'

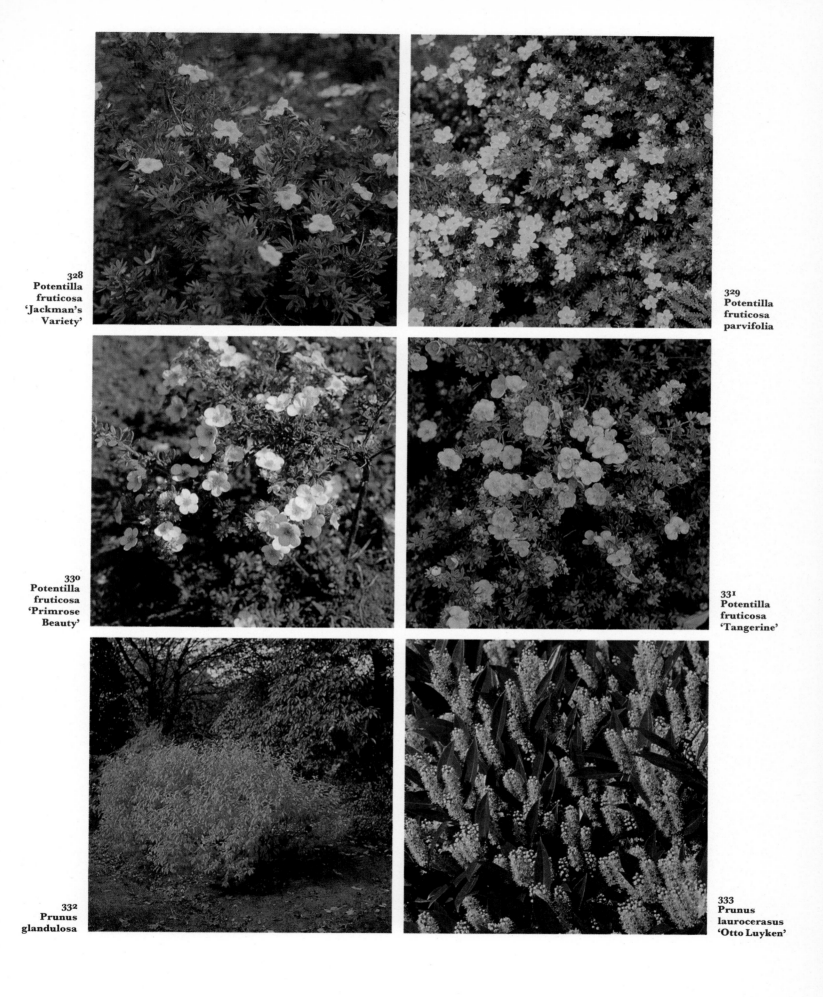

328
Potentilla
fruticosa
'Jackman's
Variety'

329
Potentilla
fruticosa
parvifolia

330
Potentilla
fruticosa
'Primrose
Beauty'

331
Potentilla
fruticosa
'Tangerine'

332
Prunus
glandulosa

333
Prunus
laurocerasus
'Otto Luyken'

334
Prunus
lusitanica
'Variegata'

335
Prunus mume
'Brightness'

336
Prunus tenella
'Fire Hill'

337
Pyracantha
atalantoides
'Aurea'

338
Pyracantha
coccinea
'Lalandei'

339
Pyracantha
'Mohave'

340
Pyracantha
rogersiana
'Flava'

341
Raphiolepis ×
delacourii

342
Rhododendron
augustinii

343
Rhododendron
calendulaceum

344
Rhododendron
calendulaceum

345
Rhododendron
griersonianum

346
Rhododendron
dauricum
'Midwinter'

347
Rhododendron
japonicum

348
Rhododendron
kaempferi

349
Rhododendron
kiusianum

350
Rhododendron
leucaspis

351
Rhododendron
lutescens

352
Rhododendron
luteum

353
Rhododendron
obtusum
'Amoenum'

354
Rhododendron
pemakoense

355
Rhododendron
racemosum

356
Rhododendron
reticulatum

357
Rhododendron
vaseyi

358
Rhododendron
viscosum

359
Rhododendron
williamsianum

360
Rhododendron
yakushimanum

361
Rhododendron
'Bluebird'

362
Rhododendron
'Blue Diamond'

363
Rhododendron
'Byron'

364
Rhododendron
'Cecile'

365
Rhododendron
'Choremia'

366
Rhododendron
'Christopher
Wren'

367
Rhododendron
'Cilpinense'

368
Rhododendron
'Coccinea
speciosa'

369
Rhododendron
'Crest'

370
Rhododendron
'Elizabeth'

372
Rhododendron
'Grosclaude'

373
Rhododendron
'Hinodegiri'

374
Rhododendron
'Hinomayo'

375
Rhododendron
'Homebush'

376
Rhododendron
'Hope Findlay'

377
Rhododendron
'Lady
Chamberlain'

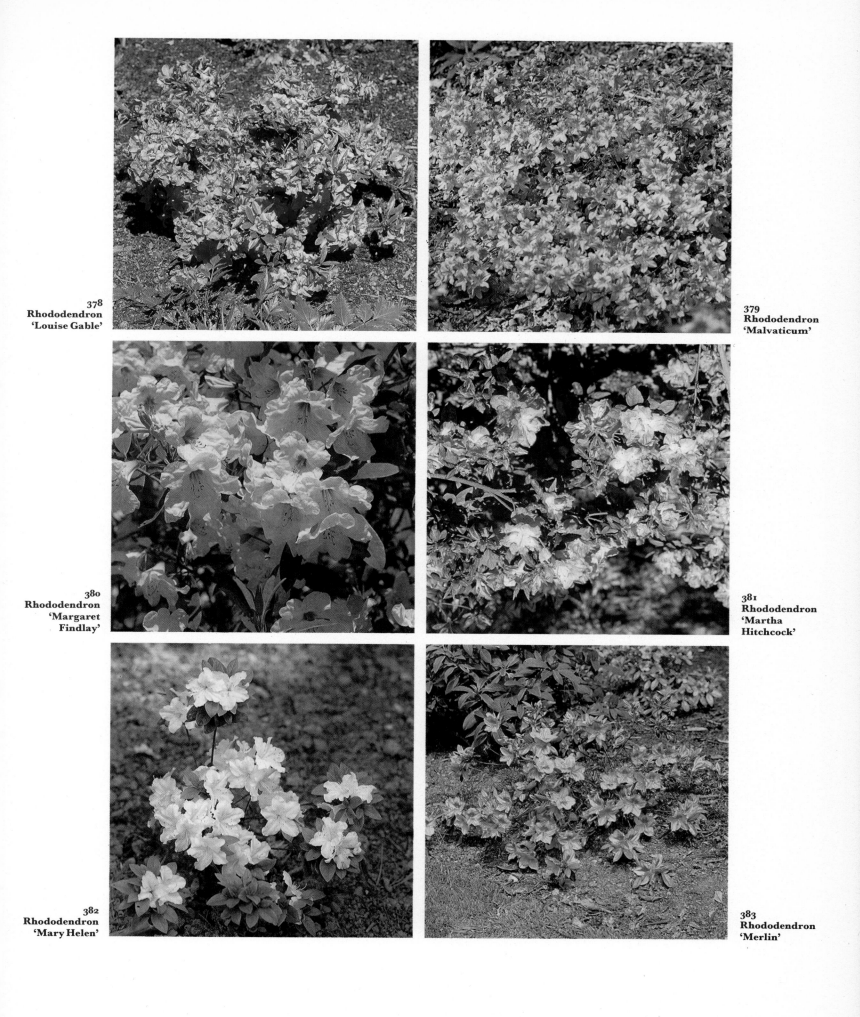

378
Rhododendron
'Louise Gable'

379
Rhododendron
'Malvaticum'

380
Rhododendron
'Margaret
Findlay'

381
Rhododendron
'Martha
Hitchcock'

382
Rhododendron
'Mary Helen'

383
Rhododendron
'Merlin'

384
Rhododendron
'Mother's Day'

385
Rhododendron
'Mrs G. W.
Leak'

386
Rhododendron
'Orange
Beauty'

387
Rhododendron
'Palestrina'

388
Rhododendron
'Praecox'

389
Rhododendron
'Queen
Elizabeth II'

390
Rhododendron
'Rasho-mon'

391
Rhododendron
'Red Rum'

392
Rhododendron
'Roman
Pottery'

393
Rhododendron
'Rosebud'

394
Rhododendron
'Seven Stars'

395
Rhododendron
'Tay'

396
Rhododendron
'Temple Belle'

397
Rhododendron
'Tessa'

398
Rhododendron
'Thames'

399
Rhododendron
'Trewithen
Orange'

400
Rhododendron
'Unique'

401
Rhododendron
'Venapens'

402
Rhododendron
'Vuyk's Rosyred'

403
Ribes
sanguineum
'Atrorubens'

404
Robinia hispida

405
Robinia
pseudoacacia
'Frisia'

406
Rosa
californica
'Plena'

407
Rosa
chinensis
mutabilis

408
Rosa davidii

409
Rosa farreri
persetosa

410
Rosa helenae

411
Rosa kordesii

412
Rosa
macrantha

413
Rosa ×
micrugosa
'Alba'

414
Rosa
multibracteata

415
Rosa ×
penzanceana

416
Rosa
virginiana

417
Rosa 'Alfred de
Dalmas'

418
Rosa
'Andersonii'

419
Rosa 'Anne of
Geierstein'

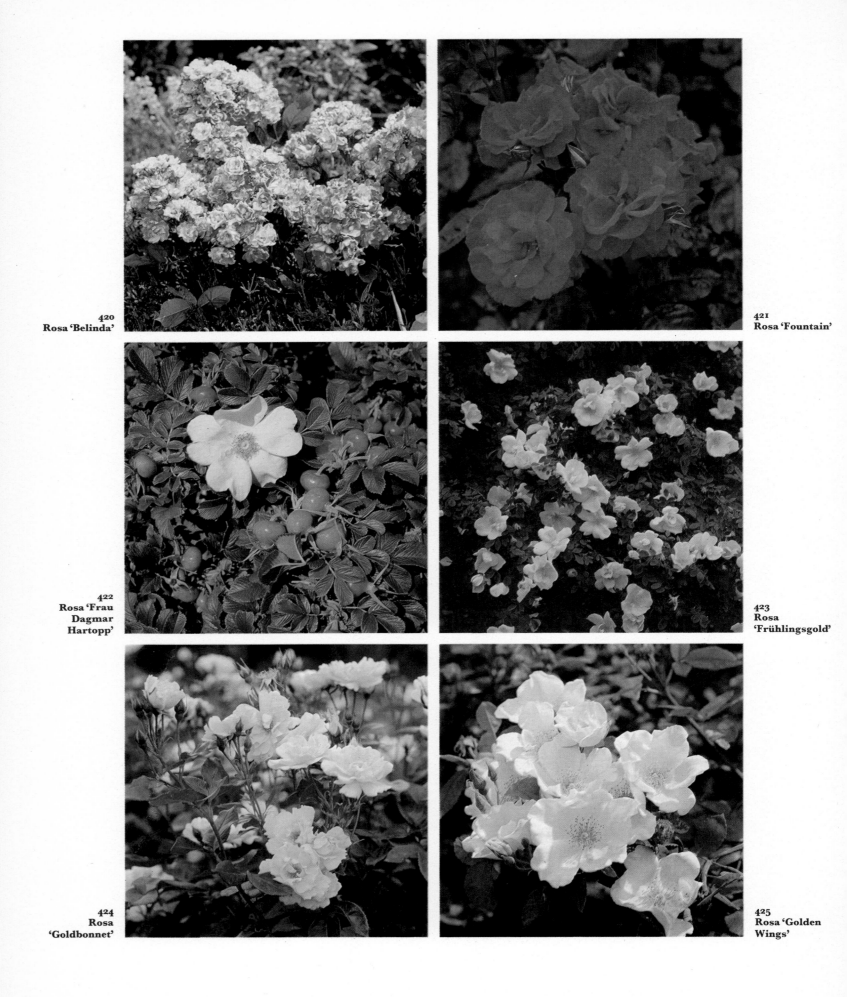

420
Rosa 'Belinda'

421
Rosa 'Fountain'

422
Rosa 'Frau
Dagmar
Hartopp'

423
Rosa
'Frühlingsgold'

424
Rosa
'Goldbonnet'

425
Rosa 'Golden
Wings'

426
Rosa
'Herbstfeuer'

427
Rosa 'Max
Graf'

428
Rosa 'Mozart'

429
Rosa
'Raubritter'

430
Rosa
'Scharlachglut'

431
Rosa
'Schneezwerg'

432
Rubus
cockburnianus

433
Rubus Tridel
'Benenden'

434
Ruta
graveolens
'Jackman's
Blue'

435
Ruta
graveolens
'Variegata'

436
Salix bockii

437
Salix
'Wehrhahnii'

438
Sambucus
racemosa
'Plumosa
Aurea'

439
Salix lanata
'Stuartii'

440
Santolina
virens

441
Sapium
japonicum

442
Sarcococca
hookerana
'Digyna'

443
Sciadopitys
verticillata

444
Senecio greyi

445
Sequoia
sempervirens
'Prostrata'

446
Skimmia
japonica

447
Skimmia
japonica
'Rubella'

448
Solanum
crispum
'Glasnevin'

449
Solanum
jasminoides
'Album'

450
Sorbus
cashmeriana

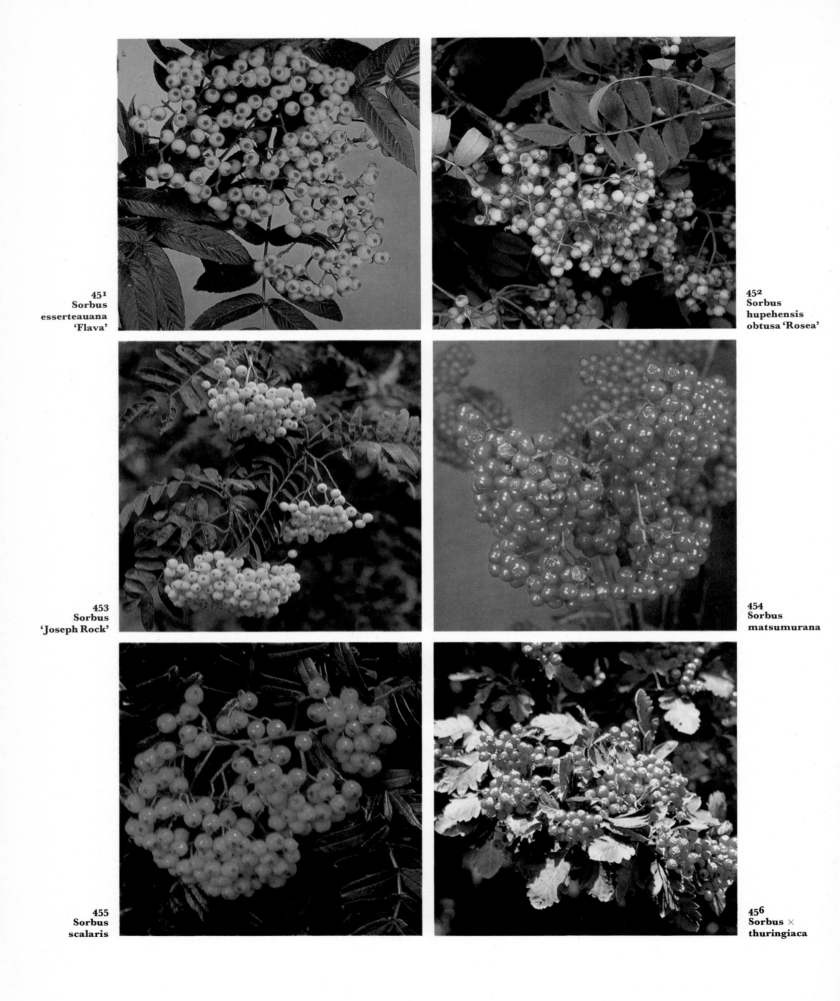

451
Sorbus
esserteauana
'Flava'

45²
Sorbus
hupehensis
obtusa 'Rosea'

453
Sorbus
'Joseph Rock'

454
Sorbus
matsumurana

455
Sorbus
scalaris

456
Sorbus ×
thuringiaca

457
Sorbus
matsumurana

458
Sorbus
vilmorinii

459
Spartium
junceum

460
Spiraea ×
bumalda

461
Spiraea
japonica
'Alpina'

462
Spiraea
nipponica
tosaensis

463
Spiraea
thunbergii

464
Stachyurus
praecox

465
Staphylea
pinnata

466
Stranvaesia
davidiana

467
Symphori-
carpos albus
laevigatus

468
Symplocos
paniculata

469
Syringa ×
hyacinthiflora
'Esther Staley'

470
Syringa
microphylla

471
Syringa ×
prestoniae
'Elinor'

472
Syringa ×
prestoniae
'Isabella'

473
Syringa
vulgaris 'Glory
of Hortenstein'

474
Syringa
vulgaris
'Monique
Lemione'

475
Syringa
vulgaris 'Mrs
Edward
Harding'

476
Syringa
vulgaris 'Paul
Thirion'

477
Syringa
vulgaris
'Vestale'

478
Thuya
occidentalis
'Ericoides'

479
Thuya
occidentalis
'Rheingold'

480
Thuya
orientalis
'Aurea Nana'

481
Thymus
carnosus

482
Ulex europaeus
'Plenus'

483
Ulmus ×
sarniensis
'Dicksonii'

484
Viburnum
alnifolium

485
Viburnum ×
bodnantense
'Dawn'

486
Viburnum
bodnantense
'Deben'

487
Viburnum
cassinoides

488
Viburnum
farreri
candidissimum

489
Viburnum
foetens

490
Viburnum
grandiflorum
'Snow White'

491
Viburnum
opulus

492
Viburnum
opulus
'Compactum'

493
Viburnum
opulus
'Xanthocarpum'

**494
Viburnum
tinus 'Eve
Price'**

495
Viburnum
'Park Farm
Hybrid'

496
Viburnum
plicatum
'Lanarth'

497
Viburnum
plicatum
'Mariesii'

498
Viburnum
sargentii

499
Viburnum
tinus

500
Weigela
'Bristol Ruby'

501
Weigela
florida
'Variegata'

502
Weigela
'Looymansii
Aurea'

503
Wisteria
sinensis

504
Yucca
filamentosa

505
Yucca flaccida
'Ivory'

506
Yucca gloriosa
'Nobilis'

The Dictionary

A

Aaron's Beard see *Hypericum calycinum*

ABELIA CAPRIFOLIACEAE ⊙

These shrubs may be propagated from summer cuttings under mist.

× *grandiflora* *(A. chinensis* × *A. uniflora)* △※
Glossy Abelia 1·5 m. (5 ft)

Origin unknown. Plant first described from a plant in the Ravelli Nurseries, Pallanza on Lake Maggiore, Italy. A medium sized shrub, semi-evergreen. Graceful in habit, this is the most ornamental of the really hardy abelias, its white and pink flowers have purplish spots and appear through July to October. Prune back half the branches to base each year. A.G.M. 1962. Z.5.

triflora **Himalayan Abelia** 3·05 m. (10 ft) ▼●

From North-west Himalaya. Introduced 1847. An erect growing but graceful shrub, deciduous. Flowers white delicately tinged with rose are scented and appear during the summer. Does not always flower freely, but when it does is very pretty. Persistent calyces surrounding fruits extend interest for some time. Z.7.

ABELIOPHYLLUM OLEACEAE ⊙

distichum **Korean Abeliophyllum** ▼※
2·45 m. (8 ft)

Korea. Introduced 1924. A beautiful early flowering deciduous shrub which grows very slowly to 90 cm.– 1·2 m. (3–4 ft) in the open garden. It flowers best on a west or south facing wall where it will, in time, reach 2·45 m. (8 ft). The white flowers are faintly tinged pink and in common with many winter flowering plants are pleasantly scented. They open in February in warm areas but up to mid-April in cool regions. An ideal plant for filling in a space at the base of other choice taller flowering shrubs on a warm wall where by pruning after flowering it can be fitted in. Such pruning keeps up a supply of new growths which when well ripened, especially after a good summer flower freely. Can be propagated by layering or cuttings of semi-hardwood growths in July in a propagating case. F.C.C. 1944. Z.5. **1**

ABUTILON MALVACEAE **Flowering Maple** ⊙

megapotamicum **Brazil Flowering Maple** ▼※
1·85–2·45 m. (6–8 ft)

From Brazil. Introduced 1864. Flowers pendulous, yellow petals with red calyx and purple anthers, freely produced in summer and autumn. A medium sized graceful shrub which requires shelter of a warm wall, where it is most attractive. In cold gardens some winter protection is necessary. Easily propagated by cuttings of young growths in spring or early summer, under mist or in a warm frame.

'Variegatum', a variegated form, the leaves being prettily mottled with yellow. Attractive outdoors but only thriving in the warmest regions.

ochensii see under *A.* × *suntense*

× *suntense* *(A. vitifolium* × *A. ochsenii)* ▼※
3·05 m. (10 ft)

A name used to cover crosses between *A. vitifolium* and *A. ochsenii*. Not fully hardy, these hybrids are of rapid growth especially if grown in a warm position, where they may attain 3·05 m. or more in two or three seasons. **2**

vitifolium **Grape-leaved Flowering Maple** ▼※
3·65 × 2·45 m. (12 × 8 ft)

Introduced from Chile in 1836. Flowers vary from pale to deep mauve. Not reliably hardy except in the warmest regions but will make a large shrub, size depending on the locality. Happiest in a sheltered sunny site, preferably with a wall at its back. Handsome with its grey-green leaves and saucer shaped flowers, it is a somewhat short lived plant. However, it grows quickly and readily from seed. Self-sown seedlings are frequently produced and occasionally these produce colour variations, and those of merit can be increased by cuttings in a warm frame. F.C.C. 1888.

'Album', a snow white form which generally comes true from seed, and is more impressive seen from a distance. **3**

Acacia,
  Common see *Robinia pseudoacacia*
  False see *Robinia pseudoacacia*
  Rose see *Robinia hispida*

ACER ACERACEAE **Maple** ⊙ ◖

palmatum **Japanese Maple** to 4·6 m. (15 ft) ▼●

Japan, central China, Korea. Introduced 1820. Flowers inconspicuous, but delicately formed leaves provide quite startling colour changes in autumn. A slow growing rounded shrub or small tree which is ideal for small gardens, but to give of its best requires a sheltered well drained site, either in sun or partial shade. There are many cultivars some of which have deservedly become very popular. *A. palmatum* can be grown from seed which should be sown in a fresh condition in autumn and in a sheltered site or a frame. Although plants can be produced from seed of cultivars, true plants are usually increased by grafting in spring under glass on seedlings of *A. palmatum*. No pruning except removal of dead or damaged wood required. A.G.M. 1969. Z.5.

'Dissectum', a green leaved form with deeply cut, finely divided leaves, very slow growing to 1·2 m. (4 ft), it only attains a few feet in several years.

Mushroom shaped until old when it becomes more rounded. A.G.M. 1956. **4**

'**Dissectum Atropurpureum**', is similar in habit but with deep purple leaves during summer. A.G.M. 1969. **5**

'**Osakazuki**', a cultivar with deeply toothed leaves, green during summer but one of the most brilliant in autumn when it becomes fiery scarlet. Grows to 1·2 m. (4 ft). A.G.M. 1969.

'**Senkaki**', **Coral Bark Maple**, during the winter months the coral red young stems are most effective, especially in sunshine. The leaves are beautiful at all stages of growth during summer, but most handsome in autumn in shades of yellow and orange. An invaluable shrub growing to about 3 m. (10 ft) and worth the good soil conditions it requires to give of its best. A.G.M. 1969. **6**

pseudoplatanus **Sycamore (U.K.),** ▼🍂
Sycamore Maple (U.S.)

'**Brilliantissimum**', a small tree, this plant is slow growing so it will not get out of hand in a medium sized garden. Specimens about 6·1 m. (20 ft) high are known but are very rare and generally it is more shrub like in size. It is worth planting because of its very distinctive colouring in spring when the young leaves are a brilliant shrimp pink. They eventually change to pale yellow and finally become green.

Adam's Needle (U.K.) see *Yucca gloriosa*
Adam's Needle (U.S.) see *Yucca filamentosa*

AESCULUS HIPPOCASTANACEAE
Horse Chestnut, Buckeye

× *mutabilis* ▼❋

First described in 1834. A large deciduous shrub which may, in time, become a small tree, producing red and yellow flowers in May and June. A group of hybrids thought to have arisen from the crossing of *A. discolor mollis* and *A. neglecta* or its shrubby form *A. neglecta georgiana*.

'**Induta**', a deciduous shrub which slowly attains some size, and was known originally as *A. rosea nana*. The rather attractive pinkish apricot flowers with yellow markings are freely borne and last for several weeks. This plant arose in Hesses' nurseries in Germany. A rare plant in cultivation. **7**

parviflora **Bottlebrush Buckeye,** ▼❋
Dwarf Horse Chestnut 2·45–4·6 m. (8–15 ft)
South east U.S. A very fine flowering shrub with red stamened, white flowers which are produced during July and August. These flower panicles are up to about 30 cm. (1 ft) long. An added asset is the foliage which becomes beautifully coloured before the leaves fall in the autumn. A.G.M. 1969.

rosea nana see *A.* × *mutabilis* '**Induta**'

Alexandrian Laurel see *Danae racemosa*
Almond,
   Dwarf Russian see *Prunus tenella*
   Dwarf Flowering see *Prunus glandulosa*
Alternated-leaved Dogwood see *Cornus alternifolia*
Althea, Shrubby see *Hibiscus syriacus*

AMELANCHIER ROSACEAE **Snowy Mespilus,**
June Berry

confusa syn. *A. canadensis* 3·65 m. (12 ft) ▼❋🍂
North America. Flowers white, freely borne in spring. A medium to large shrub which suckers, thriving best in moist situations. Leaves assume brilliant scarlet colours in autumn. An easily grown dual season shrub which does not require pruning. A.G.M. 1927. **8**

American
   Arbor-vitae see *Thuya occidentalis*
   Wayfaring Tree see *Viburnum alnifolium*
Anchor Plant see *Colletia cruciata*
Angelica Tree, Japanese see *Aralia elata*
Apple,
   Siberian Crab see under *Malus* × *robusta*
   Toringo Crab see *Malus sieboldii*
Apricot, Japanese see *Prunus mume*

ARALIA ARALIACEAE

elata **Japanese Angelica Tree** △🍂
1·85–2·45 m. (6–8 ft)
Japan, South-east Asia. Introduced about 1830. Flowers small and white in large panicles. Usually a large suckering shrub with pithy shiny stems and large leaves some 90 cm. (3 ft) long and 60 cm. (2 ft) wide. Very effective as a foliage plant and especially attractive when it flowers. No pruning is required. *A. elata* is easily

---

Abbreviations and symbols used in the text

▼	Deciduous	†	Lime hater
△	Evergreen	◍	Shade
❋	Flowers	◐	Semi shade
●	Fruit	⊙	Sun
🍂	Foliage		

A.G.M.   Award of Garden Merit, Royal Horticultural Society
F.C.C.   First Class Certificate, Royal Horticultural Society

Z1–10   The Z numbers represent the climatic zones used in the United States and provide a useful hardiness rating elsewhere. Thus Z1 is for those plants surviving coldest conditions and Z10 is the other extreme

The illustration numbers are in **bold type**.

propagated by removing small suckers, which should be potted and established in a warm greenhouse. Apt to become rampant in warm climates, such as eastern U.S. and in these regions the varieties listed below should be considered instead. The handsome variegated forms are increased by grafting on the common form, but production of suitable material is very slow. Z.3.

'Albo-marginata' see **'Variegata'**
'Aureovariegata', a cultivar in which the leaflets have irregular golden margins in spring. Later in summer it becomes similar to *A. elata* 'Variegata'. **9**
'Variegata', a form in which the leaflets have irregular margins of creamy white. A handsome and beautiful variegated shrub sometimes known as 'Albo-marginata'.

Aralia, Japanese see *Fatsia japonica*
Arbor-vitae see *Thuya*
Arbor-vitae,
   American see *Thuya occidentalis*
   Chinese see *Thuya orientalis*
   Oriental see *Thuya orientalis*

ARCTOSTAPHYLOS ERICACEAE

uva-ursi **Red Bearberry** 15 cm. (6 in.) △●
Cool regions Northern hemisphere. A creeping evergreen alpine shrub which forms a very useful ground cover plant. The flowers of the Red Bearberry which appear from April onwards, are small, pinkish and quietly attractive. These are succeeded by smooth, shining red fruits. Easily grown on any well drained soil and is ideal for furnishing sandy banks, or sprawling over boulders or tree stumps. Easily propagated by tip cuttings in a close frame in August and September. **10**

Ardoin Broom see *Cytisus ardoinii*
Arolla Pine see *Pinus cembra*

ARTEMISIA COMPOSITAE ◉

abrotanum **Southernwood, Lads Love** ▼🔄
90 cm. (3 ft)
Southern Europe. Cultivated since 16th century. Flowers dull yellow, of little beauty, infrequently produced. A great favourite particularly in cottage gardens, for its finely divided grey-green aromatic leaves. Easily propagated from summer cuttings. Can be pruned hard in spring if desired. A hardy plant. Z.5.

arborescens **Shrubby Wormwood** ▼🔄
1·2–1·85 m. (4–6 ft)
Southern Europe. Introduced 1640. Flowers bright yellow, but of secondary importance. Grown for its finely filigreed silvery foliage. Liable to succumb in severe winters so requires a warm, sunny, well drained position. Easily propagated, young plants can be over

wintered under glass as a safeguard. Z.7–8. **11**

ARUNDINARIA GRAMINEAE

variegata 90 cm. (3 ft) △🔄
Japan. Cultivated before 1863. A plant of tufted habit, generally regarded as the best of the white variegated bamboos. It is a pretty plant, useful in autumn and suitable for small gardens. Spreads quite quickly and is easily increased by division. Z.6. **12**

viridistriata syn. *Pleioblastus viridistriatus* △🔄
to 1·2 m. (4 ft)
Japan. Introduced about 1870. A very hardy and beautiful little bamboo. The narrow dark green leaves have longitudinal yellow stripes which frequently overwhelm the green. The erect purplish green canes form into small patches which, if cut back to ground level, will encourage new canes which produce the most colourful foliage.

Ash,
   Japanese Mountain see *Sorbus matsumurana*
   Mountain see *Sorbus*
   Vilmerin Mountain see *Sorbus vilmorinii*
Ashy Woadwaxen see *Genista cinerea*
Asiatic Symplocos see *Symplocos paniculata*

ATRIPLEX CHENOPODIACEAE

halimus **Tree Purslane** △/▼🔄
1·5–1·85 m. (5–6 ft)
Southern Europe. Cultivated since early 17th century. Flowers small, greenish and of little garden value. A useful silvery grey, medium sized, semi-evergreen shrub which can be used, in the background, to lighten dark-leaved plants. One of the best seaside shrubs standing salt spray well enough to be used in a protective capacity for choicer plants. It needs a light soil and indeed in the U.S. is not considered suitable for cultivation unless grown in seaside conditions or on dry sandy soil. Usually grows from 1·5–1·85 m. either way. Can be cut back in spring if desired. Can be increased by cuttings during summer in a cold frame. Z.7. **13**

AUCUBA CORNACEAE

japonica 2–3·05 m. (6½–10 ft) △🔄●
Japan. Introduced 1783. Flowers of little garden value, but succeeded by bright red fruits in female forms where pollination has taken place from a nearby male plant. A very useful shrub especially for growing in shade in conjunction with trees. Very popular early in the century, particularly in its variegated leaved forms, but it has become neglected, a whim of fashion. There are however, signs of a return to favour, not only for privacy in the garden in winter, but also for window boxes, urns and as a house plant. F.C.C. 1864, A.G.M. 1969.

Autumn Cherry see *Prunus subhirtella* 'Autumnalis'

Azalea mollis see under *Rhododendron japonicum*

Azaleas see *Rhododendron*

Azalea,
Yellow see *Rhododendron luteum*
Flame see *Rhododendron calendulaceum*
Kirishima see *Rhododendron obtusum*
Kyushu see *Rhododendron kiusianum*
Swamp see *Rhododendron viscosum*

B

Bamboo see *Sasa veitchii*
Bamboo, Sacred see *Nandina domestica*
Bamboo, White Variegated see *Arundinaria variegata*
Barberry see *Berberis*
Barberry,
Common see *Berberis vulgaris*
Darwin's see *Berberis darwinii*
Japanese see *Berberis thunbergii*
Bay, Sweet see *Laurus*
Bay Laurel see *Laurus nobilis*
Bearberry, Red see *Arctostaphylos*
Beauty Berry see *Callicarpa bodinieri*
Beauty Bush see *Kolkwitzia amabilis*
Bell Heather see *Erica cinerea*
Bells, Golden see *Forsythia*

BERBERIS BERBERIDACEAE **Barberry** ⊙

These shrubs are easily grown on any well drained soil, flowering and fruiting most freely when planted in open sunny sites. Pruning is seldom required, but old wood may be removed, or the plant reduced in size in spring.

atrocarpa 1·5 m. (5 ft) △

West Szechwan, China. Introduced 1909. Flowers light yellow in clusters in April and May. An evergreen shrub with smooth deep green foliage. Makes a fine impenetrable hedge, which will withstand close clipping. Z.7.

'Barbarossa' 1·85 m. (6 ft) ▼●

A vigorous shrub belonging to the Carminea Group of seedlings which show the influence of *B. aggregata* in their inflorescences, when crossed by chance with other species such as *B. wilsoniae subcaulialata*. This cultivar produces its red berries in pendulous profusion, arching their branches with their weight. Will not come true from seed so must be increased by cuttings. Firm young growths can be taken in August and rooted under mist or in a cold frame. **14**

darwinii Darwin's Barberry △❋🍂●
1·85 m. (6 ft)

Chile, Chiloe and Argentine. Discovered in 1835 by

Charles Darwin. Introduced in 1849. Flowers orange, tinged red, followed by striking purplish blue berries in early autumn. One of the finest evergreen early spring flowering shrubs averaging about 1·85 m. although attaining more in sheltered gardens or good soil. Prefers a soil which is reasonably moist, if poor is apt to get thin at base of plant. Can be raised from seed and will grow on chalk and limey soil. Limited in the U.S. to the south eastern states where it grows to about 90 cm. (3 ft) high. F.C.C. 1967, A.G.M. 1930. **15**

linearifolia 1·85–2·45 m. (6–8 ft) △❋

Argentine, Chile. Flowers rich orange and apricot in the spring and occasionally later in the year. A somewhat ungainly, medium sized, shrub but with the best coloured flowers in the genus. An evergreen with dark green glossy leaves which does best where sheltered from cold winds. Does well on chalk and limey soil. F.C.C. 1931.

× *lologensis* (*B. darwinii* × *B. linearifolia*) △❋🍂●
1·5–1·85 m. (5–6 ft)

Argentine, found growing with the parents in 1927. A natural hybrid. A beautiful, medium sized, evergreen shrub, intermediate between its parents but with larger flowers. **16**

× *ottawensis* (*B. vulgaris* × *B. thunbergii*) ▼●

A group of deciduous shrubs, hybrids between *B. vulgaris* and *B. thunbergii*, which were the result of a cross made early in this century at the Ottawa Experimental Station in Canada. Similar hybrids have also arisen in gardens.

'Superba', is an outstanding shrub and the best known form of this cross raised in Holland by Ruys. It is sometimes found in nursery lists as *B. thunbergii atropurpurea* 'Superba'. Growing 1·85 m. (6 ft) high or more in good soil this vigorous shrub with arching branches clothed with reddish purple leaves which turn crimson before leaf fall in autumn. It has red fruits. A.G.M. 1969. Z.4. **17**

Abbreviations and symbols used in the text

▼ Deciduous	† Lime hater
△ Evergreen	⦶ Shade
❋ Flowers	⦷ Semi shade
● Fruit	⊙ Sun
🍂 Foliage	

A.G.M. Award of Garden Merit, Royal Horticultural Society

F.C.C. First Class Certificate, Royal Horticultural Society

Z1–10 The Z numbers represent the climatic zones used in the United States and provide a useful hardiness rating elsewhere. Thus Z1 is for those plants surviving coldest conditions and Z10 is the other extreme

The illustration numbers are in **bold type**.

---

sargentiana 2·45 m. (8 ft)

West China. Introduced by Wilson 1907. A large evergreen shrub which is very hardy and well armed with inch long sharp rigid spines. The sweetly scented yellow flowers in March and April are decorative, but not spectacular and are followed by black fruits. A very useful evergreen especially in public gardens subject to vandalism. Especially ornamental in autumn when some of the leaves become scarlet. F.C.C. 1916. **18**

× *stenophylla* (*B. darwinii* × *B. empetrifolia*)
2·45 m. (8 ft)

An indispensable shrub where there is room. A natural hybrid found in a Sheffield, England nursery about 1860. Flowers golden yellow, very freely produced in April. A graceful evergreen with slender arching shoots wreathed with flowers. One of the most lovely sights in spring this berberis makes an excellent informal hedge, which should be cut back immediately after flowering. Propagated by cuttings in a cold frame in August. Many forms have been raised. F.C.C. 1864, A.G.M. 1923. Z.5 (deciduous), Z.7 + (evergreen). **19**

> **'Gracilis'**, is one of the most useful forms for small gardens. It is a graceful shrub, 90 cm. (3 ft) or so in height, with golden yellow flowers and bright green leaves.

thunbergii Japanese Barberry (U.S.)
1·2–1·5 m. (4–5 ft)

China, Japan, seen in Japan by Thunberg in 1784. Introduced to cultivation about 1874. Flowers pale yellow, suffused red, followed by bright red berries. Grown mainly for its brilliant autumn colour and berries and makes a useful hedge. F.C.C. 1890, A.G.M. 1927. Z.4.

> *atropurpurea*, arose in a French nursery around 1913, being distributed about 1926. Generally propagated from seeds this is, when grown in full sun, one of the best purple foliaged shrubs. Grows slightly taller than the type and, like it, makes a good informal hedge. A.G.M. 1932.
> **'Atropurpurea Nana'**, Little Favourite, Crimson Pygmy (U.S.), a dwarf shrub generally under 60 cm. (2 ft) in height raised in Holland about 1942. Useful for massing with its brownish red leaves, almost thornless, it also makes a nice dwarf hedge. A.G.M. 1969.
> *atropurpurea* 'Superba' see *B.* × *ottawensis* 'Superba'
> **'Aurea'**, a recent introduction, has bright yellow leaves which turn pale green by early autumn. **20**
> **'Rose Glow'**, also recently introduced, is a striking shrub. Purple leaves on young growths, are flecked and striped pink becoming purple as they mature. Odd branches revert on occasion, these should be removed.

vulgaris Common Barberry
1·85–3 m. (6–10 ft)

A deciduous shrub, a native of many parts of Europe, including Britain, north Africa and temperate areas of Asia. An introduced plant in north America it is now naturalized there. It is a useful and ornamental shrub for large gardens, quite attractive in blossom during May and even more so when in fruit. The pendulous clusters of bright red, translucent berries are very handsome and were, at one time, preserved in sugar and considered to be a delicacy. A host of wheat rust in the country.

> **'Atropurpurea'**, is a handsome shrub with vinous purple foliage which is striking in contrast to the pendulous racemes of yellow flowers. Must be grown from cuttings as plants grown from seed vary considerably in shade.

wilsoniae 90 cm. (3 ft)

Western China, discovered and introduced about 1904. Flowers small, pale yellow, followed by an abundant crops of coral red berries. An elegant, generally deciduous shrub of spreading habit, under 90 cm. (3 ft) in height. Its great value for gardens lies in its combination of autumn tints and prettily coloured berries. The true plant should be propagated by cuttings. F.C.C. 1907, A.G.M. 1969.

> *subcaulialata*, a taller variety from Western China, differing from the type in its glabrous shoots and larger leaves. Introduced in 1908. **21**

Berry,
> **Beauty** see *Callicarpa bodinieri*
> **June** see *Amelanchier*

Bindweed see *Convolvulus*
Biscay Heath see *Erica erigena*
Black Locust see *Robinia pseudoacacia*
Bladder Nut see *Staphylea*
Bladder Senna see *Colutea*
Blue
> **Blossom** see *Ceanothus thyrsiflorus*
> **Leadwort, Willmott** see *Ceratostigma willmottianum*

Bluebeard see *Caryopteris* × *clandonensis*
Bottlebrush Buckeye see *Aesculus parviflora*
Box see *Buxus*
Box, Christmas see *Sarcococca*
Bramble see *Rubus*
Brazil Flowering Maple see *Abutilon megapotamicum*
Bridal Wreath see *Spiraea* × *arguta*
Brier, Penzance see *Rosa* 'Anne of Geierstein'
Broom see *Cytisus*
Broom,
> **Ardoin** see *Cytisus ardoinii*
> **Common** see *Cytisus scoparius*
> **Morocco** see *Cystisus battandieri*
> **Mount Etna** see *Genista aetnensis*
> **Purple** see *Cytisus purpureus*
> **Scotch** see *Cytisus scoparius*
> **Spanish** see *Genista hispanica* and *Spartium junceum*
> **White Portuguese** see *Cytisus multiflorus*

Buckeye, Bottlebrush see *Aesculus parviflora*
Buckthorn, Sea see *Hippophae rhamnoides*

BUDDLEIA LOGANIACEAE
These shrubs are easily grown from seed, indeed self-grown seedlings are frequently found and it has become naturalized in some areas by this means. Seedlings show considerable variation in habit and colour and are frequently inferior to their parents. Cultivars or selected forms should be increased by cuttings. Firm young growths root easily under mist in summer, while ripe young wood can also be used in autumn on a sheltered border. They are more effective when grown in good soil.

alternifolia **Fountain Buddleia**
2·1–4·25 m. (7–14 ft)
China. Described in 1880 but not introduced until 1915. Flowers soft purple-lilac, with a delicate fragrance, from mid-May to June. A beautiful shrub 2·1 m. high which can be trained into a small elegant tree, when it is much more impressive, at double the height. The graceful arching branches should be pruned back nearly to their base immediately after flowering. Easily propagated from cuttings. A.G.M. 1924. **22**

crispa to 4·55 m. (15 ft)
Afghanistan, Himalaya and North India. Introduced 1850. Flowers lilac with orange throat, freely produced in late summer and fragrant. A medium sized shrub of 1·5 m. (5 ft) when pruned hard in March, when it will be quite at home in the mixed border. Stems and leaves are covered with a white woolly felt which enhances the appearance of the plant. May also be grown on a wall. A.M. 1961. **23**

davidii syn. *B. variabilis*
Butterfly Bush 2·1–2·75 m. (7–9 ft)
Central and western China. Discovered in 1869, introduced later. The flowers appear in late summer and are fragrant. Frequently called the Butterfly Bush because of the attraction the flowers have for butterflies, thus providing an extra bonus. A deciduous, medium sized shrub, often found naturalized. Gives best results if pruned hard in March. The species is seldom planted in gardens as there are now many superior cultivars more suitable for this purpose, a large proportion of these were raised in the U.S. A selection follows. Z.5.
  'Black Knight', 2·75 m. (9 ft), very deep purple. A.G.M. 1969.
  'Charming', 2·75 m. (9 ft), lavender pink.
  'Empire Blue', 2·75 m. (9 ft), rich violet-blue with orange eye. A.G.M. 1969.
  'Fortune', 2·75 m. (9 ft), arching spikes of lilac with orange eye. A.G.M. 1969.
  'Harlequin', 2·1 m. (7 ft), wine red flowers but with leaves conspicuously variegated creamy white.
  'Royal Red', 2·75 m. (9 ft), long spikes of wine red. A.G.M. 1969. **24**
  'White Profusion', 2·1 m. (7 ft), white, abundantly produced on side growths with rusty coloured heads of seeds following. A.G.M. 1969.**25**

globosa **Orange Ball Tree,**
Globe Butterfly Bush 3·65 (12 ft)
Chile, Peru. Introduced 1774. Flowers deep yellow, fragrant. An erect large shrub growing up to 3·65 m. (12 ft) or more in a sheltered position. The attractive foliage is semi-evergreen, except in severe winters when it becomes deciduous. Its ball like flowers are freely produced in May and June. There is a pronounced honey fragrance. Such pruning as may be required should be carried out after flowering. **26**

'Lochinch' 2·1 m. (7 ft)
A cross between *B. davidii* × *B. fallowiana*, making a medium sized shrub, more compact in habit than the *B. davidii* cultivars. The flower spikes, which appear in late summer, are lavender in colour, scented and the young leaves are soft grey. A.G.M. 1969. **27**

variabilis see *B. davidii*

× *weyerana* (*B. davidii magnifica* ×
B. globosa) 2·1–2·45 m. (7–8 ft)
An unusual hybrid, raised in 1914 by Van de Weyer, Dorset. The ball shaped flowers are orange yellow shaded with pink and mauve, and are borne on long slender panicles on the young wood during the summer months. Z.7.

Burning Bush see *Cotinus coggygria*
Bush
  Honeysuckles see *Lonicera*
  Morning Glory see *Convolvulus cneorum*
  Poppy see *Dendromecon rigida*
Bushes, Daisy see *Olearia*
Buttercup Winter Hazel see *Corylopsis pauciflora*
Butterfly Bush see *Buddleia davidii*
Butterfly Bush, Globe see *Buddleia globosa*

Abbreviations and symbols used in the text

▼ Deciduous   † Lime hater
△ Evergreen   ◍ Shade
❊ Flowers   ◐ Semi shade
● Fruit   ☉ Sun
🍂 Foliage

A.G.M. Award of Garden Merit, Royal Horticultural Society
F.C.C. First Class Certificate, Royal Horticultural Society

Z1–10 The Z numbers represent the climatic zones used in the United States and provide a useful hardiness rating elsewhere. Thus Z1 is for those plants surviving coldest conditions and Z10 is the other extreme

The illustration numbers are in **bold type**.

BUXUS BUXACEAE **Box**

sempervirens **Common Box** △◐

Europe, North Africa and western Asia. Flowers pale green in April. A large shrub, even on occasion a small tree, which produces masses of small dark green leaves. Very adaptable to pruning, it is much used for topiary work and hedges. It has given rise to a large number of forms. Z.5.

'Elegantissima', a small slow growing box, which will eventually attain 90 cm. (3 ft). The small leaves are grey-green, daintily edged cream, giving an all over matt silver effect. Attractive as a specimen shrub which retains its colour in a shady position.

'Suffruticosa', a dwarf form, much used as an edging plant in formal gardens and for edging paths, although not now so popular for the latter purpose. Can be kept down to 15 cm. (6 in.) by annual clipping; if allowed to grow naturally can attain 90 cm.–1·2m. (3–4 ft).

'Aureovariegata', a medium sized evergreen shrub of dense, bushy habit. The leaves are splashed, striped or mottled with creamy yellow. Very effective as a specimen, this form of the Common Box is very amenable to judicious pruning, in common with others, so that its size can be kept compatible with its particular situation. **28**

'Vardar Valley', introduced by Arnold Arboretum U.S., 1957, found in the Vardar Valley of the Balkans in 1935. Very hardy form, low, flat-topped, attractive throughout the winter.

C

Calico Bush see *Kalmia latifolia*
California Rose see *Rosa californica*
Californian
    Fuchsia see *Zauschneria californica*
    Lilac see *Ceanothus*
    Poppy Bush see *Dendromecon rigida*

CALLICARPA VERBENACEAE ⊙

Callicarpas may be grown from seeds and such plants show considerable variation in form. Good or named forms can be increased by rooting firm cuttings in summer under mist.

bodinieri **Beauty Berry** 1·8 m. (6 ft) ▼◐●

China, discovered by Henry 1887. Flowers although freely produced are insignificant, pink in colour. An erect deciduous shrub, which bears deep lilac fruits. Foliage assumes rosy purple shades in autumn.

giraldii, a medium sized shrub which differs from the type in having less downy inflorescences. The lilac flowers are produced in late summer and succeeded by masses of fruits which vary from lilac to purple and violet. The fruits are most generously produced where several plants are grown in close proximity and given adequate nourishment in a sunny position. Very striking in October and November. F.C.C. 1924. Z.5–6. **29**

dichotoma 1·2–1·5 m. (4–5 ft) ▼●

This is a more compact shrub with deep lilac to violet-purple fruits. Z.5–6.

japonica 1·2–1·5 m. (4–5 ft) ▼◐✳●

Oval-leaved, deciduous shrub with pale pink flowers and violet fruits.

'Leucocarpa', a white fruited form of *C. japonica*.

CALLUNA ERICACEAE ⊙ ◑

vulgaris **Heather, Ling** 90 cm. (3 ft) △✳●◐

An evergreen shrub growing from a few inches to about 90 cm. in height, according to soil conditions. Dwarf compact plants, better for garden purposes, will be produced, on poorish soil with some peat or organic matter added. Particularly beautiful in late summer and autumn, a large number of forms have arisen, some of which with coloured foliage continue the display into the winter months. Heathers thrive best in the full sun, flowering more freely and certainly providing better colour in the foliage cultivars. Pruning, if required when plants are becoming too tall and straggly, can be carried out after flowering, or in the case of foliage forms, in the spring when a light trim over with garden shears will be effective. Propagation by layering during spring or autumn will provide a limited number of plants. Where numbers are required firm young growths made into cuttings can be inserted in sandy peat in a cold frame in late summer. Seed may also be used, self sown seedlings are frequently found, but although interesting plants will be obtained, garden forms will not reproduce true plants by this method. Very useful ground cover plants, especially for banks, taller forms are useful for cutting for indoor decoration. A.G.M. 1969. Z.4.

'Alba', the well known White Heather which is greatly prized, particularly in Scotland where it is frequently credited with bringing good luck. 45–60 cm. (1½–2 ft).

'Alba Plena', a form with double white flowers. 45 cm. (1½ ft). A.G.M. 1969.

'County Wicklow', dwarf spreading form with double shell pink flowers. 23 cm. (9 in.). A.G.M. 1969.

'Darkness', a cultivar which produces beautiful crimson flowers in August and September. Growing 30 cm. (1 ft) in height it is compact in growth and is very effective when seen from some distance. **30**

'Elsie Purnell', double silvery pink flowers with more deeply coloured buds, in long sprays, useful for cutting. 75 cm. (2½ ft).

'Golden Feather', an attractive foliage plant, the golden feathery foliage changes to orange during winter months when it is most effective. 45 cm. (1½ ft). A.G.M. 1974. **31**

'**Gold Haze**', a white flowered form which has bright golden foliage throughout the year. A good plant. 60 cm. (2 ft). A.G.M. 1969. **32**

'**H. E. Beale**', long sprays of double silvery pink flowers lovely for cutting and useful as a pot plant. 60 cm. (2 ft). F.C.C. 1843, A.G.M. 1942. **33**

'**Hirsuta Typica**', stems and leaves present an attractive silvery appearance. Light mauve flowers in August and September on plants up to 45 cm. ($1\frac{1}{2}$ ft) in height. F.C.C. 1964. **34**

'**Peter Sparkes**', double, deep pink flowers in long sprays, a good late cultivar for the garden and as a pot plant. 45 cm. ($1\frac{1}{2}$ ft). A.G.M. 1969. **35**

'**Robert Chapman**', a good foliage plant, gold in spring, becoming orange and eventually red in winter with soft purple flowers. 45 cm. ($1\frac{1}{2}$ ft). A.G.M. 1965. **36**

'**Serlei**', long sprays of white flowers on an erect plant. 60 cm. (2 ft) A.G.M. 1969.

'**Serlei Aurea**', similar to above but with brighter golden foliage, which I find attractive. **37**

'**Tib**', an early cultivar, with soft reddish purple double flowers, very freely produced making quite a splash of colour. 45 cm. ($1\frac{1}{2}$ ft). **38**

Camellia, Common see *Camellia japonica*

CAMELLIA THEACEAE   ⊙ ◑ † △ ✳

'**Cornish Snow**'   3·05 m. (10 ft)
A free growing open shrub, with narrow burnished leaves, coppery coloured when young, and bearing innumerable small white flowers over a lengthy period. A.G.M. 1963. **39**

'**Inspiration**'   3·05 m. (10 ft)
A good upright grower, producing its semi-double pink flowers in masses. **40**

japonica **Common Camellia**   over 3 m. (10 ft)
Japan and Korea. Introduced 1739. A large shrub, eventually a small tree except in very favoured gardens where it will attain considerable size. One of the most valuable evergreens, with deep glossy green leaves and a much branched habit. Hardy in England and only the southern states of U.S., except in very exposed cold gardens, camellias were formerly important denizens of greenhouses in large establishments, frequently having a special house devoted to their cultivation. During this century its merits for outside planting have been recognized, especially for woodland gardens in lime free soils. Flowering in winter and early spring, a situation shaded from the early morning sun is essential to prevent frost damage to the flowers. In cold bleak gardens treatment as wall plants is desirable, where some sun is available to encourage bud formation and ripen the wood. Pruning is required only to keep plants shapely or in bounds and is best carried out immediately after flowering. Propagation from summer cuttings of short lengths of young wood, inserted in sandy peat under mist is as a rule successful. Large numbers are generally propagated from leaves with the basal bud kept intact from which the young growth arises, again under mist. Layering may also be carried out where only a few plants are required. In addition to their uses in the garden and cool greenhouse, they are ideal plants for growing in tubs, being brought indoors to enjoy the flowers. Tub plants must not be allowed to suffer from lack of moisture, or bud dropping may result. Z.7.

There are a tremendous number of cultivars, far too many, and these are being constantly added to and many represent an advance on the older cultivars. A selection only can be mentioned.

'**Adolphe Audusson**', a bushy upright plant hardy and free flowering. Well-known and proven. Large semi-double flowers, blood red with reflexed petals and a bold tuft of stamens. 3 m. (10 ft). F.C.C. 1956, A.G.M. 1969. **41**

'**Akashigata**' see *C. japonica* '**Lady Clare**'

'**Amagashita**' see *C. japonica* '**Apollo**'

'**Ama-no-kawa**', a single flowered cultivar, introduced from Japan about 1938 by Sir James Horlick. Grows well into a nice shrub producing white flowers. **42**

'**Apollo**', syn. 'Amagashita'. One of the best garden plants, a good grower, with semi-double rose red flowers on well clothed open branches. 3 m. (10 ft). A.G.M. 1969. **43**

'**Chandleri Elegans**' see *C. japonica* '**Elegans**'

'**Donckelarii**', a good garden plant, bushy, upright in growth. Large semi-double flowers, red often splashed white. 2·45 m. (8 ft). A.G.M. 1969.

'**Elegans**', syn. 'Chandleri Elegans'. A well proved cultivar of open spreading form, with large anemone form flowers of deep pink, stamens of the same colour with some white petaloids. 2·45 m. (8 ft). F.C.C. 1958, A.G.M. 1969.

'**Frau Minna Seidel**' see *C. japonica* '**Pink Perfection**'

'**Gloire de Nantes**', a medium, compact grower, well

Abbreviations and symbols used in the text

▼ Deciduous   † Lime hater
△ Evergreen   ◉ Shade
✳ Flowers   ◑ Semi shade
● Fruit   ⊙ Sun
🍃 Foliage

A.G.M.   Award of Garden Merit, Royal Horticultural Society

F.C.C.   First Class Certificate, Royal Horticultural Society

Z1–10 The Z numbers represent the climatic zones used in the United States and provide a useful hardiness rating elsewhere. Thus Z1 is for those plants surviving coldest conditions and Z10 is the other extreme

The illustration numbers are in **bold type**.

proven in gardens. Semi-double carmine rose flowers, which come very early if grown under glass. 2·45 m. (8 ft). A.G.M. 1969. **45**

'**J. J. Whitfield**', an early flowering American cultivar, producing medium sized crimson flowers, in loose paeony shape. **44**

'**Lady Clare**', syn. 'Akashigata'. An old favourite of pendulous, spreading growth. Large semi-double pink flowers with creamy petaloids among the stamens. 2·45 m. (8 ft.). A.G.M. 1969. **46**

'**Pink Pearl**' see *C. japonica* '**Pink Perfection**'

'**Pink Perfection**', syn. 'Frau Minna Seidel', 'Usu-Otome', 'Pink Pearl'. An old very free flowering Japanese camellia of vigorous erect growth. The small double flowers are very formal in outline and shell pink in colour. **47**

'**Tricolor**', syn. 'Tricolor de Sieboldii'. A well formed cultivar of compact habit, medium sized flowers, semi-bold, white striped carmine. Red or white flowers are sometimes produced on the same plant. **48**

'**Tricolor de Sieboldii**' see *C. japonica* '**Tricolor**'

'**Usu-Otome**' see *C. japonica* '**Pink Perfection**'

'**Leonard Messel**' (*C. reticulata* × *C.* × *williamsii* '*Mary Christian*') over 3 m. (10 ft)

A very fine large shrub with dark green leaves which has become popular in a very short time. An upright grower which produces large semi-double flowers in deep pink which incline towards *C. reticulata*.

'**Salutation**' (*C. reticulata* × *C. saluenensis*) 3·05 m. (10 ft)

A good shrub with matt green leaves and open growth, with rather informal semi-double flowers of a delicate silvery pink.

× *williamsii* (*C. saluenensis* × *C. japonica*) 2·45–3·05 m. (8–10 ft)

This hybrid has proved to be one of the best of garden shrubs. A particular merit is that flowering takes place throughout winter and spring months, fading flowers falling naturally and replaced in succession by further blooms of exquisite beauty. There are many excellent varieties now available.

'**Brigadoon**', an open growing shrub with large, rose pink flowers which come in a succession and are of very high quality. Quite hardy in England.

'**Donation**' (*C. saluenensis* × *C. japonica* 'Donckelarii'). A vigorous erect grower to over 3 m. (10 ft), an outstanding shrub in any company. Flowering freely over a considerable period, lovely soft pink semi-double flowers, considered by many the best camellia. Excellent as a pot or tub plant. A.G.M. 1958. **49**

'**J. C. Williams**', a good shrub, somewhat arching in growth to 2·45 m. (8 ft), consequently is better staked when young. The first clone of this hybrid to be named. The single clear pink flowers have reflexing petals and are very freely produced. F.C.C. 1942, A.G.M. 1949. **50**

'**Parkside**', a larger leaved plant of somewhat pendant habit to 2·45 m. (8 ft). Large semi-double flowers of clear rose pink.

'**St Ewe**', a shrub with good dark glossy foliage and upright habit to 3 m. (10 ft). Flowering freely over a long period, the bright rose pink single flowers are somewhat bell shaped. **51**

'**Shocking Pink**', a good upright grower. The flowers are rich pink, very formal and double, a very distinct cultivar which has impressed me.

Cape
Figwort see *Phygelius capensis*
Fuchsia see *Phygelius capensis*

CARPENTERIA PHILADELPHACEAE
California. Introduced to Europe about 1880.

californica **Evergreen Mock Orange**   ☉ △ ✳
3·05 m. (10 ft)

A beautiful evergreen shrub which requires a sunny sheltered site, preferably backed by a wall. Pure white flowers produced June and July. Fragrant. In a warm area will attain a height of 3 m. or more. The large white flowers are much enhanced by conspicuous golden anthers. Should be propagated from cuttings or layers, since seedlings are apt to be poor in type. F.C.C. 1888, A.G.M. 1935. Z.7–8. **52**

CARYOPTERIS VERBENACEAE

× *clandonensis* **Bluebeard** 90 cm. (3 ft)   ☉ ▼ ✳
This is a group of hybrids derived from *C. incana* × *C. mongholica*. **53**
The original and typical clone is:

'**Arthur Simmonds**', a small shrub 90 cm. in height which produces a crop of bright blue flowers in September and October enhanced by greyish green foliage. Should be pruned early in April nearly to the base of the previous years growth. Easily rooted from cuttings, placed in a frame during summer. F.C.C. 1941, A.G.M. 1942.

'**Heavenly Blue**', introduced and popular in the U.S. Also available in England. Somewhat more compact than *C.* × *clandonensis* 'Arthur Simmonds'.

'**Kew Blue**', a deeper blue seedling of *C.* × *clandonensis* 'Arthur Simmonds' and like its parent a first class shrub for autumn, with flowers much appreciated by bees. Z.5.

CASSINIA COMPOSITAE

fulvida 1·5 m. (5 ft)   ☉ △ ☙
New Zealand. An evergreen shrub of dense habit and slightly heath-like in appearance. Flowers white in July. May attain a height of 1·5 m. or so and is useful for a golden effect in the garden, the twigs and underleaf

being covered with yellow down. Young growths are somewhat sticky. Some pruning back in spring may be required after a severe winter.

CASSIOPE ERICACEAE

'Muirhead' 20 cm (8 in.)   ⊙†△❀
A dwarf evergreen shrub around 20 cm. in height, a hybrid between *C. lycopodioides* × *C. wardii*. Raised by R. B. Cooke, this beautiful plant like others of the group, thrives best in peaty soil which does not dry out. The much forked shoots bear masses of white, nodding flowers in spring. Will withstand intense cold but are difficult to cultivate in warm areas. F.C.C. 1962. **54**

CEANOTHUS RHAMNACEAE   ⊙
Californian Lilac
Natives of North America and, generally, none too hardy in the British Isles. Most particularly evergreen kinds are more at home on sheltered walls than in open exposed conditions but some of the hybrids are hardier and do well in open borders provided the soil is well drained and sunny conditions overhead are available. Propagation by cuttings of young growths under mist or in a propagating frame will provide plants for increase, or replacement if a mature plant has succumbed in a severe winter. Young plants grow very fast, so any losses can soon be repaired.

'Cascade' 6·1 m. (20 ft)   △❀
This is generally considered to be a form of *C. thrysiflorus*, raised by Messrs Jackman, of Woking, England. A tall arching shrub which can reach the top of a 6 m. wall but also succeeds in open positions if not too exposed. The arching sprays of powder blue flowers are copiously produced. **55**

'Gloire de Versailles' 1·5–3·05 m. (5–10 ft)   ▼❀
A deciduous *Ceanothus* which is very popular, belonging to the *C.* × *delilianus* group. This group produces flowers from July to October in large loose clusters. Pruning is required to keep the plants compact and should be carried out annually in early April. Cut back all growths made the previous season to the base. Powder blue flowers. F.C.C. 1872, A.G.M. 1925. Z.4–6. **57**

dentatus Santa Barbara Ceanothus   △❀
2·45 m. (8 ft)
California. Introduced 1848. An evergreen shrub with bright blue flowers in roundish clusters in May which are nicely set off by the very small glandular leaves. A plant of considerable charm for planting against a wall and will also succeed in the open in areas of mild climate. Z.5–9. **56**

impressus 3·05 m. (10 ft)   △❀
An evergreen shrub, with deep blue flowers borne freely during April and May. The small leaves have deeply impressed veins. This is one of the hardiest and most satisfactory *Ceanothus* but best on a wall except in mild districts. In such a situation it will attain a height of 3·05 m. F.C.C. 1957, A.G.M. 1969. **58**

'Marie Simon' c. 1·5 m. (5 ft)   ▼❀
Belonging to the same group as 'Gloire de Versailles' but is a complete change of colour, a rather pretty rose pink. All plants in this group attain a height of 1·5–3·05 m. where annual pruning is carried out.

× **mendocinensis** (*C. thyrsiflorus* × *C. velutinus laevigatus*) 1·5–1·85 m. (5–6 ft)   △❀
An evergreen shrub which has been found in Mendocino and neighbouring counties in California. In these areas *C. velutinus laevigatus* and *C. thyrsiflorus* are growing and in contact so this plant is a natural hybrid between them. The dark green glossy leaves are glaucous underneath and rather sticky. The pale blue flowers are produced in racemes in spring. **59**

thyrsiflorus Blue Blossom 6·1 m. (20 ft)   △❀
Generally considered one of the hardiest evergreen *Ceanothus* but is somewhat tall and can reach over 6 m. in height on a wall. Light blue flowers are produced in June. Introduced in 1837.
  repens, a vigorous low spreading form to 1·2 m. (4 ft), which seems reasonably hardy and extremely floriferous early in its life. A useful variety for planting under windows because of its height. It has light blue flowers in May. **60**

'Topaz' 1·5–3·05 m. (5–10 ft)   ▼❀
This belongs to the same group as 'Gloire de Versailles' but has a deeper blue-violet flower. A.G.M. 1969. **61**

Cedar,
  Japanese see *Cryptomeria japonica*
  Pencil see *Juniperus virginiana*
  Plume see *Cryptomeria japonica* 'Elegans'

Abbreviations and symbols used in the text

▼ Deciduous	† Lime hater
△ Evergreen	◗ Shade
❀ Flowers	◐ Semi shade
● Fruit	⊙ Sun
❧ Foliage	

A.G.M. Award of Garden Merit, Royal Horticultural Society
F.C.C. First Class Certificate, Royal Horticultural Society

Z1–10 The Z numbers represent the climatic zones used in the United States and provide a useful hardiness rating elsewhere. Thus Z1 is for those plants surviving coldest conditions and Z10 is the other extreme

The illustration numbers are in **bold type**.

Salt see *Tamarix pentandra*

CELASTRUS CELASTRACEAE

orbiculatus 9·15–12·2 m. (30–40 ft)　　　▼●
North-east Asia. Introduced to Kew 1870. A strong vigorous deciduous shrub which will, given the opportunity, reach the height given in an old tree. The green flowers are of little decorative value, but are followed in late autumn by the most beautiful display of fruits in which the brown capsules split open to reveal the brilliant scarlet-covered seeds. These are backed by the golden yellow inner surface of the capsules and in the early stages by the yellow autumn colour of the leaves. Fortunately, birds do not seem to find the fruits attractive so the brilliant display lasts for a couple of months into the New Year. Can be pruned hard if in a place where restriction is necessary. It is of importance to get the hermaphrodite form in which both sexes are present on the same plant. Where a suitable tree is not available it can be grown over some rough branches or on a pergola, or on a large iron 'tripod' where the stems can twine for support. Plants can easily be raised from seeds but are likely to be either male or female, and useless unless used as partners. Layering of the hermaphrodite form is safer and more reliable for small gardens. Quite hardy and easily grown and deserving of more general cultivation. Female plants can sometimes be purchased with males grafted to produce the necessary pollen. F.C.C. 1958 for hermaphrodite form. **62**

CERATOSTIGMA PLUMBAGINACEAE

willmottianum **Willmott Blue Leadwort**　　⊙▼❋
90 cm. (3 ft)
Western China. Introduced 1908. A fine garden shrub about 90 cm. in height which prefers well drained soil in full sun. The clusters of bright blue flowers are produced from July to October in profusion. The foliage assumes a reddish hue in autumn. Should be pruned annually towards the end of March cutting back almost to ground level. Does well on limestone or chalk. A.G.M. 1928. Z.8. **63**

CERCIS LEGUMINOSAE

siliquastrum **Judas Tree, Redbud**　　⊙▼❋
4·55 m. (15 ft)
East Mediterranean. Introduced 16th century. A deciduous tree, often of shrubby spreading habit, with nearly horizontal branches but sometimes in well drained soils and sunny situations attains tree size. Distinctive in appearance because of its rounded blue green leaves, it is even more distinguished when in flower in May, producing masses of bright purplish rose flowers. Remarkably, many of these are in clusters even on old branches and as these flowers are borne before the leaves, the whole tree has a haze of rosy purple mist-

like in effect. The seed pods also are purplish in hue, becoming conspicuous in July and remaining on the plant throughout the winter. A sun lover, growing well on chalk or other well drained soil, the Judas Tree does best in southern temperate climes and is readily propagated from seed. The popular name arises from the legend that it was on this tree Judas hanged himself after the Betrayal. A.G.M. 1927. **64**

'Alba', white flowers and pale green leaves.

'Bodnant', a clone with flowers of a much deeper purple from the famous North Wales garden, Bodnant. F.C.C. 1944.

CHAENOMELES ROSACEAE　　⊙◐▼❋
Flowering Quince

japonica **Japanese Flowering Quince** 1·5 m. (5 ft)
Japan. Introduced about 1869. A well known deciduous shrub, often called *Cydonia* or 'Japonica' or the two names combined. Charming with its orange flame flowers and very free, blooming March to May, it will attain a height of 1·5 m. against a wall. Will grow in the open, likes good soil and doesn't object to partial shade. May be spurred back after flowering when on a wall, otherwise prune out old useless wood, as flowers are freely produced on young wood, especially if summer pruned July to August. Flowers are followed by large fruits, yellow when ripe which can be used for preserve making. F.C.C. 1890, A.G.M. 1943.

speciosa **Flowering Quince** 1·5–3·05 m. (5–10 ft)
China. Introduced to Kew 1786. A deciduous shrub, long known as *Pyrus* or *Cydonia japonica* to gardeners and botanists, erroneously referred to as such now. Excellent as a wall shrub, where it will eventually attain a height of about 3 m. with a greater spread. Scarlet to deep red flowers from February to June, freely produced, especially if summer pruned. Can also be grown successfully in the open and as a hedge where it will average 1·5 m. in height. Several garden cultivars have arisen with different coloured flowers. The following selection are good garden plants:

'Cardinalis', crimson scarlet double flowers. 1·2 m. (4 ft). A.G.M. 1969.

'Moerloosii', thick clusters of soft pink and white flowers. 1·5 m. (5 ft). A.G.M. 1969. **65**

'Nivalis', fairly large pure white flowers. 1·2 m. (4 ft). A.G.M. 1969.

'Simonii', dwarf, with semi-double blood red flowers, a beautiful plant. 90 cm. (3 ft). A.G.M. 1924.

× **superba** (*C. japonica* × *C. speciosa*)
1·2–1·5 m. (4–5 ft)
Flowers are very freely produced on small to medium-sized shrubs. Some of these have become very popular.

'Crimson and Gold', deep crimson contrasting well with golden anthers. A.G.M. 1969. **66**

'Knap Hill Scarlet', an old orange scarlet cultivar which is well known for profusion of bloom. A.G.M. 1969.

'**Pink Lady**', an attractive spreading plant. The rose pink flowers emerge from deeper pink buds. **67**

'**Rowallane**', low spreading, with large brilliant crimson flowers, very good as a wall plant. A.G.M. 1957.

CHAMAECYPARIS CUPRESSACEAE ⊙△🐦
False Cypress

lawsoniana **Lawson Cypress** *c.* 30 m. (100 ft)
North-western U.S. Introduced 1854. This tree is much too large eventually for small gardens although it can usefully be employed to give shelter in gardens with enough room and makes an excellent evergreen hedge even in sites which are very exposed. It is really included here because many of its numerous cultivars are very slow growing, while others, although faster, can still be confined to quite small gardens because of their spreading habit.

'**Backhouse Silver**' see *C. lawsoniana* '**Pygmaea Argentea**'

'**Columnaris**', raised by Jan Spek, Boskoop, Holland about 1940. 6–7.5 m. (20–25 ft). One of the best narrow upright growing conifers for small gardens. The closely packed ascending branches have flattened sprays, glaucous at the tips and underneath. Very effective as a focal point. A tree at Wisley is 6 m. (20 ft) high and only 90 cm. (3ft) across at its widest. A.G.M. 1961. **68**

'**Ellwoodii**', in cultivation 1929. 3.7 m. (12 ft). A juvenile form which grows very slowly into a columnar bush and is very effective in winter when the grey green foliage becomes a greyish blue. Very popular both in England and the United States, for large rock gardens or as a lawn specimen. A.G.M. 1969.

'**Kilmacurragh**', 9 m. (30 ft). A narrow upright tree of great architectural value and a lovely dark green colour. Hardy and because of the branch angle very resistant to damage by snow. Resembles the Italian cypress. A.G.M. 1969.

'**Lutea**', Golden Lawson Cypress, 9–12 m. (30–40 ft). An old cultivar known before 1873 which has golden yellow foliage and large flattened sprays. The habit is stiff but with soft sprays. Rather susceptible to sunburn in certain areas. Very good for colour in winter and a useful boundary tree. A.G.M. 1955.

'**Pembury Blue**', 7.5 m. (25 ft). A very striking conifer, with the most delicate shade of glaucous blue foliage I know. Raised at Pembury in Kent, England, this is a medium sized tree broadly conical in habit. Makes a lovely hedge. A.G.M. 1969. **69**

'**Pygmaea Argentea**', 90 cm. (3 ft). A dwarf, rounded bush of very slow growth. The dark bluish green foliage is capped with silvery white tips and is of good colour in winter and summer. One of the best dwarf conifers, sometimes known as 'Backhouse Silver' and has been in cultivation since 1891. A.G.M. 1969. **70**

obtusa **Hinoki False Cypress** 90 cm. (3 ft)
'**Intermedia**', is a very small slow growing shrub with the green foliage in short, loose sprays becoming conical in shape. Z.3. **71**

pisifera **Sawara Cypress** 1.5–3 m. (5–10 ft)
'**Boulevard**', this is a juvenile form which arose in about 1934, as a sport of C. *pisifera* 'Squarrosa' in the U.S. where it is often known as 'Cyanoviridis'. It has now become a very popular conifer and suitable for any size of garden. The very light blue foliage acquires an attractive tinge of purple in winter. Can be pruned to keep it in shape and colours better in slight shade. It is at its best as a young plant. In summer, cuttings root readily under mist. Z.3. **72**

'**Plumosa Aurea Compacta**', a dwarf dense conical bush, of about 60 cm. (2 ft), with soft yellow foliage especially in spring. Feathery in appearance and a very slow grower. In cultivation in 1891. Z.3. **73**

thyoides
'**Ericoides**', a dwarf form with juvenile foliage, blue-green in summer, turning bronzy purple in winter. In cultivation in 1840 this is an attractive conifer which is soft to touch. Z.3. **74**

Cherry,
Autumn see *Prunus subhirtella* '**Autumnalis**'
Chinese Bush see *Prunus glandulosa*
Cornelian see *Cornus mas*
Rosebud see *Prunus subhirtella*
Cherry
Laurel see *Prunus laurocerasus*
Crab Apple see *Malus* × *robusta*
Chestnut,
Dwarf Horse see *Aesculus parviflora*
Horse see *Aesculus*
Chilean
Fire Bush see *Embothrium coccineum*
Lantern Tree see *Crinodendron hookeranum*
Pernettya see *Pernettya mucronata*
Potato Tree see *Solanum crispum*

Abbreviations and symbols used in the text

▼ Deciduous | † Lime hater
△ Evergreen | ⑩ Shade
✳ Flowers | ① Semi shade
● Fruit | ⊙ Sun
🐦 Foliage

A.G.M.   Award of Garden Merit, Royal Horticultural Society
F.C.C.   First Class Certificate, Royal Horticultural Society

Z1–10   The Z numbers represent the climatic zones used in the United States and provide a useful hardiness rating elsewhere. Thus Z1 is for those plants surviving coldest conditions and Z10 is the other extreme

The illustration numbers are in **bold type**.

CHIMONANTHUS CALYCANTHACEAE

praecox syn. *C. fragrans* **Winter Sweet**
2·45 m. (8 ft)
China. Introduced 1766. A deciduous shrub about 2·4 m. high and as much across. Flowers with waxy yellow outer petals, the inner ones stained purple, are produced December to January in Europe, but in U.S. Z. 4–7, February and March; Z. 8–9 December to February. They are more numerous if planted against a south or west wall where plenty of sun will ripen the growth and the plant become established. In such a situation it will attain a greater height. Most of the pruning can be done for house decoration where the delightful perfume can be enjoyed to the full. Any long growths can be shortened immediately after flowering. Propagated by layering and from seeds, seedlings generally taking several years to flower.

    'Grandiflorus', a more showy plant of a deeper yellow and a red stain, but less fragrant.
    'Luteus', a distinctive cultivar probably introduced from Japan around 1930. Clear brighter yellow waxy flowers, unstained, flowering in January, after *C. praecox*. F.C.C. 1970. **75**

China Rose see *Rosa chinensis*
Chinese
    Arbor-vitae see *Thuya orientalis*
    Bush Cherry see *Prunus glandulosa*
    Dogwood see *Cornus kousa chinensis*
    Pieris see *Pieris formosa* 'Forrestii'
    Privet see *Ligustrum sinense*
    Wisteria see *Wisteria sinensis*
    Witch Hazel see *Hamamelis mollis*

CHOISYA RUTACEAE

ternata Mexican Orange Blossom
1·5–1·85 m. (5–6 ft)
Mexico. Introduced 1825. A beautiful bright evergreen foliaged shrub of rounded shape, generally 1·5–1·85 m. in height and spread. White, scented flowers mainly in May but will flower spasmodically over a long season in a sheltered well drained position. Pruning is not generally required and it makes a pleasing informal hedge or screen. It can be increased by firm young cuttings, taken during summer and put under mist. F.C.C. 1880, A.G.M. 1969. **76**

Christmas Box see *Sarcococca*
Cider Gum see *Eucalyptus gunnii*
Cinquefoil see *Potentilla*

CISTUS CISTACEAE **Rock Rose**
Natives of southern Europe and North Africa these beautiful evergreen shrubs are not genuinely hardy so are likely to succumb in severe winters. Cuttings however are not too difficult to root under mist or in a frame and as planting is best done from pots or containers, overwintering young plants does not present too much of a problem. Preferring a situation in full sun and tolerant of chalk, they are ideal for dry banks. Drought has no terrors and they are good for seaside gardens. Pruning is generally not required. Some of the best for gardening purposes are hybrids.

× **corbariensis** *(C. populifolius* × *C. salviifolius)*
60 cm. (2 ft)
A low well furnished shrub about 60 cm. or more high, one of the hardiest *Cistus*. Flowering from June onwards, the white flowers with a yellow base are profusely produced.

crispus see *C.* × *pulverulentus*

× **cyprius** *(C. ladanifer* × *C. laurifolius)*
1·85 m. (6 ft)
An evergreen shrub of some vigour about 1·85 m. high and reasonably hardy. The attractive flowers are white with crimson blotches at the base of each petal. They are prolifically produced during June and July. Has been considered the most beautiful *Cistus* for gardens. Young branches are clammy with fragrant gum and the dull green leaves turn leaden in winter. A.G.M. 1926.

× **florentinus** *(C. monspeliensis* × *C. salviifolius)*
60 cm.–1·2 m. (2–4 ft)
Algeria, southern Europe. A natural hybrid. The white flowers which occur in May and June have a yellow basal blotch on each petal. A useful shrub for the front of borders, but it may suffer damage in a severe winter. **77**

× **loretii** *(C. ladanifer* × *C. monspeliensis)*
60 cm. (2 ft)
A hybrid which has arisen in gardens and has also been found in the wild. Dwarf in habit. The large white flowers which appear in June and July have attractive crimson blotches at the base of each petal. **78**

'Peggy Sannons' 75 cm. (2½ ft)
A small shrub of upright habit, distinctive in its grey green leaves and downy stems. The flowers produced in summer are pale pink. This is a plant which arouses admiration at the Royal Horticultural Society's Garden at Wisley, England. **79**

× **pulverulentus** syn. *C. crispus* 60 cm. (2 ft)
A compact 60 cm. shrub, said to have been introduced to England in 1656, produces its glowing purple red flowers from May to July which are offset by sage green undulating margined leaves. **80**

× **purpureus** 1·5 m. (5 ft)
Introduced in 1790. A handsome rock rose, having large rosy crimson flowers with conspicuous dark red basal blotches. The bushy rounded growth usually attains a height of 1·5 m. and as much across, even more in gardens with a favoured climate. This plant is not

generally happy in cold areas. The dull greyish leaves are scented. A.G.M. 1927. **81**

'Silver Pink' 60–90 cm. (2–3 ft)

A beautiful hybrid raised about 1910. Generally 60–90 cm. high and reasonably hardy, this plant produces clear soft silvery pink translucent flowers in clusters. A.G.M. 1930. **82**

CLEMATIS RANUNCULACEAE **Virgins Bower** ⊙ ◐

A genus comprising at least 200 species in addition to which large numbers of garden hybrids have been produced, providing gardens with a tremendous range of woody climbing plants. Many authors have waxed lyrical about the beauty of clematis and books have been devoted to it. However in this book, more general in character, only a small selection can be mentioned. Clematis like good deep soil which retains moisture in summer but heavy soils are better suited if well broken up and lightened by the addition of leaf mould or peat. Growers are not agreed whether or not lime is necessary. The European species *Clematis vitalba* which so frequently adorns hedges and trees as to be known as Travellers' Joy is invariably found on chalk or limestone but in spite of this lime does not seem essential to their welfare. The natural habit of clambering over trees and shrubs so that the plants flower in the sun but do not expose the roots and lower parts is worth some attention when planting. In open sites, a few dwarf shrubs will provide this protection. Lavender is ideal for the purpose. Clematis are rather difficult to transplant successfully and because of this are usually sold in pots so may be planted at any time, from September onwards to April is the ideal time, when the weather is reasonably mild. Pruning of clematis is regarded as difficult by many gardeners, but all benefit from pruning to a healthy pair of buds near the base of the plant when newly planted. Follow-up pruning depends on species or variety and will be detailed in the descriptions which follow. Many may be allowed to grow naturally. Clematis are more easily layered than many other plants and this method used in spring or summer will provide a limited number. Larger numbers can be produced from cuttings under mist or in a propagating frame during summer; species may be grown from seed. The method much used at one time of grafting, using seedlings as stocks has been superseded by 'mist propagation'. By growing them up through old fruit trees, shrubs or in conjunction with other plants, such as roses, quite a large collection can be grown in quite small gardens as little soil space is required. Quite beautiful floral effects can thus be created throughout the season, certainly unsurpassed by any other climbing plant.

alpina up to 2·45 m. (8 ft) ▼✿

North and Central Europe, North Asia. Introduced 1792. A lovely species with solitary blue flowers which are produced during April and May from axillary buds on the growth made the previous year. Pruning is seldom required but if it becomes necessary should be done as soon as possible after flowering.

'Frances Rivis', is a fine form of *C. alpina*, sometimes known incorrectly as 'Blue Giant', in which the flowers are larger and with more conspicuous white stamens and staminodes, making a lovely contrast to the blue. Superb scrambling over a small shrub. **83**

× **eriostemon** (*C. integrifolia* × *C. viticella*) ▼✿

A hybrid originally raised in France before 1852, but probably not in cultivation.

'Hendersonii', raised by Henderson of St John's Wood, London, England about 1830, is a beautiful clematis for the small garden of semi-herbaceous habit. Flowers profusely from the end of May to September, with deep bluish violet flowers which are borne singly. Can be supported by a few pea sticks, as it grows to a height of 1·5 m. (5 ft). Prune back to ground level in spring. **84**

× **jackmanii** (*C. lanuginosa* × *C. viticella*) ▼✿
up to 6·1 m. (20 ft)

A hybrid raised in 1858 in Messrs Jackman's Nursery at Woking, England, and still among the most popular and reliable for present day planting. The large violet purple flowers are produced very freely, particularly in July and August on the growth of the current year. Pruning therefore is best carried out in February, cutting back almost to the base of the previous year's growth. F.C.C. 1863, A.G.M. 1930. Z.5.

× **jouiniana** (*C. vitalba* × ▼✿
C. heracleifolia davidiana) c. 3·05 m. (10 ft)

A vigorous climber, a hybrid which grows up to 3·05 m. high and originated previous to 1900. Very attractive from August to October when smothered with a profusion of small white, lilac suffused flowers and very useful for covering over an old tree stump. Popular in Britain but not well-known in U.S.

'Praecox', a very similar plant but commences flowering late July. Soft lavender-blue flowers. Z.4. **85**

Abbreviations and symbols used in the text

▼	Deciduous	†	Lime hater
△	Evergreen	◍	Shade
✿	Flowers	◑	Semi shade
●	Fruit	⊙	Sun
➤	Foliage		

A.G.M. Award of Garden Merit, Royal Horticultural Society

F.C.C. First Class Certificate, Royal Horticultural Society

Z1–10 The Z numbers represent the climatic zones used in the United States and provide a useful hardiness rating elsewhere. Thus Z1 is for those plants surviving coldest conditions and Z10 is the other extreme

The illustration numbers are in **bold type**.

montana **Anemone Clematis** 9·1 m. (30 ft) ▼✳
Himalaya. Introduced by Lady Amherst 1831. The first to come to America came from China in 1900. A deciduous climber which when well established is exceedingly vigorous, especially if allowed to ramp up into a tree where it is particularly effective. Quite hardy and useful for any aspect, even a wall facing north. The white flowers are borne in great profusion during April and May on growths from the previous year so that when pruning is necessary this should be carried out after flowering. Plants on a wall should be trained with a framework of old branches from which the flowering wood can be cut back nearly to the base. On pergolas the main growths can be trained along and the flowering growths allowed to hang down, displaying a flowering curtain. A.G.M. 1930. Z.6.

> **'Elizabeth'**, a large flowered form, which when established, produces pearly pink flowers which are deliciously scented. White flowers are sometimes produced the first season after planting. A.G.M. 1969.

> **'Tetrarose'**, a form which originated in Holland with large purplish pink flowers and bronze foliage. Having twice the normal number of chromosomes it is very vigorous. Flowers in May and June. **86**

orientalis **Orange-peel Clematis** ▼✳●
to 6·1 m. (20 ft)
Northern Asia. Introduced 1731. A deciduous climber with slightly fragrant yellow flowers in August to September, followed by silky seed heads, very handsome in autumn sunlight.

> **'L.S.E. 13372'**, a remarkable form allied to *C. orientalis* and which has become known as the 'orange-peel clematis'. A vigorous climber with orange yellow flowers with sepals as thick as the skin of an orange and flowering June to October. Prune in February to 0·90–1·2 m. (3–4 ft). A.G.M. 1973. Z.6. **87**

rehderana to 7·5 m. (25 ft) ▼✳
Western China. Introduced 1898. A deciduous climber and valuable where there is room because of its late flowering, August to October, and for the delightful cowslip-like fragrance of its flowers. These are bell shaped, nodding and delicate pale yellow in colour. A.G.M. 1969. Z.6. **88**

tangutica **Golden Clematis** ▼✳●
to 4·55 m. (15 ft)
Central Asia. Introduced 1898. A species which seems closely allied to *C. orientalis*, possibly a form of it, with more bell shaped flowers. The abundant yellow flowers are very handsome, freely produced, July to October, and they are very effective in autumn especially when married up with the silky seed heads from earlier flowers. Annual pruning in February as advocated earlier for its relative *C. orientalis* gives good results and makes for convenience in a small garden where it can be trailed over another plant such as *Chamaecyparis pisifera* 'Squarrosa' or *Mahonia* × *media* 'Charity'. Z.5. **89**

texensis **Scarlet Clematis** to 3·05 m. (10 ft) ▼✳
Texas, U.S. Introduced 1868. A distinct species with red, pitcher shaped, nodding flowers from June to autumn. In colder areas is usually semi-herbaceous, being somewhat tender. It is best grown in company with other shrubs near a sheltered wall, where it can scramble up into the sun. Some winter protection is necessary. More tolerant of dry soils than many other clematis.

> **'Etoile Rose'**, a hybrid of above which can be pruned hard in February if required as it flowers on current year's growth. **90**

viticella 3·05 m. (10 ft)
Southern Europe, Western Asia. Cultivated since 16th century. A slender, deciduous climber, flowering in the summer, to early autumn. Usually represented by forms or nearly related hybrids in which the stems die back in winter so should be pruned back in February to where live buds can be seen. Z.4.

> **'Abundance'**, a form raised by Markham with masses of small lilac purple flowers from July to September. Will grow in any aspect. A.G.M. 1973. **91**

> **'Kermesina'**, raised by Lemoine, a very good free blooming hardy variety with masses of deep wine red flowers. A.G.M. 1969. **92**

LARGE FLOWERED CLEMATIS ◉▼✳

> **'Barbara Dibley'**, a large free flowering hybrid of the patens group growing 3·05 m. (10 ft) high. Violet-blue with bars of petunia purple when grown in a little shade. The removal of old flowered growths is the only pruning required. Flowers May and June and a second crop in September. **93**

> **'Comtesse de Bouchaud'**, introduced before 1915, a vigorous 3·05 m. (10 ft) variety, which produces its beautiful soft cyclamen pink flowers continuously from June to September. Prune hard in February if required. A.G.M. 1969.

> **'Hagley Hybrid'**, a variety of the *jackmanii* group growing 3·05 m. (10 ft) high, flowering from June to September. This vigorous hybrid produces abundant shell pink flowers with brown anthers. Prune hard in February. **94**

> **'Marie Boisselot'**, a variety with very fine full rounded flowers, snowy white with yellow stamens. A vigorous free-flowering plant, up to 4·25 m. (14 ft) high which will grow in any aspect. Prune hard in February for best results. **95**

> **'Nelly Moser'**, one of the best known and most popular clematis. The large pale pinkish mauve flowers with a carmine bar to each sepal are freely produced in May and June and frequently again in September. The removal of old flowering wood is the only pruning necessary. Bleaching is apt to occur in hot weather so a shady position should be selected, a north wall is ideal. 3·05 m. (10 ft). A.G.M. 1969. **96**

> **'Perle d'Azur'**, a vigorous variety up to 3·65 m. (12 ft) high, is very free flowering from June to August. The light blue flowers are of striking appearance

having broad sepals. Prune hard in February. A.G.M. 1974. **97**

'The President', a popular variety, growing up to 3·05 m. (10 ft) and producing its deep bluish purple flowers in June and July and again in September, on both old and young wood. Light pruning to remove old flowering wood is all that is required. If the base of the plant becomes bare one or two of the main growths can be looped round to cover it.

'Ville de Lyon', is a striking variety, especially if planted in front of a white wall which will contrast with the bright carmine red to reddish plum-violet flowers which deepen around the edges of the sepals and have golden stamens. Growing up to 3·05 m. (10 ft) it should be pruned hard in February for best results. **98**

'Vyvyan Pennell', a variety which produces double deep violet flowers from May to July. Flowering again in autumn when the flowers may be single lavender blue. Will grow to about 3 m. (10 ft). Prune lightly after flowering.

'William Kennet' 4·55 m. (15 ft)
A very fine large flowered hybrid whose lavender flowers have a dark centre and the sepals are distinctively crimped and waved along the edges. Flowering from June to August, it can attain a height of 4·55 m. and will grow on almost any aspect. Can be pruned back in February to basal buds of the previous year's growth or if required to fill a larger space retain some main growths for this purpose. Some of these can be looped around to cover bare basal wood. **99**

CLERODENDRON VERBENACEAE

bungei syn. *C. foetidum* 1·5–1·85 m. (5–6 ft) ▼❈
China. Introduced by Fortune 1844. A deciduous shrub, generally 1·5–1·85 m. high, but somewhat tender so apt to be cut back to ground level in severe winters. Flowers purplish rose, fragrant, in August and September. Suckers freely, but should be planted where it is unlikely to be handled. The leaves when bruised give off a heavy repulsive odour, accounting for its former name of *C. foetidum*. Can be increased from suckers. Z.7. **100**

trichotomum Harlequin Glory-bower ▼❈●
2·45 m. (8 ft)
Japan and China. In cultivation 1800. A shrubby small tree, usually grown as a shrub and, although hardy and easily grown, prefers some shelter and a sunny position. Flowers deliciously fragrant, white with maroon calyces. July to September, succeeded by turquoise berries, surrounded by the persistent calyces. Pruning is not required except to cut back the winter-killed shoots. Propagation by root cuttings is relatively easy. Apt to sucker, especially if roots are damaged by cultivation and can be increased by this means also. The leaves of this species also have an unpleasant odour if crushed. F.C.C. 1893. Z.6.

fargesii, this differs in having smaller leaves, paler and more slender smooth stems. It generally fruits more freely but retains the unpleasant odour when leaves are crushed. Introduced 1898 by Père Farges to France.

CLETHRA CLETHRACEAE

alnifolia Sweet Pepper Bush, †▼❈
Summer Sweet 1·5–1·85 m. (5–6 ft)
Eastern U.S. Introduced 1731. A deciduous shrub with pleasantly arching branches which produce terminal racemes of flowers, white, richly aromatic in August. Generally about 1·5–1·85 m. high where happy. Requires a moist lime-free soil, well laced with leaf mould to give of its best. Requires no pruning and can be increased by layering and occasionally by rooted suckers. Cuttings of firm young growth can be rooted under mist in summer. A.G.M. 1969.

'Paniculata', one of the best out-door clethras which has terminal panicles and is more vigorous in growth. It was introduced in 1770. A.G.M. 1969. Z.3.

'Rosea', a beautiful form with healthy glossy leaves which produces flowers which are tinged pink in bud and when fully open. A.G.M. 1969.

Climbing Honeysuckle see *Lonicera*
Cockspur Coral-bean see *Erythrina crista-galli*

COLLETIA RHAMNACEAE

armata 2·45 m. (8 ft) ▼❈➹
South Chile, introduced between 1880 and 1884. A deciduous shrub eventually 2·45 m. high curiously furnished with rigid, sharply pointed, spiky branchlets, apparently leafless, or with small leaves. A difficult shrub to grow yet reasonably hardy in a sunny situation, where it will flower freely. Small waxy white hawthorn

---

Abbreviations and symbols used in the text

▼ Deciduous	† Lime hater
△ Evergreen	◍ Shade
❈ Flowers	◐ Semi shade
● Fruit	⊙ Sun
➹ Foliage	

A.G.M.   Award of Garden Merit, Royal Horticultural Society
F.C.C.   First Class Certificate, Royal Horticultural Society

Z1–10   The Z numbers represent the climatic zones used in the United States and provide a useful hardiness rating elsewhere. Thus Z1 is for those plants surviving coldest conditions and Z10 is the other extreme

The illustration numbers are in **bold type**.

scented flowers in autumn, September to December. Summer cuttings can be rooted under mist.

'**Rosea**', a delightful variation, pink flowers while in bud becoming pale rose on opening. **101**

cruciata **Anchor Plant** 3·05 m. (10 ft) ▼❋🍃
South Brazil, Uruguay. Introduced 1824. A curious shrub, which can attain a height of 3·05 m., armed with two kinds of spines, one flat, rigid and triangular, the other sharply pointed and comparatively slender. Tubular yellowish white flowers produced in late summer and autumn. More frequently seen in gardens than *C. armata*, it flowers very freely after a fine summer when it is an attractive and interesting though formidable shrub of unusual appearance.

Colorado Spruce see *Picea pungens*

COLUTEA LEGUMINOSAE **Bladder Senna**

arborescens 3·65 m. (12 ft) ▼❋●
South-east Europe. Introduced 16th century. A fairly large deciduous shrub which may make itself very much at home becoming easily naturalized. Will grow on any soil which is well drained and produces its yellow peel like flowers over several months. These are followed by inflated seed pods which when squeezed explode giving a sharp report much to the delight of children. These pods are responsible for the common name of Bladder Senna and provide an abundant supply of seeds which are easily raised. Where its size must be restrained this can be done by pruning each year in March almost to the old wood. Z.5.

Common
   Acacia see *Robinia pseudoacacia*
   Barberry see *Berberis vulgaris*
   Box see *Buxus sempervirens*
   Broom see *Cytisus scoparius*
   Camellia see *Camellia japonica*
   Gorse see *Ulex europaeus*
   Ivy see *Hedera helix*
   Juniper see *Juniperus communis*
   Laurel see *Prunus laurocerasus*
   Lilac see *Syringa vulgaris*
   Myrtle see *Myrtus communis*
   Pearlbush see *Exochorda racemosa*
   Sage see *Salvia officinalis*
   Spindle Tree see *Euonymus europaeus*
   Sun Rose see *Helianthemum nummularium*
Connemara Heath see *Daboecia cantabrica*

CONVOLVULUS CONVOLVULACEAE

cneorum **Bush Morning Glory** ☉△❋🍃
60 cm. (2 ft)
Southern Europe. Cultivated since 1640. A neat ever-

green shrub about 60 cm. high and covered with silky, silvery leaves which make it an attractive plant for well drained positions in front of the shrub border or indeed as a border plant in small gardens. White flimsy funnel-mouthed flowers tinged with pink during the greater part of the summer. Not really hardy in cold areas, it can be overwintered by means of readily rooted cuttings kept in a frame or greenhouse for planting out the following spring. Touchy in Z.5 and 6, satisfactory Z.7 southward.

Coral
   Bark Maple see *Acer palmatum*
   Tree see *Erythrina crista-galli*
Coral-bean, Cockspur see *Erythrina crista-galli*
Corkbush see *Euonymus*
Corkscrew Hazel see *Corylus avellana* '**Contorta**'
Cornelian Cherry see *Cornus mas*
Cornish Heath see *Erica vagans*

CORNUS CORNACEAE **Dogwood**

alba **Red-barked** or **Tartarian Dogwood**
2·75 m. (9 ft)
Siberia to Manchuria; North Korea. Introduced in 1741. A deciduous, wide spreading well known shrub, a rampant grower in most soils, especially when moist, attaining a height of 2·75 m. Small, yellowish white flowers of little decorative value, followed by fruits white or blue tinted. Leaves provide good autumn colour but the most effective display is derived from the coloured bark of the young branches in winter. This display is enhanced if these stems are hard pruned to the base in early spring, at least in alternate years. Several varieties are available of which the following are a selection. Z.2.

   '**Elegantissima**', 1·5 m. (5 ft) has soft grey-green leaves margined creamy white with red bark in winter. Cut sprays are effective when used for home decoration. A.G.M. 1969.
   '**Sibirica**', Westonbirt Dogwood, Siberian Dogwood, is less vigorous than the type and is most successful in damp, well-cultivated soil, where it will attain 1·4 m. (4 ft) in height. The bark is bright on young growths, sealing-wax red gradually darkening as spring approaches. To attain this, pruning back to base each March is essential. A.G.M. 1969.
   '**Spaethii**', 1·2 m. (4 ft) is a striking plant for its foliage all summer, and is red-barked in winter, but less brilliantly so than *C. alba* 'Sibirica'. A beautiful plant with green leaves edged old gold, one of the most conspicuous and effective yellow variegated shrubs in gardens. F.C.C. 1889, A.G.M. 1969.
   '**Variegata**', greenish grey foliage irregularly margined creamy white, more robust than *C. alba* 'Elegantissima'. **102**

alternifolia **Alternate-leaved Dogwood**
   '**Argentea**', a very fine silver variegated shrub, put in

commerce in the U.S. before 1900. Forms a spreading tier branched bush 2·1–2·75 m. (7–9 ft) high. Z.3.

baileyi to 3·05 m. (10 ft)
East North America. Introduced 1892. An upright vigorous deciduous shrub with downy shoots which turn reddish brown before winter. A plant which grows well on light soils. The flowers are small and are succeeded by white fruits. Sometimes confused with *C. stolonifera*, but this plant is not the same. The leaves are glaucous underneath and provide brilliant colour in the autumn. **103**

'Eddie's White Wonder' (*C. nuttallii* × *C. florida*)
A hybrid raised in America by Mr Eddie. This is a beautiful shrub which will eventually grow into a small tree, flowers large white in spring. Awarded the Cory Cup by the Royal Horticultural Society, 1973. **104**

florida **Flowering Dogwood**
2·45–3·05 m. (8–10 ft)
Eastern United States. In cultivation in 1730. Not in common cultivation in England, but thriving best in south-eastern and eastern parts. Very popular in the Eastern U.S. and considered the finest November-time flowering tree. Flowers green, yellow tips, insignificant but beauty supplied by four large white petal-like bracts which expand in May. Superb autumn colour, as seen in the photograph, is attained after a fine summer. Does not thrive on chalky soils. There are pinkish or roseate forms. Z.4. **105**

kousa to 6·1 m. (20 ft)
Japan, Korea, central China. Introduced 1875. A large shrub of elegant habit which in time attains small tree size, but which dislikes shallow or chalky soils. Flowers in May and June, freely produced on erect stalks all over the spreading branches and are rendered conspicuous by the bracts, which creamy at first, become white. Beautifully formed they are followed by strawberry like fruits, and glorious bronze and crimson coloured leaves in autumn. A choice plant in gardens where soil conditions are suitable. F.C.C. 1892. A.G.M. 1969. **106**
   chinensis **Chinese Dogwood**; China. Introduced by Wilson 1907. A geographical form of a great beauty, a deciduous shrub which eventually grows into a small tree at least 3 m. (10 ft) in height. Small flowers are inconspicuous, but surrounded by four large white bracts in June, produced in such numbers as almost to hide the branches. Quite hardy, grows well in peaty soil in a sunny position and appreciates some shelter. As seen by the photographs an additional season of beauty comes along in autumn, the brilliant red colourings lasting for a month. F.C.C. 1924, A.G.M. 1969. Z.5. **107, 108**

mas **Cornelian Cherry** 3·05 m. (10 ft)
Central and southern Europe. Cultivated for centuries. A large deciduous shrub which eventually becomes a small tree. Most effective as it produces masses of bloom while still without foliage, so association with an evergreen background is an advantage. Small yellow flowers produced abundantly in February in England, early April in eastern U.S. The cherry like fruits used to be made into a preserve, but in my experience they are only borne on odd bushes. A.G.M. 1924. Z.4. **109**

stolonifera syn. *C. sericea* 1·2 m. (4 ft)
   'Flaviramea', Golden Twig Dogwood, a very effective shrub in winter, round about 1·2 m. if pruned hard each spring. The greenish yellow young growths contrast beautifully with *C. alba* 'Siberica'. Sent out by Späth in 1899. It likes a moist situation. Z.2. **110**

CORONILLA LEGUMINOSAE

glauca 3·05 m. (10 ft)
Southern Europe. Introduced 1722. An attractive evergreen shrub, which can attain a height of 3·05 m. when trained against a wall, the most suitable site except in mild areas of the country. Leaves very dainty and glaucous on a rounded bush which grows best on light well drained soils. Rich yellow flowers, produced freely April to June, periodically at other times of the year in warm sheltered positions. Little if any pruning is required, badly placed growths are best cut out in spring. Firm young growths can be rooted under mist or in a heated frame and will provide a replacement if, after a very severe winter, the plant succumbs. Probably hardy only in the warmest parts of the U.S. **111**

Corsican Heath see ***Erica terminalis***

CORYLOPSIS HAMAMELIDACEAE **Winter Hazel** ▼

glabrescens **Fragrant Winter Hazel**
4·6 m. (15 ft)
Japan. Introduced 1905. A deciduous shrub up to 4·6 m.

Abbreviations and symbols used in the text

▼	Deciduous	†	Lime hater
△	Evergreen	◍	Shade
✳	Flowers	◖	Semi shade
●	Fruit	⊙	Sun
✿	Foliage		

A.G.M.   Award of Garden Merit, Royal Horticultural Society
F.C.C.   First Class Certificate, Royal Horticultural Society

Z1–10   The Z numbers represent the climatic zones used in the United States and provide a useful hardiness rating elsewhere. Thus Z1 is for those plants surviving coldest conditions and Z10 is the other extreme

The illustration numbers are in **bold type**.

therefore only suitable for fairly large gardens. Pale yellow fragrant flowers freely borne in April on drooping racemes. Leaves slightly glaucous. Quietly beautiful. F.C.C. 1968, A.G.M. 1969. Z.5.

pauciflora Buttercup Winter Hazel †◑❋
1·5 m. (5 ft)

Japan. Introduced by Messrs Veitch 1862. A closely branched shrub, eventually reaching 1·5 m. each way, does not like lime or excessive sun, in short a woodland plant of considerable charm. Flowers creamy yellow, cowslip scented, all along the branches in March and April. Does not require pruning and may be increased by layering. F.C.C. 1893, A.G.M. 1923. Z.6. **112**

veitchiana 1·85 m. (6 ft) ❋

Central China. Introduced in 1900 by Wilson. A distinct upright shrub of about 1·85 m. in height. Primrose yellow flowers, with red brown protruding anthers, fragrant, produced in nodding spikes. A regular flowering plant, but may be injured by late frosts. Z.6. **113**

CORYLUS CORYLACEAE Hazel ▼

avellana European Hazel ❋🐦
'Contorta', the **Corkscrew Hazel**, popularly known as 'Harry Lauder's Walking Stick' is a form discovered about 1863. Growing slowly to 2·45–2·75 m. (8–9 ft) it makes a winter feature with it fantastically twisted branches and when in catkin. Floral arrangement artists also find it a useful component for indoor decoration. **114**

maxima Filbert ●🐦
'Purpurea', the **Purple-leaved Filbert**, makes a bush from 2·1 m. (7 ft) high and almost as wide. The dark purple leaves during summer are useful as a background for plants of a lighter colour. Purple catkins are produced in winter. **115**

COTINUS ANACARDIACEAE

coggygria syn. *Rhus cotinus* ⊙▼❋🐦
Smoke Tree 3·05–3·65 m. (10–12 ft)

Central and southern Europe. A highly decorative and distinctive deciduous shrub which will reach 3·05–3·65 m. in height. The flowering panicles, pinkish brown becoming grey, profusely produced in June and July. Particularly beautiful in autumn, when its leaves turn yellow, orange and bright crimson before falling. This plant has been given a number of popular names, Burning Bush, Smoke Tree and Wig Tree all in reference to the characteristic plume-like flowering panicles which persist for a considerable time. A.G.M. 1969. **116, 117**

'Notcutt's Variety', appears to be very similar to the plant mentioned below. These plants like open sunny, well drained situations and provide better colour if soil is not too rich. A.G.M. 1969. **118**

'Royal Purple', is a selected form with wine purple leaves, slightly darker than 'Notcutt's Variety', translucent in sunshine, particularly attractive in early morning sunshine and one of the finest purple-leaved shrubs. A.G.M. 1969.

COTONEASTER ROSACEAE

Species of cotoneaster may be grown quite readily from seed sown in spring either in a frame or out of doors. Hybrids will not come true to their parents but may be used for hedging etc. depending on parentage. To ensure plants true to parent, cuttings are easily rooted under mist or in a frame. *Cotoneaster* is a very important genus, its members will grow in almost any soil or situation. There is considerable variation from ground cover plants to small trees. Many are outstanding plants, especially for their fruits in autumn, and the selection which follows draws attention to some of those most suitable for garden purposes. Unfortunately, *Cotoneaster* is subject to a destructive bacterial disease called fireblight, but this seems less virulent than when it first appeared in the fifties. Affected plants show shrivelling foliage as one of the most noticeable symptoms and these shoots should be cut out as soon as seen. If pruning becomes necessary because of lack of space, it should be carried out in late March or early April.

adpressus Creeping Cotoneaster ▼❋●🐦
30 cm. (1 ft)

Western China. Introduced about 1895. This very dwarf deciduous shrub is prostrate, rising 30 cm. or so above ground level, but can in time spread several metres if allowed to grow unchecked. Flowers white tipped pink, followed by bright red fruits in autumn. The small leaves turn red in autumn, a very distinctive shrub useful in rock garden or as a border subject, ground or bank cover. Z.4.

conspicuus Wintergreen Cotoneaster △❋●
90 cm.–1·85 m. (3–6 ft)

South-east Tibet. Introduced by Kingdon Ward in 1925. This evergreen shrub is somewhat variable in habit, anything from a low spreading shrub 90 cm. high upwards to shrubs at least 1·85 m. in height forming dense mounds. Flowers white, hawthorn scented in May with red purple anthers, followed by numerous glossy scarlet fruits in autumn. One of our most valuable flowering and fruiting shrubs, excellent for banks. The more prostrate form known as 'Decorus' which received an A.G.M. 1947 and F.C.C. 1953 is regarded by Bean as a superfluous name and therefore invalid. However, in U.S. 'Decorus' is still retained. Z.6. **119, 120**

'Cornubia' 6·1 m. (20 ft) △/▼●
A semi-evergreen, large spreading shrub raised at Exbury, England which by training can be grown into a small tree over 6 m. high. The rich green leaves make a splendid foil for the enormous crop of brilliant red fruits, so profuse as to weigh down the branches. Must

be ranked as one of the finest of the larger growing cotoneasters. F.C.C. 1936, A.G.M. 1969. **121**

dammeri **Barberry Cotoneaster** ⊙ △ ❋ ●
prostrate
Central China. Introduced by Wilson 1900. The most prostrate cotoneaster, evergreen, ideal for ground cover, trailing over the ground in all directions for some 3 m. (10 ft). Useful also for sunny and shady banks, shaping itself to any contours which are present. Pure white solitary flowers with dark anthers followed in autumn by brilliant red fruits. A vigorous form named 'Skogholm' is becoming popular for ground cover. Z.5.

>   **radicans**, a variety with smaller leaves, flowers generally in pairs on longer pedicels. A.G.M. 1973.

'Exburiensis' △ ●
A tall evergreen shrub raised from a yellow fruited form of *C. frigidus* crossed with *C. salicifolius* at Exbury. Handsome when bearing a good crop of its pale orange-yellow fruits, pinkish in winter. A.G.M. 1969. **122**

horizontalis **Herring-bone** or ▼ ❋ ● ⤳
Fish-bone Cotoneaster, Rockspray to 2·75 m. (9 ft)
China. Introduced round about 1870. A deciduous shrub, probably the best known of the cotoneasters from its striking characteristic of opposite branching which gives rise to the popular names. Flowers white, suffused pink in May, very popular with bees and succeeded by an abundant crop of red berries. When planted in an open site it grows about 90 cm. high and may in time cover an area treble that in extent. Invaluable for walls with a northern or eastern exposure, it will fan out and eventually attain a height of 2·75 m. without support. Gives good autumn colour before leaf fall, is easily raised from cuttings and occasionally self sown seedlings can be found. F.C.C. 1897, A.G.M. 1925. Z.4. **123**

>   **'Variegatus'**, has leaves edged with white and is especially pretty in autumn when suffused red. Much less vigorous in growth, an ideal plant for gardens of limited size. **124**

'Hybridus Pendulus' △ ●
A hybrid of unknown parentage, which if allowed to grow naturally is a splendid plant for furnishing a bank. I have seen it trained up a wall also with a very fine effect of cascading growths with abundant fruits. White flowers June and July succeeded by a heavy crop of red fruits in autumn. Top grafted on a 1·85 m. (6 ft) stem it provides a good focal point in small gardens, especially in autumn. **125**

'John Waterer' 3·65 m. (12 ft) △ ●
A fine shrub which is a hybrid between *C. frigidus* and *C. henryanus*. Evergreen or semi-evergreen, growing up to 3·65 m. high it develops into a fine shapely large shrub or if trained to a central stem, a small tree. The arching branches are furnished with dark green willow like leaves and plentiful clusters of scarlet fruits. A.G.M. 1969. **126**

lacteus 3·05 m. (10 ft) △ ❋ ●
West China. Introduced by Forrest in 1913. An evergreen shrub which can reach a height of 3·05 m., possibly more in some gardens. However, it is easily controlled by careful pruning in spring and makes an excellent hedge. Distinctive when making its young growth by the white down which covers them and the bold olive green leaves. Milky white flowers in June and July, followed by large clusters of red berries, which ripen late and hang until January. An invaluable garden shrub which can also be trained on walls. A.G.M. 1969. Z.6. **127**

microphyllus 90 cm. (3 ft) △ ❋ ●
Himalaya, South-west China. Introduced 1824. A pleasing evergreen shrub of rounded habit and about 90 cm. in height. Leaves are very small and dark green and lustrous, a plant much used for covering low walls and banks for which purpose it is ideal being extremely hardy. White flowers, usually single, followed by round fairly large bright red fruits.

>   **thymifolius**, a smaller version, useful for the rock garden being of very close habit, but to retain this should be propagated from cuttings.

salicifolius **Willow-leaf Cotoneaster** △ ❋ ●
4·5 m. (15 ft)
China. Introduced 1908. An evergreen shrub of tall, elegant habit up to 4·5 m. high which has been the parent of several seedlings. Flowers white, small, followed by profusely borne small bright red fruits in autumn. Raised on the continent and in commerce are 'Herbstfeuer' ('Autumn Fire'), 'Parkteppich' and 'Repens' ('Avondrood'), the two latter being useful ground cover plants. The prostrate 'Herbstfeuer' can also be used to furnish banks and trained on fences or walls where its bold willow like leaves and clusters of fruits are very decorative. Z.6.

simonsii **Simon's Cotoneaster** ▼ ❋ ●
2·45 m. (8 ft)
Assam. A deciduous, sometimes semi-evergreen, stiff

Abbreviations and symbols used in the text

▼	Deciduous	†	Lime hater
△	Evergreen	⬤	Shade
❋	Flowers	◑	Semi shade
●	Fruit	⊙	Sun
⤳	Foliage		

A.G.M.   Award of Garden Merit, Royal Horticultural Society
F.C.C.   First Class Certificate, Royal Horticultural Society

Z1–10   The Z numbers represent the climatic zones used in the United States and provide a useful hardiness rating elsewhere. Thus Z1 is for those plants surviving coldest conditions and Z10 is the other extreme

The illustration numbers are in **bold type**.

growing upright shrub which generally grows about 2·45 m. high. Flowers white in June and July, much visited by bees. It makes an excellent hedge and is popular for this purpose, usually up to 1·85 m. and very decorative also when some of the leaves have fallen and the berries can be more easily seen. Z.5.

Cotoneaster,
  Fish-bone see *Cotoneaster horizontalis*
  Herring-bone see *Cotoneaster horizontalis*
  Simon's see *Cotoneaster simonsii*
  Willow-leaf see *Cotoneaster salicifolius*
  Wintergreen see *Cotoneaster conspicuus*
Cotton, Lavender see *Santolina*
Crab Apple,
  Cherry see *Malus × robusta*
  Siberian see under *Malus × robusta*
  Toringo see *Malus sieboldii*
Cranberry Bush, European see *Viburnum opulus*
Cream Honeysuckle see *Lonicera etrusca*
Creeping
  Cotoneaster see *Cotoneaster adpressus*
  Juniper see *Juniperus horizontalis*
  Willow see *Salix repens*
Crimson Pygmy see *Berberis thunbergii* **'Atropurpurea Nana'**

CRINODENDRON ELAEOCARPACEAE   ◍†△❋

hookeranum syn. *Tricuspidaria lanceolata*
3–9 m. (10–30 ft) **Chilean Lantern Tree**
Chile. Introduced by Lobb in 1848. An evergreen shrub around 3 m. in height, but which in time and in very mild areas will become a small tree up to some 9 m. high. In colder areas it is best planted on a wall where it will get protection and I have seen it grown as an informal hedge. Where it succeeds it is one of our choicest shrubs, but demands lime free soil and a little shade. Crimson, lantern like flowers, freely produced in May. Can be propagated from cuttings of half-ripened wood in a heated propagating frame. Better known to older gardeners under its synonym. F.C.C. 1916. **128**

Crossed-leaved Heath see *Erica tetralix*

CRYPTOMERIA TAXODIACEAE   △🍂

japonica **Japanese Cedar**
  'Elegans', Plume Cryptomeria, Plume Cedar
a remarkably beautiful tree which may reach a height of 6 m. (20 ft) in favoured gardens but is usually much less. The soft feathery juvenile foliage is retained permanently and turns rust-bronze during winter. It sometimes becomes top heavy and suffers from snow damage, but can be pruned to prevent this. It withstands pruning very well and makes a very fine and unusual hedge. Z.5. **129**

'Globosa', a small dense bush, very neat and compact in habit with adult type foliage which becomes brownish-red in winter. In cultivation since 1923. Z.5. **130**
'Vilmoriniana', very slow growing globular bush, very neat habit. A popular dwarf conifer which will attain a height of 30 cm. (1 ft) in ten years. Assumes reddish purple colours during the winter months. A.G.M. 1973.

Currant, Flowering or **Winter** see *Ribes sanguineum*
Cydonia see *Chaenomeles japonica*
Cydonia japonica see *Chaenomeles speciosa*
Cypress,
  False see *Chamaecyparis*
  Golden Lawson see *Chamaecyparis lawsoniana* **'Lutea'**
  Hinoki False see *Chamaecyparis obtusa*
  Lawson see *Chamaecyparis lawsoniana*
  Sawara see *Chamaecyparis pisifera*

CYTISUS LEGUMINOSAE **Broom**   †◉❋
There is considerable variation in the group of shrubs generally known as 'brooms', some about 20 cm. (8 in.) high, others growing to 3 m. (10 ft) plus. Few, if any, plants grown in gardens are more generous with their flower production and, as they will grow in poor sandy or peaty soils, they are invaluable. Sunny open sites suit them best and they will succeed on any well drained soil if not too limey. They dislike root disturbance so that established plants are difficult to move. Nurserymen generally grow them in pots or containers to overcome this difficulty.

  Pruning of the more compact kinds is seldom required but the larger ones and particularly those bred from *C. scoparius*, will be kept more compact and manageable if flowered shoots are cut by two thirds immediately after flowering. Pinching out the tips of strong growth in early summer also helps. Pruning into old hard wood is undesirable. Brooms are easily increased by seed sown in spring in a cold frame, seedlings being transplanted singly into pots while still small. Hybrids or garden forms will not come true and must be propagated by cuttings taken in August and placed under mist. Many plants are grafted on to seedling stocks of broom or laburnum in spring under glass. In general brooms are not long lived plants so it is fortunate they grow quickly.

albus see *C. multiflorus*

ardoinii **Ardoin Broom**   *c.* 20 cm. (8 in.)
Golden yellow flowers, pea like in clusters April and May. A very pretty little shrub, quite dwarf and hardy in Britain, but in U.S. not above Z. 7, and flowering very freely, excellent for the rock garden. If growing near other brooms should be propagated by cuttings as it hybridizes readily through insect agency. Z.7.

***battandieri* Morocco Broom** 3·05 m. (10 ft) ▼
Morocco. Introduced about 1922. A remarkable deciduous shrub with distinctive trifoliate leaves which have a silky silver sheen. Flowers in erect racemes, golden yellow and pineapple scented in June and July. Generally hardy except in very cold areas where it is well worth a place on a sheltered wall and where it will grow 3 m. high, occasionally more. In such a situation old flowering growths should be removed and replaced by the vigorous upright growths which spring from the base. F.C.C. 1934, A.G.M. 1938. Z.6. **131**

× ***beanii*** *(C. ardoinii × C. purgans)*
22·5 × 90 cm. (9 in. × 3 ft)
Originated at Kew in 1900 in seedlings of *C. ardoinii*. This small semi-prostrate shrub 22·5 cm. high, 90 cm. across is one of the prettiest dwarf brooms, very useful as a ground cover or rock garden plant. Brilliant golden yellow flowers in May, smothering the plant. F.C.C. 1955, A.G.M. 1969. Z.5. **132**

× ***kewensis*** *(C. ardoinii × C. multiflorus)*
30 cm. × 1·2 m. (1 × 4 ft)
A hybrid, from Kew, England, in 1891. One of the most beautiful dwarf brooms, 30 cm. high and 1·2 m. across. Pale creamy yellow flowers which smother young growths April and May. Ideal for ground cover or a large rock garden, prune after flowering. A.G.M. 1951. **133**

multiflorus syn. *C. albus* 1·85 m. (6 ft)
White Spanish or **White Portuguese Broom**
Spain, Portugal, north-west Africa. Cultivated by Philip Miller 1752. An upright medium-sized shrub, 1·85 m. high, occasionally more. This species has long been known and is still catalogued as *C. albus*. White flowers in May in feathery sprays. A most useful hardy shrub, easily grown from seed and reaching its full beauty in three or four seasons. A parent of several garden hybrids. A.G.M. 1926. Z.6.

× ***praecox*** *(C. multiflorus × C. purgans)*
Warminster Broom 1·2 m. (4 ft)
A fine broom about 1·2 m. high which produces cascading masses of cream and yellow flowers. A very effective plant for massed effect and very beautiful. Some people find its heavy odour unpleasant so in such cases it is unwise to plant it close to the house. Easily increased by cuttings under mist. Bean (8th Ed. page 823) considers the typical and original clone should be known as *C.* × *praecox* 'Warminster'. It appeared among seedlings of *C. purgans* in Wheeler of Warminster's Nursery about 1867. The other parent is now known to be *C. multiflorus*. Fertile seed is set but does not come true but from which some good cultivars have been raised. A.G.M. 1933.

'Allgold', of Dutch origin, produces a densely cascading fountain of long-lasting soft golden yellow flowers in April and May. Growing up to 1·5 m. (5 ft) in height pruning after flowering will keep it suitable for the small garden. A.G.M. 1969, F.C.C. 1974. **134**

'Goldspear', raised by Arends in Germany is another fine cultivar which grows erectly to about 90 cm. (3 ft) high. The deep golden yellow flowers are freely produced. Good for the small garden. **135**

'Hollandia', has the same tumbling fountain like effect as *C.* × *praecox* but flowers are purplish red and soft rose.

'Warminster' see under ***C.* × *praecox***

'Zeelandia', a cultivar over 1·85 m. (6 ft) in height with pale yellow standards, wings flushed lilac red, the overall effect being lilac-pink.

***purpureus* Purple Broom** 30 cm. (1 ft)
Central and South-east Europe. Introduced 1792. A charming very distinct dwarf shrub just over 30 cm. high, not often seen in gardens but a very useful ground cover plant under thinly planted shrubs. Purple flowers produced abundantly in May on the previous year's growth. By cutting out flowering shoots when over, basal growths spring up and will supply next season's crop. Easily propagated from seed. In Europe it is often grafted high on *Laburnum* stock. Z.5. **136**

***scoparius* Common** or **Scotch Broom** ▼
1·85 m. (6 ft)
Europe. A deciduous shrub varying in height according to where it is growing, but generally about 1·8 m. Rich glowing yellow flowers freely produced in May and June. A well known shrub, familiar for its wonderful display especially in the north of Scotland where hillsides present a glowing golden picture. It is a parent of many garden varieties. Easily propagated from seed. A.G.M. 1969.

'Andreanus', a form found in Normandy in the wild about 1884. A beautiful cultivar with rich brownish wing petals and the standard mainly yellow. Valuable in the garden but also valuable because of the part it has played in the production of new cultivars. F.C.C. 1890.

'Burkwoodii', a vigorous plant with deep crimson wings edged yellow, and cerise standards. A well known hybrid. **137**

Abbreviations and symbols used in the text

▼ Deciduous	† Lime hater
△ Evergreen	◍ Shade
❋ Flowers	◐ Semi shade
● Fruit	⊙ Sun
Foliage	

A.G.M. Award of Garden Merit, Royal Horticultural Society
F.C.C. First Class Certificate, Royal Horticultural Society

Z1–10 The Z numbers represent the climatic zones used in the United States and provide a useful hardiness rating elsewhere. Thus Z1 is for those plants surviving coldest conditions and Z10 is the other extreme

The illustration numbers are in **bold type**.

'**Cornish Cream**', an attractive 1·2 m. (4 ft) plant with cream flowers. A.G.M. 1969.

'**Early White Spire**', is very similar to *C. multiflorus* in general appearance and effect but grows to a greater height. A good cultivar for cutting purposes.

'**Golden Sunlight**', a robust form around 1·5 m. (5 ft) in height with rich yellow flowers. A.G.M. 1969.

'**Joan Clark**', a very tall variety about 3 m. in height, named after the raiser, bright in appearance with orange yellow standards, flushed red and orange yellow wings. A new variety. **138**

'**Johnson's Crimson**', introduced in 1940, is a fine hybrid about 1·2 m. (4 ft) in height. Small velvety crimson flowers are freely produced on gracefully sprayed growths. **139**

'**Lena**', a branch sport found on 'Burkwoodii' about 1940 by Charles Coates and named after his wife. A very fine plant particularly for small gardens, being very compact around 60 cm. (2 ft). Flowers orange red and yellow are freely produced. **140**

'**Luna**', raised by Firma Arnold, Holstein, Germany, is a fine cultivar about 1·5 m. (5 ft) high, producing yellow and white flowers in profusion. **141**

prostratus, a distinctive prostrate spreading shrub found in the wild in different parts of Europe, in which the leaves and young growths are covered with dense silky hairs. It produces large yellow flowers. It breeds true from seed and is a very useful plant for the large rock garden. If grafted high onto *Laburnum* understock, branches grow pendulous. **142**

sulphureus, also found occasionally in the wild, the cream flowers are tinted red in the bud, on a flat compact plant. A.G.M. 1969

D

DABOECIA ERICACEAE †△❋

cantabrica Connemara or **Irish Heath**
60 cm. (2 ft)

Western Europe, including Ireland. This evergreen shrub about 60 cm. in height has a charm of its own and is valuable because of its long flowering season. Flowers rosy purple from June to November. Its requirements are similar to heather and it is suitable for inclusion in the heather garden. Best on peaty soil free from lime. Trimming over with shears after flowering or in spring will keep plants more compact in habit and more effective. Can be raised from seed, but selected varieties should be raised from cuttings of firm young growth under mist or in a propagating frame during summer. A.G.M. 1930. Z.5.

'**Alba**', 60 cm. (2 ft), with pure white flowers was found in Connemara about 1832. A very floriferous form with light green leaves and hardier than the type. A.G.M. 1969. **143**

'**Atropurpurea**', 60 cm. (2 ft), deeper red purple flowers than the type. A.G.M. 1969. **144**

'**Bicolor**', 60 cm. (2 ft), a variable form in flower. On the same plant there may be white, purple and white and purple flowers. A.G.M. 1969.

'**William Buchanan**' *(D. azorica × D. cantabrica)* to 30 cm. (1 ft)

A spontaneous hybrid between *D. azorica* and *D. cantabrica* which arose around 1953 in W. Buchanan's garden in Glasgow, Scotland. A beautiful plant of dwarf habit, free flowering a mass of rich red flowers. **145**

Dagger, Spanish see *Yucca gloriosa*
Daisy, Tree see *Olearia*
Daisy Bushes see *Olearia*

DANAE LILIACEAE

racemosa **Alexandrian Laurel** 1·2 m. (4 ft) ◑△●
Asia Minor to Persia. Introduced 1713. This is a delightful evergreen, with some resemblance to the bamboos in habit. It prefers a semi-shaded spot with moist soil and is very useful for cutting in the winter months when its polished green leaves make a delightful setting for cut flowers, remaining fresh for a considerable time. The bisexual flowers are small and of little decorative value but are succeeded by orange red fruits after a hot summer. Can be grown from the seeds when these are available, otherwise by division in spring.

DAPHNE THYMELAEACEAE

'**Albert Burkwood**' see under *D.* × *burkwoodii*

× *burkwoodii* *(D. caucasica × D. cneorum)* △/▼❋
90 cm. (3 ft)

A hybrid raised by Albert Burkwood in Surrey, England. An excellent shrub which may be evergreen, semi-evergreen or deciduous which grows vigorously to 90 cm. and at least as much across. Soft mauvish pink flowers, sweetly scented and freely produced from May to June. Bean, 8th edition, considers this clone should be distinguished as 'Albert Burkwood' to separate it from the very similar plant 'Somerset'.

'**Somerset**', as mentioned is very similar but somewhat larger and regarded by some as the better plant. Both are more easily grown than many daphne's and are longer lived plants. **146**

cneorum **Rose Daphne, Garland Flower** △❋
30 cm. (1 ft)

Central and southern Europe. In cultivation 1752. A great favourite when it can be established successfully, this dwarf evergreen shrub is usually under 30 cm. in height, but can spread triple that distance when happy. Rich rose pink flowers, sweetly scented and freely produced in April and May. Certainly one of the best shrubs for the rock garden if a moist root run can be ensured. It does not seem to object to lime. The layering of outside shoots by placing stones on them seems to contribute to successful culture. Easily rooted from cuttings in late summer. A.G.M. 1927. Z.4.

'Eximia', a more procumbent form, larger in leaf and flower, considered to be the best with deeper pink flowers. F.C.C. 1967.

collina 45 cm. (1½ ft) △✻
Southern Europe to Asia Minor. Introduced 1752. Evergreen up to 45 cm. a highly suitable shrub for the rock garden, very slow growing and like many daphnes not long lived. Purplish rose flowers, fragrant, produced during April and May. A.G.M. 1974. Z.7.

***mezereum* Mezereon, February Daphne** ▼✻●
90 cm. (3 ft)
Europe, Siberia and Asia Minor. A popular deciduous shrub growing over 90 cm. high and as much across. Flowers purplish red with a delicious fragrance in January to March. The erect growths are covered with flowers on the leafless wood of the previous year, followed by poisonous berries of a showy scarlet in autumn. Can be grown from seeds which may have to be protected from birds, indeed self sown seedlings are frequently found. These are worth growing on as old plants are apt to die suddenly. Thrives in chalk or limey soil. Good colour forms on occasion are found amongst seedlings and these can be increased by root cuttings. A.G.M. 1929. Z.4. **147**

'Alba', a white flowering form which flowers earlier than the type and comes true from seed. The fruits are yellow.

× ***neapolitana*** 90 cm. (3 ft) △✻
This upright branched, evergreen shrub is one of the easiest daphnes to grow and is now generally considered to be a natural hybrid of uncertain parentage. The sweetly scented rosy purple flowers pale as they age. They are borne in profusion from April to June. Usually about 90 cm. high, this is one of the most useful and beautiful plants which likes lime in the soil. A.G.M. 1969.

***odora* Winter Daphne** 90 cm.–1·2 m. (3–4 ft) △✻
China, Japan. Introduced from the latter country in 1771. An evergreen shrub 90 cm. to 1·2 m. high and with a wider spread. Reddish purple flowers, very fragrant, bloom in February and March and into April in U.S. Reputedly somewhat tender it is usually planted in sheltered places where it commences to bloom very early in mild winters. Well worth some protection because of its delightful fragrance and handsome appearance. Not fussy regarding soil it can be increased by cuttings of fairly firm young growths in July under mist, or by layers. Z.7.

'Aureomarginata', is a form in which the leaves have faint yellow margins, but which grows more strongly and is hardier than the type. This may be the same as 'Marginata', of U.S. which is more popular than the species. A.G.M. 1974. **148**

retusa 60 cm. (2 ft) △✻●
Western China, east Himalaya. Introduced by Wilson 1901. A dwarf slow growing evergreen shrub which has a close, neat and sturdy habit. The flowers are produced in May and June in crowded clusters and are rosy purple outside while inside they are sparkling white flushed purple. A very hardy plant, suitable for the smallest of gardens, it has a pleasing lilac like fragrance and bright red fruits. A.G.M. 1946. **149**

tangutica 90 cm.–1·5 m. (3–5 ft) △✻
West China. Introduced by Wilson about 1908. A dwarf evergreen shrub of sturdy habit and rounded in shape, closely allied to *D. retusa*, but differing in its longer, more acute leaves. The rosy-purple flowers, produced in March and April, are white stained purple inside in terminal clusters, with a few clusters sometimes later in the season. Fragrant in common with most members of the genus, this is quicker and freer in growth than *D. retusa*. **150**

Daphne,
February see ***Daphne mezereum***
Rose see ***Daphne cneorum***
Winter see ***Daphne odora***
Darwin's Barberry see ***Berberis darwinii***

DECAISNEA LARDIZABALACEAE ◐/⊙ ▼✻●❧

fargesii 2·75 m. (9 ft)
China. Introduced by Pere Farges in 1895. A distinctive and unusual shrub, generally about 2·75 m. in height but of narrow upright habit. The large pinnate leaves are handsome in appearance. Sprays of greenish yellow flowers are followed by remarkable pod-like fruits, blue in colour with a greyish bloom. It thrives in rich loamy soil, is hardy but apt to suffer damage in exposed places while growths are still young. Propagate by seeds which can be sown under glass in spring. **151**

Abbreviations and symbols used in the text

▼	Deciduous	†	Lime hater
△	Evergreen	◍	Shade
✻	Flowers	◐	Semi shade
●	Fruit	⊙	Sun
❧	Foliage		

A.G.M. Award of Garden Merit, Royal Horticultural Society
F.C.C. First Class Certificate, Royal Horticultural Society

Z1–10 The Z numbers represent the climatic zones used in the United States and provide a useful hardiness rating elsewhere. Thus Z1 is for those plants surviving coldest conditions and Z10 is the other extreme

The illustration numbers are in **bold type**.

DENDROMECON PAPAVERACEAE △ ✻ ☙

rigida **Californian Poppy Bush, Bush Poppy**
3 m. (*c.* 10 ft)
California. Introduced about 1854. A fairly large ever-green shrub with narrow glaucous leaves, a beautiful plant which requires the shelter of a wall, except in warm climes, and some added protection in cold winters. Bright yellow, poppy like flowers, produced over a long period in summer. It requires well drained soil. Prune back to 60 cm. (2 ft) after flowering. Can be propagated by cuttings of firm summer growth in very sandy mix in a slightly heated frame. Resents moving so must be planted from a pot. Z.9. **152**

DESFONTAINIA POTALIACEAE △ ✻ ☙

spinosa 3·05 m. (10 ft)
Chile, Peru. Introduced in 1843 and again 1925–6. An evergreen shrub which will in time in gardens where it succeeds attain about 3 m. in height and as much across. Funnel-shaped scarlet, yellow mouthed, flowers from July to October. Generally it succeeds in mild areas, but on occasion in more exposed gardens also. Easily mistaken for a holly until it produces its remarkable flowers. Doesn't like limey or hot shallow soils. The flower colour of the later introduction varies in being scarlet shading to orient red.

DEUTZIA PHILADELPHACEAE ▼ ✻
An important group of shrubs, especially for newcomers to gardening, thriving in any reasonably good soil and providing plenty of bloom, given a reasonably good supply of moisture. Pruning is very simple as they flower on shoots produced the previous year, consequently removal of growths after flowering is all that is required. To shorten growths entails loss of bloom and should only be done for reasons of space. Propagation also is easy, partially ripened shoots can be rooted in June or July with a little heat under mist, while ripened growths can be rooted outside in a sheltered border if inserted in late October.

× *elegantissima*
A plant of garden origin about 1909. Flowers borne in June, a delicate pink in bud, white tinted rose on the inside of the petals, a bushy graceful plant. A.G.M. 1954. **153**
'**Rosealind**', a more recent hybrid of this group from the Slieve Donard Nursery Co., is a lovely clone growing from 1·2–1·5 m. (4–5 ft) in height. The flowers are a rich carmine pink colour.

gracilis **Slender Deutzia** 75–90 cm. ($2\frac{1}{2}$–3 ft)
This parent of many hybrids is a species originating in Japan from where it was introduced about 1840. A handsome plant, sometimes caught by late frosts in cold areas. Has been much used for forcing, its pure white flowers being at their best unsullied under glass.

× *hybrida*
This is a group of hybrid deutzias which are of considerable value as garden plants and several have been named. A selection follows:
'**Contraste**', 1·5 m. (5 ft), soft lilac pink, outside of petals deep purple.
'**Joconde**', 1·5 m. (5 ft), a very fine shrub with very large flowers shaded rose purple on outside petals, inside white.
'**Magicien**', 1·5 m. (5 ft), a large flowered form, deep pink, with some purple on reverse side of petals. A.G.M. 1969.
'**Mont Rose**', rosy pink to purple is regarded as the type of this group which can grow to 1·5–1·85 m. (5–6 ft) in height. A late bloomer. A.G.M. 1957.
'**Perle Rose**', 1·5 m. (5 ft), soft rose pink flowers borne in June.

longifolia 1·5 m. (5 ft)
This is a handsome medium sized shrub about 1·5 m. high, from western China introduced in 1905. It produces large clusters of white faintly tinted pinkish purple flowers in June and July.
'**Veitchii**', is a superior form in which the larger flowers are a rich lilac pink. Z.6.

× *magnifica* **Showy Deutzia** 1·85 m. (6 ft)
Raised by Lemoine and put into commerce in 1909. A magnificent shrub producing rather dense panicles of double white flowers. A.G.M. 1926. Z.5.

× *rosea* 90 cm. (3 ft)
Another group of hybrids raised by Lemoine about 1895 and growing to a height of 90 cm. and well suited to small gardens. Z.4.
'**Carminea**', is the most popular of the group and is an attractive plant, put into commerce in 1900. The arching branches carry a profusion of rosy pink flowers which are more deeply coloured on the outside of the petals and in the bud stage. A.G.M. 1969. **154**

scabra 3·05 m. (10 ft)
This large shrub, sometimes attaining a height of 3 m. is a native of Japan and China and was introduced in 1822. Flowering in late June this species escapes frost damage and is a most reliable garden plant producing masses of its white flowers. Removal of old growths after flowering can reduce the size of this shrub where this may be necessary.
'**Flore Pleno**', has double white flowers, suffused with rosy purple on the outside of the petals. Sometimes known as 'Plena'.
'**Pride of Rochester**', is a similar clone. F.C.C. 1863.

setchuenensis 1·85 m. (6 ft)
Central and western China. Usually represented in gardens by *D. setchuenensis corymbiflora*, an equally beautiful and more floriferous form which grows to about 1·85 m. high. This is a strikingly beautiful shrub in gardens where it succeeds. It is not quite hardy

enough for very exposed gardens although I have seen it flowering well in a colder and more northerly garden than I would have expected. The small stellate white flowers are produced in clusters virtually in hundreds and open successively over a considerable period from June to August. Adequate ripening of the wood is of paramount importance for this plant. Z.6.

Deutzia,
    Showy see *Deutzia* × *magnifica*
    Slender see *Deutzia gracilis*
Dickson's Golden Elm see *Ulmus* ×
    sarniensis 'Dicksonii'
Diervilla see under *Weigela*

DIPELTA CAPRIFOLIACEAE

floribunda 3·05 m. (10 ft)   ▼※
A native of central and western China and discovered in 1875 but not introduced to Britain and U.S. until 1902. A large deciduous shrub reaching some 3 m. in height, possibly more in sheltered gardens. Fairly hardy and easily grown in most soils in an open position. Quite handsome when in full bloom, the weigela-like flowers, pink flushed yellow in the throat are borne in great profusion. Old flowering stems can be cut away, leaving the new non-flowering shoots for next season's crop. May be increased by cuttings under mist during June and July. Z.5.

DISANTHUS HAMAMELIDACEAE

cercidifolius 2·45–3·05 m. (8–10 ft)   ◐†➤
Japan. Introduced 1893. A deciduous shrub which thrives best in semi-woodland conditions on lime free soil, adequate moisture and some shade. The small purplish flowers are produced in October but have no decorative importance. However, when happy, this shrub with its Judas tree *(Cercis)* like leaves is of great value for its autumn colouring of wine red and purplish orange and is indeed of great beauty. F.C.C. 1970. Z.6–7. **155**

Dogwood,
    Alternated-leaved see *Cornus alternifolia*
    Chinese see *Cornus kousa chinensis*
    Flowering see *Cornus florida*
    Golden Twig see *Cornus stolonifera*
      'Flaviramea'
    Red-barked see *Cornus alba*
    Siberian see *Cornus alba* 'Sibirica'
    Tartarian see *Cornus alba*
    Westonbirt see *Cornus alba* 'Sibirica'

DRIMYS WINTERACEAE   △※

winteri **Winter's Bark** to 6·1 m. (20 ft)

Southern South America. Introduced 1827. A handsome large evergreen shrub which in sheltered gardens may become a tree. It really requires, and is worthy of, a sheltered position where the fragrant creamy white flowers are generally produced in May. Z.8. **156**

Dwarf
    Flowering Almond see *Prunus glandulosa*
    Horse Chestnut see *Aesculus parviflora*
    Russian Almond see *Prunus tenella*
Dyer's Greenwood see *Genista tinctoria*

E

Early
    Dutch Honeysuckle see *Lonicera*
      periclymenum 'Belgica'
    Forsythia see *Forsythia ovata*

EDGWORTHIA THYMELAEACEAE

chrysantha syn. *E. papyrifera* **Paper Bush**   ▼※
1·2 m. (4 ft)
A deciduous shrub, native to China, generally about 1·2 m. high which has been cultivated in Japan for a long time where it is used for the manufacture of a high class paper. The slightly fragrant pendulous flowers are produced in clusters towards the ends of branches in March and are a rich cowslip yellow. Can only be grown successfully in sheltered gardens, but, withstands more exposure in mild or maritime districts. **157**

ELAEAGNUS ELAEAGNACEAE Oleaster

× *ebbingei* (*E. macrophylla* × *E. pungens*)   △
3·05 m. (10 ft)
A seedling found by S. D. A. Doorenbos at The Hague,

Abbreviations and symbols used in the text

▼	Deciduous	†	Lime hater
△	Evergreen	◍	Shade
※	Flowers	◐	Semi shade
●	Fruit	⊙	Sun
➤	Foliage		

A.G.M. Award of Garden Merit, Royal Horticultural Society
F.C.C. First Class Certificate, Royal Horticultural Society

Z1–10 The Z numbers represent the climatic zones used in the United States and provide a useful hardiness rating elsewhere. Thus Z1 is for those plants surviving coldest conditions and Z10 is the other extreme

The illustration numbers are in **bold type**.

Holland in 1929, and which has rapidly become popular because of its fast growth, splendid for providing shelter, even near the sea. Will attain a height of 3 m., possibly more but can be controlled by pruning. Inconspicuous flowers in autumn and not likely to be noticed except for their pronounced fragrance. Berries ripen in spring. A.G.M. 1969.

   'Gilt Edge', a form in which the leaves are edged with gold. Z.6.

macrophylla to over 2·45 m. (8 ft)

Korea and Japan. Introduced 1879. A hardy evergreen shrub which grows in time to a considerable size but will withstand some pruning in spring. It is the largest leaved of the oleasters and one of the most handsome, particularly in spring when the young leaves are silvery all over, later becoming green on the upper side. The flowers produced in autumn are small, silvery white but very fragrant. Berries ripen the following spring. It is valuable for hedging or shelter belts particularly in maritime areas. A.G.M. 1969. Z.7.

pungens to 4·55 m. (15 ft)

Native of Japan. Introduced 1830. A vigorous evergreen which grows to 4·55 m. in height, very useful as a shelter plant. Produces fragrant flowers in autumn. Berries ripen in spring. Z.6.

   'Aurea', leaves margined in deep yellow.

   'Dicksonii', a wider golden margin with some leaves nearly all golden, a slow growing form.

   'Fredericii', a form with small narrow leaves of pale yellow, thinly margined glossy green. Grows to 1·5 m. (5 ft) **158**

   'Maculata', the most popular form because of its richer colouring. The gold centre in each leaf is variable in size and shape but is effectively bright in winter, particularly when sunny. Certainly one of the most pleasing of foliage shrubs, and being of moderate growth, to 2·45 m. (8 ft), easily accommodated. Can be kept restricted by cutting for indoor decoration, its leaves are a delight in floral arrangements. Like many variegated shrubs some growths are liable to revert to the green type, such growths should be removed at the point of origin. Cuttings of firm young growths can be rooted under mist in summer. F.C.C. 1891, A.G.M. 1969. **159**

Elder see *Sambucus*
Elder,
   Red-berried see *Sambucus racemosa*
   Water see *Viburnum opulus*
Elm see *Ulmus*
Elm,
   Dickson's Golden see *Ulmus* × *sarniensis* **'Dicksonii'**
   Jersey see *Ulmus* × *sarniensis*
   Wheatley see *Ulmus* × *sarniensis*

EMBOTHRIUM PROTEACEAE

coccineum **Chilean Fire Bush**

to 9·15 m. (30 ft)

Chile, South America. Introduced by Lobb 1846. An erect semi-evergreen shrub or small tree which only reaches the height mentioned in the gardens where very favourable climatic conditions prevail, warm temperate weather. In such areas this is a priceless treasure, providing during May and June the most glorious display of brilliant orange scarlet flowers fully justifying its common name of Chilean Fire Bush. Can be propagated by seed or from suckers.

   lanceolatum, the semi-deciduous, hardy form collected by Comber in 1926–7, in the Norquinco Valley and by which name this plant is sometimes known. Grows to about 5·45 m. (18 ft). In this plant the racemes are so close the whole plant becomes a graceful column of blazing scarlet during May and June, a wonderful sight. Well worth a sheltered sunny site which retains moisture in summer. Best planted from a pot or container and kept to the same depth when it will grow rapidly, to about 4·5 m. (15 ft), if kept moist. No pruning required normally, but can be pruned after flowering to keep the plant shapely or to restrict it in size. F.C.C. 1948. **160**

   'Flamenco', a seedling from above raised at Bodnant, North Wales and named in 1960. This is a very fine form quite distinct in flower from its parent and much more orange red in colour. **161**

English
   Ivy see *Hedera helix*
   Laurel see *Prunus laurocerasus*

ENKIANTHUS ERICACEAE   †

campanulatus **Redvein Enkianthus**

c. 2·75 m (9 ft)

Japan. Introduced by Maries 1880. A deciduous shrub which dislikes lime, indeed requires similar conditions to rhododendrons. The pendulous, bell shaped flowers, are pale creamy yellow tipped red and borne in great profusion in May. The subtle beauty of its flowers is later surpassed for garden effect by the red and gold of its foliage in autumn. A.G.M. 1932. Z.4. **162**

perulatus **White Enkianthus**

1·5–1·85 m. (5–6 ft)

Japan. Introduced about 1870. A compact, deciduous shrub with masses of pitcher-shaped white flowers which appear in April, before the leaves, on glabrous stalks in terminal clusters. One of our most consistent shrubs for autumn colour when its leaves turn yellow and red. Z.5. **163**

Enkianthus,
   Redvein see *Enkianthus campanulatus*
   White see *Enkianthus perulatus*

ERICA ERICACEAE **Heath** △

Evergreen shrubs which are increasing considerably in popularity because they cover the ground rapidly. They are easily established, thus saving a great deal of labour in the garden. An open sunny position is preferable but slight shade is tolerated. They thrive in sandy peat or loamy soils but appreciate the addition of moist peat or leaf mould at planting time. Most are best planted in small groups of five or so, according to the size of the garden, whether it be in a 'heather' garden or in conjunction with shrubs or other subjects. Most heaths dislike lime, the exceptions being *Erica* × *darleyensis*, *E. herbacea (carnea)*, and *E. mediterranea* which can be grown in alkaline soils but do not like pure chalk, plus *E. terminalis*, which has been known to grow well on chalk.

arborea **Tree Heath** 3·05 m. (10 ft) † ❀ ✿

Native of southern Europe, north and east Africa and Caucasus. Introduced 1658. A bushy shrub, sometimes attaining a height of 3 m., but only in favourable climatic conditions when it may reach considerably more. The fragrant white globular flowers are borne in great profusion in early spring. Z.7.

'Alpina', a handsome evergreen shrub with bright green foliage on an upright plant, not so tall as *E. arborea*, at 1·5–2·1 m. (5–7 ft). Slow to reach blossoming, the flowers are a dullish white, but are scented and freely produced when well established. Dislikes lime. A.G.M. 1933, **164**

'Gold Tips', a form in which the tips of the young growth are touched with gold, noticeably in spring sunshine, similar to *E. arborea* 'Alpina'. **165**

australis **Spanish** or **Southern Heath** † ❀
1·85 m. (6 ft)

This native of Spain and Portugal is best suited in sheltered gardens where its rosy purple flowers will proclaim it as one of the showiest Tree Heaths. F.C.C. 1962, A.G.M. 1969.

'Mr Robert', a delightful white form which is apparently hardier. A.G.M. 1941.

carnea see *E. herbacea*

cinerea **Bell Heather, Twisted Heath** † ❀

A common but beautiful plant growing on the moors of Britain and also found in western Europe. A low densely woven shrub, flowering from June to August. Z.5.

'Atrorubens', a distinct form, long sprays of rich red flowers. About 15 cm. (6 in) high. **166**

'Cevennes', mauvish pink flowers on erect growths flowering over a long period. About 23 cm. (9 in) high. **167**

'Eden Valley', pinkish lilac flowers, fading to white at the base. About 15 cm. (6 in) high. A.G.M. 1969.

'Hookstone White', white flowers borne profusely on long stems over a long period. About 23 cm. (9 in.) high. **168**

× *darleyensis* 45 cm. (1½ ft) ❀

A hybrid which occurred about 1890 at Darley Dale Nurseries, Derbyshire, England, showing characters intermediate between *E. herbacea* and *E. erigena*. A natural companion to *E. herbacea* but of stronger growth, growing 45 cm. high. An invaluable garden plant, flowering from November to May.

'Arthur Johnson', long dense sprays of rosy magenta flowers, very attractive in flower arrangements. About 60 cm. (2 ft) high. A.G.M. 1969. **169**

'Darley Dale', this is the type plant of the group, and is deservedly popular; delicate pink flowers; thrives on poor soil. About 60 cm. (2 ft) high. A.G.M. 1924. **170**

'George Rendall', a very fine form which has rich pink flowers, produced over a long period and has attractive foliage in spring of bright golden yellow for a few weeks. A.G.M. 1969. **171**

'Silberschmelze', a sport of 'Darley Dale', which originated in Germany. A most useful sweet scented plant with delicate white flowers, growing to about 4·5 cm. (1½ ft). A.G.M. 1969.

erigena syn. *E. mediterranea* **Biscay** or ❀
Mediterranean Heath 1·5 m. (5 ft)

A dense bushy shrub 1·5 m. or more in height, found in southern France, Spain, Portugal and Northern Ireland, and which appears to have been in cultivation in 1648. One of the best spring flowering shrubs, providing colour and fragrance. Flowers from March to May. Rich rosy red flowers and although lime tolerant will not thrive in shallow, chalky soils. **172**

'Superba', a good form with pink flowers. A.G.M. 1974.

herbacea syn. *E. carnea* **Winter, Snow** or ❀
Spring Heath 23 cm. (9 in.)

A native of the Alps, the Apennines and some eastern European mountains, this is a popular and widely planted shrub. In February and March the plants are masses of rosy red flowers providing a brilliant effect in what is often the worst time of year for colour in the garden. More familiarly known over many years as *E.*

Abbreviations and symbols used in the text

▼	Deciduous	†	Lime hater
△	Evergreen	◍	Shade
❀	Flowers	◑	Semi shade
●	Fruit	☉	Sun
✿	Foliage		

A.G.M. Award of Garden Merit, Royal Horticultural Society
F.C.C. First Class Certificate, Royal Horticultural Society

Z1–10 The Z numbers represent the climatic zones used in the United States and provide a useful hardiness rating elsewhere. Thus Z1 is for those plants surviving coldest conditions and Z10 is the other extreme

The illustration numbers are in **bold type**.

carnea most gardeners will regret that a change of name has been found necessary. Trimming over with shears as soon as the flowers have lost colour will keep the plants dwarf and tidy. Ideal for ground cover. A.G.M. 1924.

'December Red', a cultivar which flowers from December to March. Rather badly named being pink and very similar in growth to 'Springwood White'. **173**

'King George', bright rosy red, similar to *E. herbacea* but coming into flower much earlier, dark leaves low growing. According to Bean, 8th Ed. Vol. II page 106, often wrongly called 'Winter Beauty,. A.G.M. 1927.

'Praecox Rubra', deep rosy red early to mid season, lovely low habit of growth.

'Ruby Glow', a large flowered form of deep rose with bronzed foliage and low tufted growth. One of the richest coloured ericas. A.G.M. 1969.

'Springwood Pink', clear rose pink with an abundant trailing habit, excellent for ground cover. Flowers January to March in England, to May in U.S. A.G.M. 1940.

'Springwood White', generally considered to be one of the best heaths, certainly the finest white, habit similar to 'Springwood Pink'. A.G.M. 1940. **174**

'Vivellii', deep, carmine red flowers, with very dark bronzy foliage in winter, deep green in summer. A very fine cultivar with dwarf tufted growth in flower January to March. A.G.M. 1969. **175**

lusitanica **Portugal** or **Spanish Heath**   †※
1·5 m. (5 ft)
A fine tree heath with some resemblance to *E. arborea* but flowering earlier and having paler foliage. When seen together they are quite distinct. A plant which is particularly valuable in the milder counties of south-west England, and in the U.S., coastal California, from Santa Barbara south, flowering in great profusion during March and April, earlier in mild weather. **176**

mediterranea see *E. erigena*

terminalis **Corsican Heath** 1·2–2·45 m. (4–8 ft)   ※
A native of the western Mediterranean region and has become naturalised in Northern Ireland. The rosy pink flowers are produced from June to September on a bushy, erect shrub of pleasing habit. The spent blooms are not without value becoming a warm russet colour. A desirable shrub which is more lime tolerant than other heaths and will also thrive in acid soils.

tetralix **Cross-leaved Heath**   †※🍂
to 45 cm. (1½ ft)
A native of northern and western Europe, frequently found in wet moors. Flowering June to October. Z.3.

'Alba Mollis', a distinctive plant with a somewhat frosted appearance, due to the whitish down on stems and leaves. Flowers white. 23 cm. (9 in.) high. **177**

'Con Underwood', an attractive cultivar of compact growth. Crimson urn-shaped flowers are enhanced by greyish foliage. 23 cm. (9 in.) high.

vagans **Cornish Heath** over 30 cm. (1 ft)   †※
A native of Cornwall, England, and south-western Europe. A low spreading shrub over 30 cm. in height, particularly handsome in late summer and autumn and still attractive in winter when the spent flowers catch the sun. Cutting over in spring before growth recommences, just below the old flowers will keep the plants more compact in habit. Will thrive in most soils other than heavy clay and lime. Z.5.

'Cream', has white flowers in long racemes, taller than the type. 60 cm. (2 ft.).

'Holden Pink', mauve pink flowers profusely produced in September and October on compact plants. 45 cm. (1½ ft).

'Lyonesse', is probably the best white Cornish Heath, up to 90 cm. (3 ft), with pure white flowers with protruding brown anthers which are quite distinctive. A.G.M. 1969.

'Mrs D. F. Maxwell', has large spikes of deep cerise freely produced on spreading plants. One of the finest heaths. 45 cm. (1½ ft). A.G.M. 1969. **178**

'St Keverne', a cultivar which has become very popular in gardens where its clear rosy flowers are appreciated. 45 cm. (1½ ft). A.G.M. 1927. **179**

× *veitchii* 1·5 m. (5 ft)   †※🍂
A hybrid tree heath which appears to be between *E. arborea* and *E. lusitanica*. The result is a beautiful shrub with plumes of fragrant white flowers in spring and attractive bright green foliage. Not a plant for exposed gardens. Only suitable for the warmest parts of U.S. **180**

ERYTHRINA LEGUMINOSAE   ⊙

crista-galli **Coral Tree, Cockspur Coral-Bean** ※
1·5 m. (5 ft)
Introduced 1771. A spectacularly beautiful semi-woody plant from Brazil which requires a sheltered position as a wall shrub except in gardens of very favoured climates. In others it is generally cut back to ground level during winter but survives if the crown is protected. The very large wax like flowers are deep scarlet red and produced in large terminal racemes during late summer. Z.9. **181**

ESCALLONIA ESCALLONIACEAE   ⊙△※
This is mainly represented in gardens by hybrid, evergreen shrubs which not only grow quickly but are hardier than generally supposed. Most are as useful for hedges as indeed they are for shrub borders, and particularly so in maritime areas and the milder counties. They appreciate good soil and sunny positions. Pruning is not often required except where grown as hedges, these can be trimmed back as soon as the flowers are over. Overgrown bushes may be cut hard back in April. Cuttings are easily rooted during summer under mist or in a propagating frame.

'Apple Blossom' 1·2 m. (4 ft)
An attractive, slow growing shrub, suitable for small

gardens, around 1·2 m. in height. Clear pink flowers with a white base. A.G.M. 1951.

'C. F. Ball' up to 3 m. (10 ft)
A well known seedling from *E. rubra macrantha*, a vigorous grower with crimson flowers, excellent for seaside planting.

'Crimson Spire' 1·85 m. (6 ft)
A self sown seedling, and very upright in growth. Has proved an excellent subject for hedges growing quickly to 1·85 m. and producing good crimson flowers.

'Donard Brilliance'
An excellent shrub for small gardens, flowering profusely on pendulous branches. If cut back after flowering, another display of the large rosy crimson flowers will be produced.

'Donard Seedling' 1·5 (5 ft)
A vigorous shrub, 1·5 m. in height, producing its white, suffused pink, scented flowers freely from pink buds. Bushy arching growth and useful as a flowering hedge. A.G.M. 1969

'Edinensis' 1·5 m. (5 ft)
A fine arching shrub, neat in habit up to 1·5 m. in height, spangled with clear pink flowers. A.G.M. 1969.

'Gwendolyn Anley'
A small shrub of bushy habit with flesh pink flowers. Very hardy. A.G.M. 1969.

'Langleyensis' to 2·5 m. (8 ft)
A strong, elegant shrub with rose-pink flowers. A.G.M. 1926.

macrantha see *E. rubra macrantha*

'Peach Blossom'
Very similar in habit to *E.* 'Apple Blossom', thus suitable for small gardens, clear peach pink flowers. A.G.M. 1969.

rubra macrantha 3 m. (10 ft)
Introduced about 1846 from the island of Chiloe and generally known as *E. macrantha*. Well known in many seaside towns where it is much used for hedges and as a shelter belt. In such favoured climes it is a handsome shrub with fine large glossy leaves which set off the rosy red flowers to perfection. In inland gardens it is apt to suffer damage in a severe winter. A dense shrub it can grow up to 3 m. in height. The parent of many hybrids some of them able to withstand more frost.

'Slieve Donard' 2·1 m. (7 ft)
A very hardy medium sized compact shrub. It produces large panicles of white flushed pink flowers in June. Can be used for hedging where its glossy foliage is seen to advantage. **182**

EUCALYPTUS MYRTACEAE **Gum Tree**
A large genus of evergreen trees mainly natives of Australia. Very fast growing and tolerant of most soils with the possible exception of chalk. Can in general, only be grown from seed and these are better potted up and planted out in the spring. Cuttings with a heel have, on occasion, been successfully rooted. Grown naturally the eucalyptus are outside the scope of this book but as the production of the juvenile foliage is prolonged by regular pruning, they can be accommodated in small gardens. The lovely blue grey foliage is of great value for house decoration as well as for colour effect in the garden.

gunnii **Cider Gum** 1·5–1·85 m. (5–6 ft)
A native of Tasmania and one of the hardiest. Allowed to grow naturally will become a very large tree, but pruned hard annually in April will make a lovely bush around 1·5–1·85 m. in height. **183**

perriniana **Spinning Gum**
Easily distinguished by its circular leaves which at first clasp the stems in pairs, but eventually become free and spin around in the wind. Very effective when kept as a bush by regular pruning, and also good for cutting.

EUCRYPHIA EUCRYPHIACEAE

cordifolia 4·55 m. (15 ft) △ ✳
Introduced 1851 from Chile. This is an evergreen which may reach tree size in specially favourable climates but more likely to be seen around 4·55 m. Pure white flowers with numerous yellow anthers are produced but in general this species although tolerant of chalk is only happy in a moist mild climate. Z.8.

glutinosa 3·05 m. (10 ft) † ▼ ✳ ●
Chile. Introduced by Pearce 1859. A large deciduous shrub with pinnate leaves, which in time will attain the stature of a small tree. The large, scented, white single

---

Abbreviations and symbols used in the text

▼	Deciduous	†	Lime hater
△	Evergreen	⬤	Shade
✳	Flowers	◖	Semi shade
●	Fruit	☉	Sun
➥	Foliage		

A.G.M.   Award of Garden Merit, Royal Horticultural Society
F.C.C.   First Class Certificate, Royal Horticultural Society

Z1–10   The Z numbers represent the climatic zones used in the United States and provide a useful hardiness rating elsewhere. Thus Z1 is for those plants surviving coldest conditions and Z10 is the other extreme

The illustration numbers are in **bold type**.

flowers with prominent stamens, are borne profusely in July and August singly or in pairs from the end of each shoot. The leaves turn all shades of red and yellow in the autumn, to add to the beauty of this most valuable late flowering plant, which succeeds best in moist, lime free soil. F.C.C. 1880, A.G.M. 1935. Z.8.

    'Flore Pleno', the double flowered form which appears amongst seedlings but is not generally regarded as being an improvement on the type plant. **184**

× intermedia (*E. glutinosa × E. lucida*)   †△✳
A small evergreen tree of great beauty of foliage, with variable leaves which may be single or trifoliate on the same plant. A spontaneous hybrid between *E. glutinosa* and *E. lucida* and of interest being a Chilean species crossed with a Tasmanian one. This appeared in a garden, at Rostrevor, County Down, Northern Ireland. Z.8.

    'Rostrevor', the original form of the cross mentioned above and the plant in general cultivation. A free growing small tree. The fragrant flowers are white, of a perfectly formed bowl shape with a central tuft of stamens. The slender branches are upright forming a broad column and are smothered in August and September with the beautiful flowers. **185**

× nymansensis   †△✳
'Nymansay', 9 m. (30 ft), a famous large evergreen shrub or small tree, which can attain 9 m. or more in favourable localities but is more frequently seen at less. A superb plant raised about 1915, its large cup shaped flowers are scented and freely produced when grown in a sunny position with adequate moisture at the roots. Can be easily propagated from July cuttings under mist or by layering. F.C.C. 1926, A.G.M. 1973. Z.8.

EUONYMUS CELASTRACEAE **Spindle Tree, Corkbush**

A very useful genus of plants for the garden but with flowers of little ornamental value. This is however compensated for by foliage in the evergreen kinds, with added value as ground cover in some cases. The deciduous kinds have considerable value as fruiting shrubs, especially when several are grown in a group, while others are notable for their fine autumn colours.

    Easily cultivated in any reasonable soil including chalk. Close watch used to be necessary to prevent aphis or caterpillar damage. Spraying with a systemic insecticide as a late spring routine will act as a preventative. The evergreens are generally easily increased from cuttings in summer, under mist, or in a propagating frame. Likewise deciduous kinds, while those which fruit may be grown from seeds. Layering can always be used where only a few plants are required and the creeping kinds frequently root as they spread thus providing an easy means of increase.

alatus   1·2 m. (4 ft)   ▼

A deciduous shrub from China and Japan, of medium size generally about 1·2 m. and slow in growth. Easily recognized by the corky wings on the twigs, this is one of the best shrubs for providing an autumn display of colour. A.G.M. 1932.

europaeus **Common Spindle Tree**   ▼•
over 3 m. (10 ft)
A native of Europe. It is a deciduous shrub which sometimes grows into a small tree, especially in hedges, where it frequently produces attractive crops of scarlet capsules which opens to orange-covered seeds. Grows well in chalk or lime. A.G.M. 1969. **186**

    'Red Cascade', a selected form in which the arching branches are often almost bent double with the weight of large rosy red fruits. A.G.M. 1969.

fortunei **Winter Creeper** (juvenile forms)   △•
1·2–1·5 m. (4–5 ft)
A species which is generally represented in gardens by *E. fortunei radicans*, a creeping, trailing or climbing evergreen shrub from Japan, which has two forms, juvenile and with age the adult form. The latter forsakes the trailing or creeping form and becomes shrubby with no apparent inclination to trail or climb. Grows higher against a wall. A.G.M. 1969. Z.5.

    'Carrierei', the adult state of *E. fortunei radicans* just referred to above and which grows into a low spreading shrub producing green tinted flowers and fruit.

    'Colorata', distinctive because its leaves turn a beautiful crimson purple in autumn, remain so during winter and become green again in spring. An effective ground cover plant.

    'Emerald Gaiety', a new cultivar from U.S. with rounded green leaves strikingly variegated white. **187**

    'Emerald 'n' Gold', also from the U.S. very striking colour during winter months with golden variegation. Useful for ground cover. **188**

    'Silver Queen', is often regarded as the best of the shrubby forms, and reported to be a sport of 'Carrierei', a colourful plant with creamy yellow leaves in spring becoming green margined creamy white in summer. **189**

japonicus   3·05–4·55 m. (10–15 ft)   △❧
From Japan. Introduced 1804. A large densely branched shrub with lustrous leaves which in sheltered gardens may grow into a small tree. One of the best evergreens for hedges and especially useful for coastal planting. Not hardy enough for northern gardens. Hedges should be trimmed in April. Z.8.

    'Albomarginatus', green leaves with a narrow white edging.

    'Ovatus Aureus', very popular in England, the leaves having a broad irregular margin of creamy yellow blending into the green centre. Most colourful if grown in full sun, and easily propagated by cuttings under mist. Is also useful as a pot plant for indoor decoration, particularly in winter months. Aureo-variegatus 'Yellow Queen' of U.S. is very close to 'Ovatus Aureus'. **190**

EUPHORBIA

characias 90 cm.–1·2 m. (3–4 ft) △

Mediterranean area. A sub-shrubby evergreen plant with stems which arises from below ground and bearing blue green leaves on the upper half, the lower half ringed with scars of the fallen leaves. These terminate in panicles of bright greenish yellow bracts with conspicuous purplish brown glands making up the inflorescence. The latter feature is the main distinction between this and the closely allied species, *E. wulfenii* which is frequently confused with it. There are intermediate types also probably the result of chance crosses which add to the confusion. All, however, are decorative plants when growing, on well drained soils and do well on chalky soils. Can be increased from seed, indeed self sown seedlings frequently appear, by division or from cuttings taken after flowering. In common with the other members of the spurge family, if cut or broken the younger parts of the plant exude a milky sap. **191**

wulfenii see under *E. characias*

European
 Bladder Nut see *Staphylea pinnata*
 Cranberry Bush see *Viburnum opulus*
 Hazel see *Corylus avellana*
Evergreen Mock Orange see *Carpenteria californica*

EXOCHORDA ROSACEAE Pearlbush

× ***macrantha*** *(E. korolkowii × E. racemosa)* ▼✳
3·05 m. (10 ft)

A large deciduous shrub raised about 1900 by Lemoine of Nancy, France by crossing *E. korolkowii* with *E. racemosa*. The result is a shrub of considerable beauty similar in habit to *E. racemosa* and producing abundant racemes in May from every bud of the previous years growth.

 'The Bride', a very attractive form, raised in America by the United States National Arboretum. The plant photographed is of medium size, but may justify the appellation large, in a few years time. **192**

racemosa **Common Pearlbush** †▼✳
to 3·05 m. (10 ft)

Northern China. Introduced by Fortune 1849. A beautiful white flowered deciduous shrub which becomes rather dense if not thinned out after the flowering in May, treatment which will produce much finer racemes. Will grow on any good well drained soil but does not like lime. Can be propagated from firm young growths under mist in summer. Z.4.

F

FABIANA SOLANACEAE ⊙△✳

imbricata 1·85–2·45 m. (6–8 ft)

Bolivia, Argentina, Chile. Introduced 1838. Reintroduced 1925–27. An evergreen shrub not unlike heath in appearance which succeeds best in a warm sheltered position where the soil is well drained. The funnel-shaped white flowers are freely produced in June and so that where happy it is of considerable beauty. No pruning is required and it can be propagated under mist from firm young growths during summer. Z.9. **193**

 'Prostrata', a similar but smaller shrub, somewhat hardier with pale lilac tinted flowers.
 'Violacea', similar to the type plant except in colour of the flowers which are pale blue-mauve and it is somewhat hardier. F.C.C. 1932.

False
 Acacia see *Robinia pseudoacacia*
 Cypress see *Chamaecyparis*
 Cypress, Hinoki see *Chamaecyparis obtusa*

FATSIA ARALIACEAE △☙

japonica **Japanese Aralia** 1·85–3·05 m. (8–10 ft)

Japan. Introduced 1838. A handsome evergreen shrub, quite hardy in warmer gardens, but preferring a semi-shaded sheltered position where it will provide a striking display in October. The milky white flowers, of globose formation, are produced in branching panicles handsomely offset by the large glossy palmate leaves. If the flowers are cut off as soon as they appear, the leaves grow even larger. Well known as a pot plant for house decoration it is being increasingly used in tubs or other containers because of its architectural qualities. Can be

---

Abbreviations and symbols used in the text

▼ Deciduous	† Lime hater
△ Evergreen	⦾ Shade
✳ Flowers	◐ Semi shade
• Fruit	⊙ Sun
☙ Foliage	

A.G.M. Award of Garden Merit, Royal Horticultural Society
F.C.C. First Class Certificate, Royal Horticultural Society

Z1–10 The Z numbers represent the climatic zones used in the United States and provide a useful hardiness rating elsewhere. Thus Z1 is for those plants surviving coldest conditions and Z10 is the other extreme

The illustration numbers are in **bold type**.

propagated by cuttings of firm young growths in a heated propagating frame. Pruning is not generally required but where plants have outgrown their position they may be cut back in April. Plants for house decoration of *F. japonica* are often grown from imported seed. F.C.C. 1966, A.G.M. 1969. **194**

'Variegata', has large blotches of white on the tips of the leaf lobes and on the margins. Z.7. **195**

February Daphne see *Daphne mezereum*
Figwort, Cape see *Phygelius capensis*
Filbert see *Corylus maxima*
Filbert, Purple-leaved see *Corylus maxima* '*Purpurea*'
Firethorn, Gibb's see *Pyracantha atalantioides*
Fish-bone Cotoneaster see *Cotoneaster horizontalis*
Flame Azalea see *Rhododendron calendulaceum*
Flannel Bush see *Fremontodendron californicum*
Flowering
    Almond, Dwarf see *Prunus glandulosa*
    Currant see *Ribes sanguineum*
    Dogwood see *Cornus florida*
    Maple see *Abutilon*
    Maple, Brazil see *Abutilon megapotamicum*
    Maple, Grape-leaved see *Abutilon vitifolium*
    Nutmeg see *Leycesteria formosa*
    Quince see *Chaenomeles*
    Quince, Japanese see *Chaenomeles japonica*

FORSYTHIA OLEACEAE **Golden Bells** ▼ ✳

A most popular and well known early spring flowering deciduous shrub. Not fastidious as regards soil but they are gross feeders and it is essential to provide sufficient nutrients before planting for good results. Excellent plants for the shrub border, they also provide an effective screen or may be used as an informal hedge. They are also much used for home decoration, and well budded branches can be cut in January or February, placed in water in a glasshouse, or in the home and will provide welcome colour in advance of those growing outside. Forsythias are easily propagated by summer cuttings under mist, or in a frame or by hard wood cuttings in a sheltered border outdoors in late autumn.

Pruning may be done by removal of branches for forcing thus thinning out the shrub or removal of a few old growths after flowering. Severe pruning will result in excessive young growths which will not flower. In some areas birds will destroy the flower buds and preventory measures will be necessary. Those planted close to inhabited buildings are less likely to suffer than if planted in remote areas of the garden.

'Beatrix Farrand' to 3 m. (10 ft)
A tall growing shrub, distinctive in the large size of its canary-yellow flowers and also because it produces a crop of viable seeds. The name is now considered incorrect but the plant is widely available under this name in Britain and from Gulf Stream Nurseries, Virginia, U.S. **196**

× *intermedia*
A group of hybrids between *F. suspensa* and *F. viridissima*, flowering in late March and April, first observed and described in Germany before 1885. This is an important group for garden decoration and several forms have been selected and given cultivar names. Z.4.

'Spectabilis', is probably the best known and most impressive and is especially valuable for its massed effect of brassy golden yellow. Grows to 2·45–3·05 m. (8–10 ft). Raised by Spaeth and introduced shortly before 1906. A.G.M. 1923, F.C.C. 1935. **197**

'Lynwood' to 2·45 m (8 ft)
This lovely shrub, perhaps the best forsythia is a bud-sport of *F.* × *intermedia* 'Spectabilis' found in Northern Ireland and introduced in 1935. The large deep yellow flowers are freely produced all along the branches up to a height of 2·1–2·45 m. A.G.M. 1956, F.C.C. 1966. **198**

ovata **Early Forsythia** 1·5 m. (5 ft)
Korea. Introduced by Wilson 1918. A deciduous shrub, which does not quite equal those already described in garden effect but is earlier in flower, early March, or April U.S. and has a charm of its own. More compact in growth, the bright yellow flowers associate well with forms of *Erica herbacea*. A.G.M. 1947. Z.4.

'Tetragold', a valuable new cultivar flowering in February to March. Its deep yellow flowers are produced on a 90 cm. (3 ft) high plant, very suitable for the small garden.

suspensa **Weeping Forsythia** ◑
2·45–3·05 m. (8–10 ft)
China. Introduced 1833. A rambling deciduous shrub flowering in March to April, to May in U.S., often trained on a wall where it can be very effective, even on the more difficult north facing wall. Very useful for sprawling over banks or fences as it is very hardy and tolerant of most conditions where it can be given sufficient space. On walls where it may attain a height greater than stated some pruning of the growths when the flowers have faded will keep better control. Z.5.

atrocaulis is a form with deep purple young stems and fairly large pale lemon flowers which I value highly for its decorative qualities when cut. **199**

'Nymans Variety', a sport from *F. suspensa atrocaulis,* a very beautiful cultivar with soft yellow flowers, produced on an erect growing shrub with purplish bronze branches and late in flowering.

Forsythia,
    Early see *Forsythia ovata*
    Weeping see *Forsythia suspensa*

FOTHERGILLA HAMAMELIDACEAE †✳❧

major 1·85–3·05 m. (6–10 ft)
Allegheny Mountains, U.S. Introduced 1780. A slow growing deciduous shrub which will take a number of

years to reach the greatest height given, so is quite suitable for any garden of fair size. The erect, creamy white spikes have a feathery appearance produced by the white filaments and yellow anthers (the flowers have no petals). They are profusely borne in April and May and are sweet scented. The hazel like foliage provides brilliant shades of yellow, orange and red before falling. Grows on well drained, lime free soils, and appreciates plenty of leaf mould. This species now covers plants previously grown as *F. monticola*. Can be propagated from cuttings of firm young shoots in June and July under mist, with some bottom heat. A.G.M. 1946, F.C.C. 1969. **200, 201**

Fountain Buddleia see ***Buddleia alternifolia***
Fragrant
  Snowball see ***Viburnum* × *carlcephalum***
  Viburnum see ***Viburnum carlesii*** and ***V. farreri***
  Winter Hazel see ***Corylopsis glabrescens***
Fremontia see ***Fremontodendron***

FREMONTODENDRON syn. *Fremontia* ⊙△✳
STERCULIACEAE

californicum **Flannel Bush** 3·05–6·1 m. (10–20 ft)
California, Arizona. Introduced about 1851. This long and cumbersome name replaces the more familiar *Fremontia*, known to many gardeners. An evergreen or partly deciduous shrub which will attain a height of 6 m. on a sheltered wall, the only situation in which it is likely to survive generally in cooler climes than its native habitat. Easily grown from seed it quickly attains some size on well drained soil and produces its large golden calyxed flowers freely all summer, there are no petals. F.C.C. 1866. Z.7 or 8.

'Californian Glory', a very vigorous hybrid between the above plant and *F. mexicanum* is even more valuable because of the size of its flowers and greater production of them over a long season. Some success has been achieved by rooting tip cuttings under mist, but vegetative propagation is not very easy. It resents root disturbance, therefore young plants should be grown in pots until planted permanently. A glorious plant, worthy of the sheltered position it requires in most gardens or in a large cool greenhouse. **202**

mexicanum see under ***F. californicum***
  'Californian Glory'

French Lavender see ***Lavandula stoechas***

FUCHSIA ONAGRACEAE ⊙◍▼✳
Many of the fuchsias grown in gardens are of hybrid origin and an extensive list could be given if space permitted. The short list which follows will at least draw attention to some which are worth planting, especially for garden display in late summer and autumn. Z.10.

'Army Nurse'
Raised by Hodges in 1947. A profuse producer of medium sized semi-double flowers. These have carmine sepals and tube and a violet blue corolla which has slight flushes of pink. A vigorous upright grower, it is quite hardy in the more temperate climates and stands up extremely well to summer storms, generally coming through unscathed. **203**

'Chillerton Beauty' to 1·2 m. (4 ft)
Grows to 1·2 m. in mild areas. Pale rose-pink with violet purple corolla. Flowers small but prolifically produced. A.G.M. 1973.

'Drame'
Raised by Lemoine in 1880. A fairly hardy plant in temperate areas. It is said to be a seedling of the very hardy *F.* 'Riccartonii' from which, no doubt, this characteristic has been derived. The fairly large flowers are freely produced and have scarlet sepals which contrast strongly with the violet purple corolla and show up very well against the yellowish green foliage. **204**

'Enfante Prodigue' 1·2 m. (4 ft)
A plant with semi-double flowers carmine with purple corolla. An upright bushy grower which is also known as 'Prodigy'. **205**

'Madame Cornelissen' 1·2 m. (4 ft)
Another 1·2 m. cultivar with distinctive semi-double flowers, rich crimson calyx with white corolla. A.G.M. 1969.

magellanica to 3·05 m. (6 ft)
South America. Introduced about 1823. An attractive deciduous shrub, flowering between June and October and varying considerably in size according to the situation in which it is growing. It may attain considerably more than the height mentioned in very sheltered positions in the more favoured climatic areas. This species and its forms can be grown outside in most warm temperate areas, especially if well drained. If

Abbreviations and symbols used in the text

▼	Deciduous	†	Lime hater
△	Evergreen	◍	Shade
✳	Flowers	◐	Semi shade
●	Fruit	⊙	Sun
❧	Foliage		

A.G.M. Award of Garden Merit, Royal Horticultural Society
F.C.C. First Class Certificate, Royal Horticultural Society

Z1–10 The Z numbers represent the climatic zones used in the United States and provide a useful hardiness rating elsewhere. Thus Z1 is for those plants surviving coldest conditions and Z10 is the other extreme

The illustration numbers are in **bold type**.

planted, as all fuchsias should be, a few inches below soil level and the crowns further protected, in exposed gardens, with soil, peat or any other handy material, they will survive. Growths may be cut to ground level in March and new growths from below ground level will grow quickly and commence flowering. Increase is easy, cuttings root readily under mist or in a frame. A few young plants can be overwintered for replacement in very exposed gardens. Z.5–6.

'Alba' see *F. magellanica molinae*

gracilis, is a graceful shrub with slender growths carrying large numbers of small scarlet and purple flowers. A.G.M. 1930.

molinae, an albino variant generally known as *F. magellanica* 'Alba' and occasionally seen growing in gardens but unfortunately, it is not free flowering.

'Variegata', ♠, a sport from *F. magellanica gracilis*, with green leaves margined creamy white, slightly flushed with pink, quite a handsome plant all through the summer months. A.G.M. 1969.

'Versicolor', ♠, like the plant above, a sport from the same source but of quite different appearance. The silvery grey leaves are margined with creamy white with coppery-pink tints in the centre. The young flowers are flushed crimson violet, especially when growing in full sun. A very attractive foliage plant, on occasion a growth reverts to the original parent and should be removed at the source. A.G.M. 1969. **206**

'Mrs Popple' 1·2 m. (4 ft)
Scarlet with deep purple corolla. Upright grower which flowers freely. A.G.M. 1958. **207**

'Mrs W.P. Wood' 60–90 cm. (2–3 ft)
A vigorous upright grower with small flesh pink flowers and white corolla. Much freer in bloom than *F. magellanica molinae* which it resembles but the flowers are deeper in colour. A.G.M. 1969.

'Phyllis' 75–90 cm. (2½–3 ft)
An old cultivar of unknown origin discovered and introduced by Brown in 1938. Quite hardy except in cold exposed gardens and produces its deep rose red flowers with exceptional freedom. Sometimes carries a crop of seed pods which are also quite decorative.

'Phyrne'
A cultivar introduced by Lemoine, France 1905. Double flowers whose white corolla is veined and blotched carmine, sepals and tube cerise. Bushy, free flowering in mild areas, not suitable for cold gardens. **208**

'Prodigy' see **F. 'Enfante Prodigue'**

'Riccartonii' 1·85–2·45 m. (6–8 ft)
The most common hardy fuchsia and which can be seen growing as a hedge in coastal districts of England. The parentage of this fine plant does not seem to be known but it is believed to have been raised about 1830 at Riccarton, Scotland. Bright scarlet sepals with purple or violet corolla. Can attain 1·85–2·45 m. A.G.M. 1927.

'Tom Thumb' 38 cm. (1¼ ft)
A very free flowering dwarf with rosy scarlet calyx and violet petals. A charming cultivar. A.G.M. 1969.

Fuchsia,
Californian see *Zauschneria californica*
Cape see *Phygelius capensis*
Fuchsia flowered Gooseberry see *Ribes speciosum*
Furze see *Ulex*

G

Garden Sage see *Salvia officinalis*
Garland
Flower see *Daphne cneorum*
Wreath see *Spiraeax arguta*

GARRYA GARRYACEAE △

elliptica **Silk-Tassel** 2·45–4·55 m. (8–15 ft) ❋● ♠
California, Oregon, U.S. Introduced 1828. A handsome evergreen shrub, especially in areas of mild climatic conditions. In more exposed gardens it is seen to best advantage on a wall where it will thrive even on a northern aspect. The male and female flowers are produced, during November to February, on separate plants, the former only usually being offered for sale as these produce the long and best catkins. These are freely produced, silver jade green in colour touched with pale yellow as pollen is released. If the female can be grown in conjunction with the male an effective display of purplish brown fruits will result, not without some decorative value.

Little pruning is required except to keep the plant within the limits of space on a wall, indeed removal of small branches for floral arrangements will do most of what is required. Cuttings of firm young growth can be rooted under mist in July or August. The resulting plants should be grown in pots or containers as transplanting is resented. A.G.M. 1960 to the male form. Z.8. **209**

'James Roof', a strong vigorous male form, with large leathery leaves and remarkably long catkins raised near Berkeley, California.

GENISTA LEGUMINOSAE ▼

aetnensis **Mount Etna Broom** ❋
3·65–4·55 m. (12–15 ft)
Sardinia, Sicily. This is usually a very tall shrub but is sometimes seen as a small tree with a single trunk, with little foliage but numerous, bright green rush-like branches. The fragrant golden yellow flowers are freely produced during July and August. A very graceful plant and useful for the back of a border where it will show up

without unduly shading other plants. Its growths should be shortened after flowering for the first two years to induce a more bushy habit. This broom should be securely staked for support. A.G.M. 1923, F.C.C. 1938. **210**

cinerea **Ashy Woadwaxen** to 3·05 m. (10 ft)
Spain, south-west Europe, northern Africa. Cultivated early this century. A tall deciduous shrub, not as common in cultivation as its merits warrant. The long slender branches are covered with fine silky hairs when young which combined with grey green leaves are a beautiful and elegant foil to the golden yellow flowers produced in June and July. These occur 'en masse', later than most other brooms and are fragrant. Does well in poor soil, altogether a desirable plant. A.G.M. 1933. Z.7. **211**

hispanica **Spanish Gorse** or **Broom**
60–90 cm. (2–3 ft)
South-west Europe. Introduced 1759. The Spanish Gorse is a deciduous shrub forming dense prickly mounds smothered with bright yellow pea shaped flowers, brilliant in their mass effect in May and June. Ideal for hot, sunny, well drained sites in soils of moderate quality where flower production reaches a higher level. I have seen this plant used to good effect in large troughs where its spines protect it from damage to some extent. A.G.M. 1969. Z.6.

lydia 60 cm. (2 ft)
East Balkans and west Asia Minor. Introduced 1926. A delightful deciduous shrub with typical broom like pendulous growth, which has quickly become popular in England. A most suitable plant for small gardens, ideal for trailing over a low wall or furnishing a bank. The rich yellow flowers are produced so freely, during May and June, as to hide the growths if planted in a sunny position. The plants can be kept compact in habit by pruning as soon as flowering is over. It may not be a long lived plant but can easily be propagated from cuttings taken in July or August. A.G.M. 1946, F.C.C. 1957. Z.4.

pilosa **Silky-leaf Woadwaxen**
30–45 cm. (1–1½ ft)
West and central Europe and British Isles. A dwarf deciduous shrub which gradually builds up its slender twiggy growths to the height given. The bright yellow flowers in May are massed over the mats of silvery leaves. Ideal for dry walls or sunny banks in well drained soil.

sagittalis **Winged Broom** 30 cm. (1 ft)
Central and southern Europe. In cultivation 1588. A dwarf prostrate shrub which is evergreen in appearance by virtue of its broadly winged flattish stems. The leaves are few and very scattered. The pretty yellow flowers are closely packed and freely produced in June. A useful edging plant, ideally placed on a dry wall where its unusual stems attract attention. Z.2. **212**

tinctoria **Dyer's Greenweed** to 60 cm. (2 ft)
Europe, western Asia. A low semi-prostrate deciduous shrub common on poor gravelly soils, flowering June to September. Hardiest of the genistas. Not so valuable in gardens as the following forms. Z.2.

'**Plena**', has more numerous petals than the plant above so is more brilliant in the garden, indeed it is a superb dwarf semi-prostrate shrub but which can only be propagated by cuttings. A valuable plant for small gardens. A.G.M. 1969.

'**Royal Gold**', is a more erect form growing to 60 cm. (2 ft) in height. The golden yellow flowers are freely produced in terminal and axillary racemes throughout the summer months. A.G.M. 1969.

Gibb's Firethorn see *Pyracantha atalantioides*

GLEDITSIA LEGUMINOSAE

triacanthos **Honey Locust**
'**Sunburst**', a beautiful striking form of the Honey Locust which originated in the United States, where it was patented in 1954, and has now become very popular. It is best suited to sandy soils and in hot conditions it will grow into a medium sized tree, possibly around 6 m. (20 ft) high. Thornless, this deciduous tree has elegant frond-like leaves which are bright yellow when young, presenting an unique appearance of being covered with flowers, becoming pale yellow in autumn. Worthy of consideration for planting in towns where hot dry conditions prevail and the site is well drained. **213**

Globe Butterfly Bush see *Buddleia globosa*
Glory-bower Harlequin see *Clerodendron bungei*
Gold Flower see *Hypericum* × *moseranum*
Golden
 Bells see *Forsythia*

Abbreviations and symbols used in the text

▼ Deciduous   † Lime hater
△ Evergreen   ◍ Shade
✳ Flowers   ◐ Semi shade
● Fruit   ☉ Sun
❧ Foliage

A.G.M. Award of Garden Merit, Royal Horticultural Society
F.C.C. First Class Certificate, Royal Horticultural Society

Z1–10 The Z numbers represent the climatic zones used in the United States and provide a useful hardiness rating elsewhere. Thus Z1 is for those plants surviving coldest conditions and Z10 is the other extreme

The illustration numbers are in **bold type**.

Clematis see *Clematis tangutica*
Lawson Cypress see *Chamaecyparis
    lawsoniana* 'Lutea'
Privet see *Ligustrum ovalifolium* 'Aureum'
Twig Dogwood see *Cornus stolonifera*
    'Flaviramea'
Gooseberry, Fuchsia flowered see *Ribes
    speciosum*
Gorse,
    Common see *Ulex europaeus*
    Spanish see *Genista hispanica*
Grape, Oregon Holly see *Mahonia
    aquifolium*
Grape-leaved Flowering Maple see
    Abutilon vitifolium
Greater Periwinkle see *Vinca major*
Greenwood, Dyer's see *Genista tinctoria*

GRISELINIA CORNACEAE

littoralis

New Zealand. Introduced about 1850. An evergreen shrub which will grow into a small tree in areas with mild climatic conditions. Has been much planted in seaside areas for screening purposes for which it is excellent. The densely produced apple green leaves are very handsome but apt to suffer from frost in cold inland or northern gardens.

'Variegata', a striking form in which the leaf margins are golden becoming white with age. A useful tub plant for sheltered courtyards.

Guelder Rose see *Viburnum opulus*
Gum Tree see *Eucalyptus*
Gum,
    Cider see *Eucalyptus gunnii*
    Spinning see *Eucalyptus perreniana*

H

× *HALIMIOCISTUS* CISTACEAE

45 cm. (1½ ft)
Hybrids between *Cistus* and *Halimium* which grow in well drained soil in full sun and are reasonably hardy. They usually flower between June and September. Easily propagated from summer cuttings under mist, a few young plants will ensure that losses in severe winters can be overcome. Evergreen.

sahucii

Found wild in France, and introduced about 1929 has been found a very satisfactory free flowering garden plant. The 2·5 cm. (1 in.), saucer shaped white flowers are borne in great profusion. The dense growth of deep green foliage, provides excellent ground cover on light soils in a sunny position. A.G.M. 1969. **214**

wintonensis

An attractive dwarf shrub with grey foliage which originated in Hillier's nursery, Winchester, England. The beautiful pearly white flowers have a crimson maroon blotch near the base, giving each flower a startling area of colour with the base stained yellow. An admirable plant for a well drained spot in the garden, especially if in full sun. Flowering in May and June the flowers remain open until the afternoon. **215**

HALIMIUM CISTACEAE

ocymoides 60–90 cm. (2–3 ft)

Spain and Portugal. Introduced before 1800. An erect evergreen shrub which is hardy except in exceptionally severe winters. The flowers, which appear in May and June, are striking and rather pretty, of bright yellow in contrast to black purple basal blotches. The whole plant is furnished with small grey leaves. Propagation by summer cuttings under mist. A.G.M. 1932. Z.7.

HAMAMELIS HAMAMELIDACEAE
Witch Hazel

Completely hardy, the witch hazels require good rich soil, unlikely to dry out during summer and preferably lime free. Pruning is seldom necessary unless for reasons of space, when branches can be removed or pruned back after flowering. A few small branches in the house will be much appreciated, especially for their scent in inclement weather. Plants may be raised from seed which is notoriously slow to germinate and even then takes years to attain flowering size, only to find many are inferior to the parent. Good clones in particular are in consequence spring grafted under glass by nurserymen on to a seedling stock, usually *H. virginiana*. Amateurs who may only require an odd plant may produce one by layering in the spring.

× *intermedia* (*H. japonica* × *H. mollis*)

A group of hybrids between *H. japonica* and *H. mollis*, the original plant described being *H. mollis* pollinated by *H. japonica*. Several clones have arisen in cultivation only two of which are mentioned here.

'Diane', a red flowered form which came from the Kalmthout Arboretum, Belgium. The large leaves provide a bonus of autumn colour. **216**

'Jelena', a free flowering vigorous plant. The flowers are bright coppery orange in effect when seen in winter sunshine. Raised at Kalmthout and worth planting for its fine autumn colouring. Z.5.

mollis Chinese Witch Hazel

China. First introduced 1879, later by Wilson 1907. The most popular and widely planted witch hazel in England, and sharing popularity with *H. virginiana* in U.S. A deciduous shrub which will, in favoured gardens, attain the size of a small tree. The rich golden yellow flowers are richly scented and produced frequently by Christmas Day in England and they are almost weather proof. They flower from December to March. The larger roundish leaves die off yellow in autumn. F.C.C. 1918, A.G.M. 1922. Z.5.

'Goldcrest', a late flowering form raised at Bodnant, North Wales. The large flowers of rich golden yellow are suffused with crimson at the base and are richly scented. The leaves colour yellow in autumn. **217**

'Pallida', my own favourite witch hazel. The soft, slightly greenish, yellow flowers are borne densely along the bare stems of this fine shrub and demand attention even in the dullest winter day. Raised in the Royal Horticultural Society's Garden, Wisley. The leaves differ from those of *H. mollis* in form but also colour yellow in autumn. Sweetly scented, a few twigs in flower can bring delight into the house. F.C.C. 1958, A.G.M. 1960. **218**

Hardy Tamarisk see *Tamarix pentandra*
Harlequin Glory-bower see *Clerodendron bungei*
Harry Lauder's Walking Stick see *Corylus avellana* 'Contorta'
Hazel,
   Corkscrew see *Corylus avellana* 'Contorta'
   European see *Corylus avellana*
   Winter see *Corylopsis*
   Witch see *Hamamelis*
Heath,
   Biscay see *Erica erigena*
   Connemara see *Daboecia cantabrica*
   Corsican see *Erica terminalis*
   Cornish see *Erica vagans*
   Cross-leaved see *Erica tetralix*
   Mediterranean see *Erica erigena*
   Portugal see *Erica lusitanica*
   Snow see *Erica herbacea*
   Spanish see *Erica australis* and *E. lusitanica*
   Tree see *Erica arborea*
   Twisted see *Erica cinerea*
   Winter see *Erica herbacea*
Heather,
   Bell see *Erica cinerea*
   White see *Calluna vulgaris* 'Alba'

HEBE SCROPHULARIACEAE ▼
This is a large genus of evergreen shrubs most of which are natives of New Zealand. Once included with the herbaceous species under the name *Veronica*, and still better known as such. Some are neat and compact in form and useful as ground cover plants and grow readily on well drained soils, while others have a long flowering season which makes them worthwhile in the garden. Some are damaged, or may succumb, in severe winters in cold areas. They are however, very easily increased by cuttings taken any time during the summer and put in a propagating frame or under mist. A few young plants can readily be overwintered in a frost free frame to replace any losses which may occur.

albicans
A dwarf greyish-green evergreen shrub with white flowers in summer and which seems to be reasonably hardy. Its botanical status seems somewhat doubtful, in Bean's 8th Ed., Vol. II, p. 323, it is considered close to *H. amplexicaulis*. It is a variable plant. Z.9. **219**

'Autumn Glory' 60 cm. (2 ft)
A well known hybrid possibly of *H. pimeleoides*. An open shrub about 60 cm. high which flowers almost continuously from June onwards. The deep purplish blue flowers are borne in short, dense racemes. Fairly hardy in mild gardens when planted on well drained soil which is not too rich. A.G.M. 1969.

'Carl Teschner' 23 cm. (9 in.)
A dwarf shrub 23 cm. high, hardy in mild climates, which has recently come to notice as a ground cover plant, a purpose for which it is splendidly adapted. Growing freely the short racemes of small violet flowers smother the dainty very dark green foliage in July and August. Said to be *H. elliptica* × *H. pimeleoides*. A.G.M. 1969. **220**

carnosula 30 cm. (1 ft)
A dwarf shrub with greyish green shell like leaves, about 30 cm. in height. Native of South Island, New Zealand, it is a pleasing plant and reasonably hardy in mild climates. White flowers July and August.

'Fairfieldii'
A shrub which resembles *H. hulkeana* with panicles of delicate lavender flowers, but is a dwarfer, sturdier plant than that beautiful species of which it may be a hybrid. Worth a well drained position near a sunny wall. **221**

'Great Orme' 60 cm. (2 ft)
A compact shrub which in my garden grows about 60 cm. high. The bright pink flowers are freely produced in long racemes. It is reasonably hardy in mild climates. A.G.M. 1961. **222**

Abbreviations and symbols used in the text

▼	Deciduous	†	Lime hater
△	Evergreen	◖	Shade
✳	Flowers	◑	Semi shade
●	Fruit	⊙	Sun
➴	Foliage		

A.G.M. Award of Garden Merit, Royal Horticultural Society
F.C.C. First Class Certificate, Royal Horticultural Society

Z1–10 The Z numbers represent the climatic zones used in the United States and provide a useful hardiness rating elsewhere. Thus Z1 is for those plants surviving coldest conditions and Z10 is the other extreme

The illustration numbers are in **bold type**.

'Midsummer Beauty' 1·2 m. (4 ft)
A hybrid, fairly hardy, which grows to about 1·2 m. (4 ft) high and at least as much across. The light blue-purple flowers are produced in large numbers throughout the summer months.

pinguifolia
    'Pagei', a low shrub about 30 cm. (1 ft) high growing into clumps over 60 cm. (2 ft) across when planted in well drained soil and a sunny position. White flowers are freely produced in May and spasmodically afterwards. A very beautiful plant, excellent for ground cover, the mats of greenish grey leaves are most effective at all seasons, not least during the winter months. A.G.M. 1969.

speciosa **Showy Hebe**
Generally represented in gardens by hybrids or cultivars which are particularly colourful in autumn but are usually seen at their best in seaside gardens. Easily propagated they are of value for filling gaps and even as pot plants. Z.10.
    'Alicia Amherst', a beautiful hybrid, also known as 'Veitchii' but wrongly. The large deep purple flowers are freely produced from August onwards on plants with handsome dark green foliage. **223**
    'Andersonii', is seldom grown nowadays, its variegated sport being much more popular, especially for bedding schemes. Vigorous, growing up to nearly 1·85 m. (6 ft) with bluish-violet flowers.
    'Andersonii Variegata', is an attractive plant with leaves broadly margined and splashed ivory white. Arising before 1856. It is too tender to survive except in very favoured areas.
    'Simon Delaux', a smallish spherical shrub with racemes of rich crimson flowers. **224**
    'Veitchii' see under *H. speciosa* **'Alicia Amherst'**.

Hebe, Showy see *Hebe speciosa*

HEDERA

helix **Common** or English Ivy
    'Conglomerata', a dwarf, upright, slow growing non-climbing form of the Common Ivy with its leaves in two ranks. Makes a nice feature on a raised bed, especially during the winter months when the beauty of its evergreen leaves is more evident. Can be grown equally well in woodland in conjunction with an old tree stump or a large boulder where it will produce an effective picture. Quite self-supporting. I have never seen it over 60 cm. (2 ft) in height, but will attain a greater width in course of time. F.C.C. 1872. Z.6. **225**

HELIANTHEMUM CISTACEAE **Sun Rose**

lunulatum
A dwarf matt evergreen plant found in Italy. The small

bright yellow flowers have a small orange stain at the base of each petal. Best suited in well drained soil in full sun. Easily propagated from cuttings in summer in a propagating frame. Z.7. **226**

nummularium **Common Sun Rose**
15–23 cm. (6–9 in.)
Helianthemums seen in gardens are mainly hybrids and varieties of *H. nummularium*. Low evergreen shrubs which thrive in well drained open sunny situations. The flowers only last one day and are generally at their best in the forenoon, often not opening at all in dull days. Flowering in late May and June the young growths are best trimmed back after flowering. Most grow from 15–23 cm. high. Z.6.
    'Afflick', flowers brilliant deep orange, green foliage. **227**
    'Amy Baring', butter yellow. Compact, green foliage. A.G.M. 1969.
    'Jubilee', double flowered primrose yellow, dark green foliage. A.G.M. 1969.
    'Rhodanthe Carneum' see under **'Wisley Pink'**.
    'The Bride', creamy white, small yellow blotch, low compact grower with grey foliage. A.G.M. 1969.
    'Watergate Rose', deep pinkish red, orange tinted centre and glaucous foliage. A.G.M. 1969.
    'Wisley Pink', pale pink with orange centre, a beautiful shade. Grey foliage. The cultivar 'Rhodanthe Carneum' is evidently the same thing. **228**
    'Wisley Primrose', bright primrose yellow. A compact vigorous cultivar with grey foliage. A.G.M. 1969. **229**

HELICHRYSUM COMPOSITAE

splendidum to 90 cm. (3 ft)
Africa, Ethiopia to the Cape. An evergreen shrub with white felted narrow leaves growing into a rounded plant, especially if assisted by regular pruning. Yellow flowers are produced in clusters on the ends of the young growths but it is of more value for foliage effect. It has proved reasonably hardy grown in well drained soil in full sun. Hard pruning in April is recommended followed by another trim in July. Can be propagated by cuttings. Z.10. **230**

Herring-bone Cotoneaster see *Cotoneaster horizontalis*

HIBISCUS MALVACEAE

syriacus **Rose of Sharon** (U.S.), **Shubby Althea**
3·05 m. (10 ft)
East Asia. Date of introduction unknown but probably cultivated in the British Isles for 250 years. A deciduous shrub rather erect and bushy in growth, and flowering August to September. Generally quite hardy, in colder gardens it can only be flowered as a wall plant, even in

warmer gardens its flowers open better in warm sunny weather. When such conditions prevail it is very beautiful, particularly the single flowered forms. Double flowered cultivars open less successfully in bad weather. Well drained soil of moderate quality suits it best, combined with a sunny situation. Where space is limited hard pruning in March can be practised or it can be grown as an ornamental hedge and pruned into shape. Propagation by cuttings under mist is successful or layering in spring where only a few plants are required. The following list is a limited selection of some of the best cultivars. Z.5.

'Ardens', pale pinkish-purple, a dark red-brown blotch at base, semi-double.

'Blue Bird', rich mauve blue with a deeper eye, single. Raised in France and originally called 'Oiseau Bleu'. A.G.M. 1969. **231**

'Diana', extra large white flowers, a recent introduction of great promise, single. **232**

'Duc de Brabant', deep pinkish purple, double.

'Hamabo', a single flowered clone with delicate pale pink flowers and conspicuous crimson markings in the throat. A good plant which associates well with 'Blue Bird'. A.G.M. 1969. **233**

'Oiseau Bleu' see **'Blue Bird'**

'Red Heart', extra large white flowers with distinct maroon eye, single. **234**

'William R. Smith', snowy white flowers with beautifully frilled petals, single. Raised in U.S. A.G.M. 1969. **235**

'Woodbridge', a very large rosy crimson flower with carmine eye, single. Raised in England. A.G.M. 1969. **236**

Himalayan
> **Abelia** see *Abelia triflora*
> **Honeysuckle** see *Leycesteria formosa*

Hinoki False Cypress see *Chamaecyparis obtusa*

HIPPOPHAE ELAEAGNACEAE ▼

rhamnoides **Sea Buckthorn** to 4·55 m. (15 ft) Temperate Asia, Europe including British Isles. A deciduous shrub which can reach tree size in favourable areas, very distinct in appearance with its narrow silvery leaves and (where both sexes are grown) bright orange fruits which cluster thickly on the branches until February. Few if any fruiting shrubs remain attractive for so long; the birds do not appreciate the berries as they are intensely acid. Will grow well on any soil even on sand and is ideal for seaside shelter or hedges but will also grow inland. May be propagated by seed. Layering is best where a particular sex is required, seedlings do not disclose their sex until they flower. Group plantings of one male to 5 or 6 females will ensure pollination, the pollen being wind borne. Most suitable for boundary hedging, the fierce thorns render it impenetrable but for the same reason it is unsuitable for small gardens, near the house. Z.3.

Hobble Bush see *Viburnum alnifolium*
Holly see *Ilex*
> **Grape, Oregon** see *Mahonia aquifolium*
> **Mahonia** see *Mahonia aquifolium*

Holly-leaf, Sweetspire see *Itea ilicifolia*
Honey Locust see *Gleditsia triacanthos*
Honeysuckle,
> **Bush** see *Lonicera*
> **Climbing** see *Lonicera*
> **Cream** see *Lonicera etrusca*
> **Early Dutch** see *Lonicera periclymenum* 'Belgica'
> **Himalayan** see *Leycesteria formosa*
> **Late Dutch** see *Lonicera periclymenum* 'Serotina'
> **Swamp** see *Rhododendron viscosum*
> **Tellman** see *Lonicera × tellmanniana*
> **Trumpet** see *Lonicera sempervirens*
> **Winter** see *Lonicera fragrantissima*
> **Yellow-net** see *Lonicera japonica*

Horse Chestnut see *Aesculus*
House Hydrangea see *Hydrangea macrophylla*

HYDRANGEA HYDRANGEACEAE ▼ ※

arborescens to 3·05 m. (10 ft) Eastern U.S. Introduced 1736. A deciduous shrub of loose habit, quite hardy and flowers freely in flattish cormybs July to September. The mainly fertile flowers are a dull white and not nearly so attractive for garden decoration as the following form. Z.4.

'Grandiflora', the form most common in cultivation and a much more decorative garden plant. A common name in the U.S. for this clone is Hills of Snow. The pure snowy white flowers are large and sterile, produced in globular heads which are frequently pendulous because of their weight. One of the best hydrangeas and quite hardy. A.G.M. 1969.

Abbreviations and symbols used in the text

▼	Deciduous	†	Lime hater
△	Evergreen	⦾	Shade
※	Flowers	◖	Semi shade
•	Fruit	⊙	Sun
☙	Foliage		

A.G.M.   Award of Garden Merit, Royal Horticultural Society

F.C.C.   First Class Certificate, Royal Horticultural Society

Z1–10   The Z numbers represent the climatic zones used in the United States and provide a useful hardiness rating elsewhere. Thus Z1 is for those plants surviving coldest conditions and Z10 is the other extreme

The illustration numbers are in **bold type**.

aspera to 3·65 m. (12 ft)

Himalayas, west China, Java and Sumatra. A deciduous shrub frequently little more than half the height mentioned which is only attained in favoured gardens. A somewhat variable species, the better forms are very beautiful and valuable because of their late flowering in August and September. In one group the grey-green leaves are an admirable foil for the large heads of bright blue flowers which are surrounded by a ring of large lavender or pink florets. One of the few hydrangeas which flourishes and retains its lovely colour on chalk or lime as well as other soils. It also prefers a somewhat dryer soil especially in the winter months when good drainage is essential to the welfare of young plants. Z.7. **237**

heteromalla to 6·1 m. (20 ft)

Himalayas, China. Introduced 1821. A deciduous shrub which may attain small tree size. Flowers in broad corymbs are white with conspicuous white ray florets during July and August. The dark green leaves, in most forms, are whitish on the underside. **238**

macrophylla House Hydrangea

1·85 m. (6 ft)

The most popular hydrangeas are without doubt those derived from *H. macrophylla* of which there are literally hundreds of garden varieties. Most of these have been bred for the pot plant trade, and consequently are unsuitable for garden cultivation as most only flower on terminal buds which, except in sheltered areas, may be killed by spring frost. There are however, some cultivars which will in this event flower from axillary buds and these are very suitable and valuable, flowering as they do after the spring and early summer shrubs are over. Growing outside, especially in favoured areas (near the sea in England) these hydrangeas will form large shrubs reaching at least 1·8 m. in height and as much across and can for convenience be divided into two groups. The largest of these with bold globular flower heads of infertile flowers are known as the hortensias. The lesser group, also growing into similar plants, have inflorescences much akin to the wild plants with a centre of fertile flowers ringed with a few infertile ray flowers, these have become popularly known as lacecaps.

Both groups, with the exception of those that are white flowered, are peculiar in that they are subject to colour changes in accord with the nature of the soil. Crimson varieties remain so in neutral soil but become violet on acid soil, likewise a pure blue on acid soil will become pink on neutral soil. Blueness can be induced or intensified by top dressing with alum or a commercial hydrangea colorant, a type of treatment used very effectively by pot plant growers.

The hortensias have a wide colour range from white to pink, red and blue or combinations of these colours which alter according to the soil. Many change to metallic coppery shades of great beauty which are used even when dead for floral arrangements. The faded flower heads are, in general, best left on the plant until spring when they should be removed taking care to leave the buds underneath as these will produce the next crop of flowers. Young unflowered growths are easily rooted under mist and should be grown in pots, overwintered in a frame and planted the next year.

HORTENSIA GROUP

'Altona', cherry pink or mid-blue when treated, turning to lovely metallic colours in autumn. Likes shade.

'Ayesha', a distinct plant. The greyish pink flowers have cup shaped florets with a distinct resemblance to a lilac and are slightly fragrant.

'Benelux', a well known variety with nice rounded heads and fairly large florets of a good pink. **239**

'Generale Vicomtesse de Vibraye', a fine cultivar which is frequently abbreviated to 'Vibraye'. Vivid rose pink but in acid soil or, when treated, clear blue. One of the hardiest and most free flowering at 1·5 m. (5 ft). **240**

'Hamburg', a deep rose becoming purplish in acid soils, large individual florets and one of the best varieties for colour lasting into November, the flowers turning a deep metallic purple. **241**

'Madame Emile Mouilliere', probably the finest white; large florets with serrated petals. Will grow up to 1·85 m. (6 ft). **242**

'Parsifal', deep rosy red becoming violet purple on acid soils, frequently displays strange colours according to type of soil. The beautifully shaped flowers have notched edges. **243**

LACECAP GROUP

More suitable for natural plantings than those of the Hortensia group.

'Bluewave', a vigorous shrub up to 1·85 m. (6 ft) which likes shade. Beautiful heads of blue fertile flowers with a ring of large ray florets, rich blue on acid soils otherwise varying in shades of pink. F.C.C. 1965. **244**

'Lanarth White', a compact early flowering shrub up to 90 cm. (3 ft). The flattened flower heads of pink or blue fertile flowers are ringed round with white ray florets. A superb cultivar for small gardens. A.G.M. 1973. **245**

'Lilacina', a vigorous shrub up to 1·5 m. (5 ft) the purplish blue fertile flowers are surrounded by rich pink florets with serrated edges, a beautiful cultivar.

'Maculata', a medium sized erect shrub. The flower heads have a few white ray florets. Leaves attractive because of a broad creamy white margin. **246**

paniculata Panicle Hydrangea

3·05–3·65 m. (10–12 ft)

Japan, China. Introduced 1861. A deciduous shrub of which the normal wild form has never become common in cultivation. The form generally grown has dense terminal panicles of fertile and large creamy white sterile florets appearing during July and August. The panicles can be increased in size by pruning in April down to the basal eyes of the previous years growth. A.G.M. 1936. Z.4.

The illustrations of the following varieties of *H. paniculata* have been placed out of specific alphabetical order in order to keep the illustrations of the *H. serrata* varieties close to the *H. macrophylla* Lacecap group because of their usually similar flower form.

'Grandiflora', a form introduced from Japan 1862 and one of the most spectacular large shrubs. It is popular in America, entrenched under the name 'Hydrangea P.G.'. If pruned hard in April and weak shoots removed very large panicles can be obtained especially if assisted by feeding. To my mind these huge panicles are out of place in the garden and more naturally grown plants are much more pleasing in effect. This can be obtained by moderate pruning and some thinning. Nearly all flowers in this form are sterile, white at first fading to purplish pink. F.C.C. 1869, A.G.M. 1969. **250**

'Praecox', a form with smaller panicles with both fertile and sterile florets, which commences to flower early in July, several weeks before 'Grandiflora' and growing quickly to 2·45 m. (8 ft) in height. A.G.M. 1960. **251**

'Tardiva', is a very late flowering form, September or even early October, thus of great value for extending the season. Grows into a large plant 1·85–2·45 m. (6–8 ft) in height. **252**

serrata 90 cm. (3 ft)
Japan. South Korea. Introduced 1843. A dwarf deciduous shrub which flowers August to September. Generally represented in gardens by cultivars of which the following are a selection. The illustrations of these appear following the *H. macrophylla* Lacecap group being somewhat similar in flower form. Z.5–6.

'Bluebird', an early flowering, upright shrub of slender growth 0·90–1·2 m. (3–4 ft) in height. The lacecap type with outer florets of soft pink or clear blue and similar colouring on the central disc, varying according to soil conditions on acid soil can be a lovely sky blue. A.G.M. 1969. **247**

'Grayswood', an attractive shrub with flattened corymbs of blue fertile flowers which are surrounded by ray florets, white at first, becoming pink with age and eventually, if subjected to sun, deep crimson. **248**

'Grayswood White', an attractive seedling raised at Grayswood, Surrey, England. Not as yet in general cultivation, but a welcome addition from a very fine garden. **249**

'Preziosa', a handsome shrub eventually reaching 1·2 m. (4 ft). The young stems are reddish brown and leaves have a purple tinge when young. The attractive globular heads of flower are more akin to the hortensia type, rosy pink at first deepening to reddish crimson in autumn. F.C.C. 1964.

'Rosalba', a small erect shrub which is usually about 90 cm. (3 ft) in height. This cultivar has long been an inhabitant of gardens and has ray flowers which, white at first, become blotched with crimson.

HYPERICUM GUTTIFERAE   ⊙/◑

The shrubby species, varieties and hybrids of *Hypericum* are very accommodating plants. Of easy culture in any reasonable well drained soil and not too fussy about always being in full sun. They are of considerable value as they flower over a long season in late summer and throughout autumn when few shrubs remain in bloom. All are easily increased from summer cuttings under mist or in a propagating frame. Many produce seeds which can be sown in spring but may not come true to the parents.

calycinum **Rose of Sharon** (U.K.),   △/▼◑❁
Aaron's Beard 45 cm. (1½ ft)
Europe, Asia Minor. Introduced 1676. A dwarf, almost evergreen shrub which readily adapts to a wide range of climatic conditions so that in England it has become naturalized in some areas. A most useful plant for dry banks or half-shade under trees but should not be planted in conjunction with choice plants which it will overwhelm. The large golden flowers are enhanced in beauty by a conspicuous central tuft of golden stamens. Hard shearing in spring just before new growths appear will keep the plants tidy and more effective as ground cover.

elatum see *H.* × *inodorum*

forrestii 1·5 m. (5 ft)   ▼/△❁➼
A hardy almost deciduous shrub which colours well in autumn. The saucer shaped golden yellow flowers are profusely borne in summer and autumn. It is not so popular since the advent of *H.* 'Hidcote', which may be a seedling from it. A.G.M. 1924.

'Hidcote' 1·5 m. (5 ft)   △/▼❁
A hardy, almost evergreen shrub up to 1·5 m. in height, perhaps more, and at least as much across, producing its large golden yellow shallowly saucer-shaped flowers in masses from July to October. Fruits are rarely set and its origin is not certain but it is one of the most popular of our hardy shrubs. A.G.M. 1954. Z.5. **253**

Abbreviations and symbols used in the text

▼	Deciduous	†	Lime hater
△	Evergreen	◍	Shade
❁	Flowers	◑	Semi shade
●	Fruit	⊙	Sun
➼	Foliage		

A.G.M.   Award of Garden Merit, Royal Horticultural Society
F.C.C.   First Class Certificate, Royal Horticultural Society

Z1–10   The Z numbers represent the climatic zones used in the United States and provide a useful hardiness rating elsewhere. Thus Z1 is for those plants surviving coldest conditions and Z10 is the other extreme

The illustration numbers are in **bold type**.

× *inodorum* (*H. androsaemum* ×
H. hircinum) syn. *H. elatum* 1·5 m. (5 ft)
An upright shrub, up to 1·5 m. but less if pruned hard in spring. A hybrid which occurs in the wild where *H. androsaemum* and *H. hircinum* are growing near each other. In cultivation by mid 18th century it varies somewhat, some forms inclining to one parent more than the other. It has become naturalized in some moister areas. Formerly known as *H. elatum* and still appearing in catalogues under that name. The small pale yellow flowers are borne in cymes at the ends of the shoots, followed by reddish fruits.

'Elstead', is a selected form of the above of dwarfer habit, and is particularly pretty when the later flowers open in conjunction with the brilliant salmon red fruits which succeed the earlier flowers. It is unfortunate that in some gardens a rust disease causes problems especially if the plant is grown in full sun. **254**

× *moseranum* (*H. calycinum* ×
H. patulum) **Gold Flower** 45 cm. (1½ ft)
A good dwarf shrub about 45 cm. high, raised at Versailles, France, about 1887. A good ground cover plant with arching red stems. The golden yellow flowers have overlapping petals, with striking reddish anthers and are borne at the ends of the shoots. A most attractive plant which can be grown in the smallest of gardens and will flower from July to October. On the Pacific coast (U.S.) does well as low undergrowth beneath eucalyptus trees. F.C.C. 1891. Z.7. **255**

'Tricolor', a charming form suitable for the smallest garden where a sheltered position can be given. The green leaves are edged with pink and white making a show in which the small yellow flowers are lost. **256**

olympicum 30 cm. (1 ft)
A neat little shrub about 30 cm. high with grey green leaves and bright yellow flowers. From the Balkan peninsula and Anatolia. A.G.M. 1936. Z.7.

'Citrinum', is even more beautiful, with pale lemon yellow flowers.

HYSSOPUS

aristatus 45 cm. (1½ ft)
Pyrenees. A semi-evergreen shrub which thrives in light, well drained soil in full sun. Aromatic, its rich blue flowers are freely produced and very popular with bees during July and August. An excellent plant for edging or underplanting other shrubs, associating particularly well with roses. More compact in habit than *H. officinale*, the Hyssop of the Bible. Prune back fairly hard in April every year. Summer cuttings root easily in a frame. Z.7.

ILEX AQUIFOLIACEAE **Holly**
The hollies are a large and varied genus of which the evergreen forms are best known in gardens, indeed these provide some of the most handsome trees and shrubs hardy over the greater part of the British Isles. Growing well in most garden soils, particularly if neutral or slightly acid and seemingly caring little if in full sun or slight shade. Fruits are not so freely borne in shade. Tolerant also of conditions in town or coastal gardens, and excellent for hedging. Usually male and female flowers are borne on separate plants, so that in order to obtain the bonus of handsome fruits, both sexes must be planted. Transplanting can only be carried out successfully if young plants have been grown in containers or where a good ball of soil has been kept round the roots. I always like to plant either in September before root action has ceased or in April and May when roots are again moving.

Certainly, I think it is best to avoid transplanting during very wet weather.

The common holly, *I. aquifolium*, may be raised from seed, self sown seedlings are frequently found in woodland gardens where this plant is frequently grown. Cultivars can be rooted under mist in summer, as they, in many cases being sports, will not come true from seed.

Hollies grown as hedges are best trimmed in spring and will tolerate quite severe pruning. Specimen plants or those encroaching on other plants may be pruned in July and August.

× *altaclarensis*
'Golden King', a fine golden variegated evergreen in which the almost smooth edged leaves have a rich golden margin which contrasts strongly with the deep green centre of the leaf. In spite of its name, this is a female plant which produces red fruits if pollinated by a male.

Broadly spreading and bushy in habit will eventually attain 3·1 m. (10 ft) in height and is also useful for hedging. A.G.M. 1969.

'J. C. van Tol', an almost spineless evergreen with deep shining olive green leaves. A self-fertile plant which not only bears regularly good crops of red berries but is a useful pollinator of other varieties. Stands clipping well, so makes an excellent specimen for formal gardens or for hedging. Left to grow naturally is bushy and rather spreading in habit. A.G.M. 1969.

'Lawsoniana', a holly with large dark green leaves which generally are spineless and have a large yellow splash in the centre. A sport from *I.* × *altaclarensis* 'Hendersonii' it was raised in Edinburgh, Scotland shortly before 1869. A female form it tends to revert back to its parent. Such green shoots should be removed at source. Will grow into a small tree, but can be pruned to keep it within the size required. F.C.C. 1894. Z.6. **257**

aquifolium

One of the most popular evergreens for British gardens particularly so at Christmas when berried sprays are used a good deal for decorative purposes. Cultivars vary widely in form and habit and are tolerant of soil conditions and shade.

'Argenteomarginata', a name which refers to a group with silver variegated leaves and male and female forms. The latter fruit freely and are somewhat pyramid like in habit, attaining eventually, some 6 m. (20 ft) in height. Good also for hedging. A.G.M. 1969.

'Madame Briot', a colourfully variegated female form with leaves which are spiny, blotched and margined deep yellow, contrasting with the handsome purple stems. Attains 3·65 m. (12 ft) A.G.M. 1969.

'Pyramidalis', a form with close pyramidal growth when young but widening with age. The leaves are most heavily spined at the base of this free fruiting plant. A.G.M. 1969.

'Silver Queen', another confusingly named form, being a male with green, grey mottled leaves which are strongly margined white. A.G.M. 1969.

crenata 90 cm.–1·2 m. (3–4 ft)

Introduced from Japan about 1864. This is an evergreen shrub with small leaves and a close habit generally about 90 cm.–1·2 m. (3–4 ft) high. The dull white flowers are succeeded by black fruits. A somewhat variable species.

'Golden Gem', is a particularly good form for small gardens, whose yellow leaves are most attractive during the winter months. Very compact in habit.

Irish Juniper see *Juniperus communis*

ITEA ITEACEAE

ilicifolia Holly-leaf Sweetspire
2·75 m. (9 ft)

West China. Introduced around 1890. An evergreen shrub with holly like leaves, charming in late summer when crowded with pendulous 15–30 cm. (6–12 in.) racemes of greenish white flowers. A handsome foliage plant easily increased from cuttings of moderately ripened growths. Z.9. **258**

Ivy,
 Common see *Hedera helix*
 English see *Hedera helix*

J

Japanese
 Angelica Tree see *Aralia elata*
 Apricot see *Prunus mume*
 Aralia see *Fatsia japonica*

Barberry see *Berberis thunbergii*
Cedar see *Cryptomeria japonica*
Flowering Quince see *Chaenomeles japonica*
Maple see *Acer palmatum*
Mountain Ash see *Sorbus matsumurana*
Snowball see *Viburnum plicatum*
Jasmine see *Jasminum*
Jasmine Nightshade see *Solanum jasminoides*

JASMINUM OLEACEAE Jasmine, Jessamine

nudiflorum Winter Jasmine
3·65–4·55 m. (12–15 ft)

China. Introduced by Fortune 1844. A deciduous scrambling shrub, the Winter Jasmine must be one of the most valuable shrubs ever introduced into gardens. Deservedly popular it can often be seen growing in the most uncongenial surroundings and yet producing its bright golden yellow flowers during the most miserable and dreary months of the winter, November to February. It is frequently grown on a wall where its main growths should be spaced out and securely fastened. Side shoots can then be pruned after flowering if not already removed for home decoration. Not a climber by nature it will make itself at home on a bank or more naturally will flop down over a retaining wall, this being its natural disposition. Can be easily layered or grown from cuttings. A.G.M. 1923. Z.5.

× stephanense (J. beesianum × J. officinale)
Stephan Jasmine 6·1 m. (20 ft)

A hybrid raised in France and put into commerce about 1921 by Lemoine. The same hybrid has been found in Yunnan, China, where the parent species are found. A climber of considerable vigour which can reach 6 m. or so where space is available, it can be very beautiful when allowed this freedom. The leaves of vigorous shoots are frequently variegated. The fragrant flowers are soft pale pink, and are borne in terminal clusters. These are produced in profusion in May (U.S.), June and July. Z.7. **259**

Abbreviations and symbols used in the text

Symbol	Meaning	Symbol	Meaning
▼	Deciduous	†	Lime hater
△	Evergreen	◍	Shade
✳	Flowers	◖	Semi shade
●	Fruit	☉	Sun
➤	Foliage		

A.G.M.   Award of Garden Merit, Royal Horticultural Society
F.C.C.   First Class Certificate, Royal Horticultural Society

Z1–10   The Z numbers represent the climatic zones used in the United States and provide a useful hardiness rating elsewhere. Thus Z1 is for those plants surviving coldest conditions and Z10 is the other extreme

The illustration numbers are in **bold type**.

Jersey Elm see *Ulmus* × *sarniensis*
Jerusalem Sage see *Phlomis fruticosa*
Jessamine see *Jasminum*
Judas Tree see *Cercis siliquastrum*
June Berry see *Amelanchier*
Juniper,
    Common see *Juniperus communis*
    Creeping see *Juniperus horizontalis*
    Irish see *Juniperus communis* 'Hibernica'
    Shore see *Juniperus conferta*

JUNIPERUS CUPRESSACEAE **Juniper** △

communis Common Juniper

Temperate parts of northern hemisphere, including British Isles. A very variable species, a shrub of spreading habit sometimes reaching the size of a small tree. Common on chalk downs or limestone hills it is found in many parts of the British Isles while in U.S. it extends in the north from Atlantic to Pacific. A very accommodating plant of which there are many variations, the prostrate forms are becoming very popular as ground cover plants and the upright slender columns of the Irish Juniper are frequently seen in gardens.

    'Compressa', a dwarf compact upright column which may after many years attain a height of 60–90 cm. (2–3 ft.). Very often used in sink gardens, a miniature Irish Juniper, and splendid for any small garden. In cultivation from about 1855.

    'Depressa Aurea', an excellent cultivar whose leaves and young growths are golden yellow in early summer. Will eventually attain 90 cm. (3 ft) in height and treble that distance in width. In cultivation since about 1887. **260**

    'Hibernica', Irish Juniper, is a narrow conical tree which may reach 2·75 m. (9 ft.) seldom more and is frequently a feature in formal gardens. In cultivation from about 1838. Easily accommodated in quite small gardens.

    'Repanda', was found in Ireland and introduced about 1934. A low spreading juniper 25 cm. (10 in.) in height it will in time spread to 2·75 m. (9 ft.), but can be pruned if this space is not available. The branches which spray outwards in all directions are furnished with deep green leaves which sometimes become slightly tinged with bronze in winter. An excellent evergreen ground cover plant when grown in a sunny position. **261**

conferta Shore Juniper 30 cm. (1 ft)

Japan. Introduced by Wilson 1914. Especially valuable as ground cover or for coming over a wall. Fairly fast growing it will spread over 3·65 m. (12 ft) across in time but withstands pruning very well if in danger of encroaching. The large patches of very bright apple green, prickly leaves are most attractive in winter. Z.5. **262**

'Grey Owl' 90 cm.–1·2 m. (3–4 ft)

A delightful medium sized hybrid shrub with attractive silver grey foliage on widely spreading branches. It is thought to be a hybrid between *J.* *virginiana* 'Glauca' and *J.* *chinensis* 'Pfitzerana' which originated in 1938. A nice plant to isolate as an accent plant. **263**

horizontalis Creeping Juniper

North-eastern North America. In cultivation 1830. Very variable the Creeping Juniper is a dwarf shrub, some forms with long procumbent branches which given time extend a considerable distance. The leaves are variable in colour from glaucous green to blue, often purple in winter. A fine species for ground cover especially when planted in conjunction with green forms to provide a contrast. Can be pruned back, especially when young to encourage dense, compact growth. A.G.M. 1969. Z.2.

    'Bar Harbor', a dwarf spreading evergreen, generally under 60 cm. (2 ft.) in height but eventually triple this width across. The name appears to be given to plants found growing wild in Maine, U.S. The branches hug the ground closely and the short ascending branchlets are furnished with glaucous steel blue scale like leaves. In cultivation since 1930 this fine form has been found well within reach of salt spray in its homeland so is an obvious candidate for seaside planting. **264**

× *media*

A variable hybrid whose origin has not, as yet, been agreed upon by botanists. There is some agreement that a number of clones included in this group may have been of hybrid origin but have been selected from wild material. Z.4.

    'Hetzii', a medium to large wide spreading shrub, growing to about 1·85 m. (6 ft) in height and of greater width. The main branches arise at an angle of 60 degrees and are furnished with glaucous mainly adult foliage. Useful as a specimen shrub. **265**

squamata 60 cm. (2 ft)

Himalaya, China. Introduced 1824. A low evergreen shrub which spreads over the ground with branchlets rising above. A variable species with awl shaped pale green leaves and nodding tips to the shoots which is better furnished if pruned hard occasionally.

    'Blue Star', a low bush with a lovely dense habit and fairly large awl-shaped leaves. Beautiful silvery blue, this comparatively new cultivar appears to be a very desirable plant which has sported from *J.* *squamata* 'Meyeri' and is very slow in growth.

virginiana Pencil Cedar

    'Skyrocket', is a spectacular extremely narrow columnar clone, the most pencil-shaped of all the columnar conifers. Found as a seedling in the wild and in cultivation in 1949. The blue grey foliage is very pleasing and it has already attained a height of over 4·55 m. (15 ft.). Ideal for breaking up flat-planting schemes or as a focal point in gardens. It resists wind very well and is easily accommodated in any size of garden. A.G.M. 1973. **266**

K

KALMIA ERICACEAE   ⊙△

latifolia **Calico Bush, Mountain Laurel**   †◐❋
to 3·05 m. (10 ft)
Eastern North America. Introduced 1734. The Calico Bush is a beautiful slow growing evergreen shrub for lime free soils, thrives best in moist cool peaty soil, and possibly a little shade. Pruning is not required and propagation can be done by seeds sown in sandy peat in spring in a frame but will not necessarily breed true. Cuttings of young growths can also be rooted under mist in July or August. In June the flowers are crowded in rounded clusters, terminating the previous year's growth and vary in colour from pale to bright pink. A magnificent shrub where soil conditions are suitable. A.G.M. 1948. Z.4. **267**

> **'Clementine Churchill'**, a strain developed at Sheffield Park, Sussex, England. The best red flowered *Kalmia*. It has been successfully propagated by cuttings, but is very difficult to obtain as yet. A.G.M. 1969.

KERRIA ROSACEAE

japonica **Kerria** to 1·85 m. (6 ft)   ⊙/◐▼❋
China, Japan. Introduced 1834. A graceful deciduous shrub whose arching branches are wreathed in April and May with slightly cup shaped rich yellow flowers reminiscent of buttercups. This is a quite hardy and easily grown shrub in any reasonable garden soil, thriving in full sun or partial shade. It is usually possible to increase by digging out offsets between October and April, while cuttings may be rooted under mist in June or July. Pruning out of old flowering growths will encourage strong new shoots to flower the following year. A.G.M. 1928. Z.4. **268**

> **'Aureo-vittata'**, branches are striped yellow and green, an exciting sight in winter.
> **'Pleniflora'**, syn. 'Flore Pleno', is a much more familiar garden plant than the above and of quite different habit. Stouter branches, a taller and more vigorous shrub than the type, it shows little of its dense twiggy character. The flowers are rich yellow but fully double like pompons, providing a gay brassy effect in spring. Introduced in 1804 from China. A.G.M. 1928.

Kirishima Azalea see *Rhododendron obtusum*
Kohutu see *Pittosporum tenuifolium*

KOLKWITZIA CAPRIFOLIACEAE

amabilis **Beauty Bush** 2·45 m. (8 ft)   ⊙▼❋
West China. Introduced 1901 by Wilson at the Arnold Arboretum, Boston, Mass. U.S. A deciduous shrub of great beauty when a good form is grown. Very hardy, thriving in any average soil, but prefers a sunny position. This fine shrub produces soft pink flowers touched with yellow in the throat during May and June. Thinning out of some old growths will provide room for younger growths to flower the following year. Increase by cuttings of younger growths in July and August under mist or in a propagating frame. Z.4.

> **'Pink Cloud'**, a seedling from above raised at the garden of the Royal Horticultural Society, Wisley, England in 1946 from seeds received from the Morton Arboretum, Illinois, U.S. A very floriferous form with flowers of a deeper pink, a very beautiful shrub well worth planting. F.C.C. 1963, A.G.M. 1965. **269**

Korean
  Abeliophyllum see *Abeliophyllum distichum*
  Lilac see *Syringa velutina*
Kumazasa see *Sasa veitchii*
Kyusha Azalea see *Rhododendron kiusianum*

L

Lads Love see *Artemisia arbrotanum*
Lance-leaf Phillyrea see *Phillyrea decora*
Late Dutch Honeysuckle see *Lonicera periclymenum* 'Serotina'
Laurel see *Laurus*
Laurel,
  Alexandrian see *Danae racemosa*
  Bay see *Laurus nobilis*
  Cherry see *Prunus laurocerasus*
  Common see *Prunus laurocerasus*
  English see *Prunus laurocerasus*
  Mountain see *Kalmia latifolia*
  Portugal see *Prunus lusitanica*

Abbreviations and symbols used in the text

▼	Deciduous	†	Lime hater
△	Evergreen	◐	Shade
❋	Flowers	◑	Semi shade
●	Fruit	⊙	Sun
	Foliage		

A.G.M.   Award of Garden Merit, Royal Horticultural Society
F.C.C.   First Class Certificate, Royal Horticultural Society

Z1–10   The Z numbers represent the climatic zones used in the United States and provide a useful hardiness rating elsewhere. Thus Z1 is for those plants surviving coldest conditions and Z10 is the other extreme

The illustration numbers are in **bold type**.

LAURUS LAURACEAE **Laurel, Sweet Bay** △🐦

nobilis **Bay Laurel** to 12·2 m. (40 ft)
Mediterranean region. In cultivation 1562. An ever-green shrub which can attain tree size in sheltered areas, but is probably better known as a tub plant flanking hotel entrances or town houses, a purpose for which it is well suited as it stands clipping well and can be trimmed into formal shapes. Commonly known as Bay Laurel or Sweet Bay it is in favour in cooking for flavouring and could well be used as a feature in the herb garden. This is the true laurel used to make wreaths for poets of distinction or crowns for triumphant heroes. Plants grown in tubs are frequently housed in cool greenhouses during winter and are apt to attack by scale insects which cause sooty mould on the leaves. Control can be obtained by spraying with Malathion or a systemic insecticide. Thriving in coastal areas it can be used for hedges or shelter belts. Z.7.

Laurustinus see *Viburnum tinus*

LAVANDULA LABIATAE **Lavender** ⊙△✳🐦

Evergreen shrubs which have long been cultivated and certainly since the mid 16th century. All lavenders thrive best in light soils in full sun and benefit from a dressing of lime where acid conditions prevail. Flower stalks should be cut back in early autumn and pruning of the plants to keep them compact in spring, taking care not to cut back into old wood. Cuttings are easily rooted under mist during summer or by using ripened growth later in a cold frame. Few plants equal lavender for fragrance in the garden during the flowering period. In spite of the long history of lavender in cultivation its nomenclature is still in a confused state botanically. For garden purposes however, and this is the main purpose of this book, it is suggested in Bean, 8th Ed., Volume II, page 532 that as the majority of commercial varieties have clonal names, these can be used in conjunction with the generic name *Lavandula*, omitting any specific names. What follows is a short selection of these clones, under this system.

    'Alba', a robust form with grey green leaves and white flowers produced in late July. 60 cm. (2 ft).
    'Folgate', a more compact form with grey green leaves and lavender blue flowers, freely produced in early July, A.M.T. 1963, 45 cm. (1½ ft).
    'Hidcote', **'Nana Atropurpurea'**, a compact form with narrow grey green leaves and rich purple flowers flowering in June and July. This is a very fine lavender, silvery in appearance and very popular in gardens. 45 cm. (1½ ft), A.G.M. 1965. **270**
    'Loddon Pink', a compact form with narrow grey green leaves and pale pink flowers in early July. 45 cm. (1½ ft).
    'Nana Atropurpurea' see **'Hidcote'**
    'Twickel Purple', a fairly compact form with broader grey green leaves with spreading spikes of rich purple flowers, very fragrant. 60 cm. (2 ft)

stoechas **French** or **Spanish Lavender**
60–90 cm. (2–3 ft)
South-west Europe. A very aromatic, evergreen shrub 60–90 cm. in height when grown in dry sunny positions in sheltered gardens. The dark purple flowers which are borne in dense purple heads with characteristic 'stacked' bracts are in strong contrast to the very grey foliage. Not a reliable plant in cold gardens. Z.9–10.

LAVATERA MALVACEAE ⊙✳

olbia 1·2–2·45 m. (4–8 ft)
Western Mediterranean. Introduced before 1570. A very useful soft-stemmed shrub particularly for reason-ably sheltered gardens where it will thrive in relatively poor soil. It has a long flowering period, producing pinkish-purple blooms, often through July to December or when cut by frost. Although not a plant with a long expectancy of life it is so easily propagated from young growth under mist or in a frame during summer that a few plants for replacement should be readily available. Overwintered in pots in a frame or greenhouse it is convenient plant for gapping up a herbaceous border where its quick growth will soon fill up. The form known as 'Rosea' is more pleasing in colour. Prune in April to young growths at the base of old wood. Z.9.

Lavender see *Lavandula*
Lavender, French see *Lavandula stoechas*
Lavender Cotton see *Santolina*
Lawson
    Cypress see *Chamaecyparis lawsoniana*
    Cypress, Golden see *Chamaecyparis lawsoniana* **'Lutea'**
Leadwort, Willmott Blue see *Ceratostigma willmottianum*
Lesser Periwinkle see *Vinca minor*

LEYCESTERIA CAPRIFOLIACEAE ⊙◐✳●

formosa **Himalayan Honeysuckle, Flowering Nutmeg** 1·85–2·45 m. (6–8 ft)
Himalayas, China. Introduced 1824. A half woody, deciduous shrub with arching, bottle green shoots which are covered with a glaucous bloom in early stages of growth. Easily grown and not particular as to soil. It will grow in shade but flowers more freely in sunny situations. From July to October the white flowers contrast with the claret purple bracts and are succeeded by reddish purple fruits which are relished by birds. Pheasants in particular are fond of them so that it has been planted in England in woods or pheasant coverts. Easily grown from seed. Established plants should preferably be pruned almost to the ground each fall or in March. Z.7. **271**

LIGUSTRUM OLEACEAE **Privet**

All privets can be readily rooted from cuttings, under mist in summer if this is considered necessary or in a sheltered outdoor site or frame in autumn.

ovalifolium **Oval-leaf** or **California Privet** △/▼
to 4·55 m. (15 ft)

Japan. Introduced U.S. 1847. An overplanted hedging shrub, semi-evergreen except in very severe winters when it will become deciduous. It is not without merit in difficult situations, as it will thrive in poor soils, in towns where few if any other shrubs will succeed and withstands clipping well. The smell of the white flowers is disliked by many people while others delight in it. Z.5.

'Aureum', Golden Privet, is almost as well known for the same purpose as the above but is slower growing and will not attain the same height. It has been much reviled in some quarters but is a much brighter plant and has much merit for brightening up dull corners where few plants will thrive. Pruned fairly hard in spring and allowed to grow naturally afterwards (unclipped) it can produce a striking colour effect especially in a sunny position. The young growths with their rich golden bordered leaves are very useful for floral arrangements.

sinensis **Chinese Privet** to 6 m. (20 ft) ▼/△✳●

China. Introduced 1852. A deciduous shrub which may in mild winters retain many of its leaves. In most gardens it will only attain half the height mentioned, and is a remarkably free flowering shrub in July. The white flowers are produced in great feathery masses and give off a heavy perfume which is not to everyone's liking. These are succeeded by dark purple fruits which arouse interest in the winter months. A popular shrub, with its varieties, in the south eastern states of U.S. Z.7. **272**

Lilac see *Syringa*
Lilac,
   Californian see *Ceanothus*
   Common see *Syringa vulgaris*
   Korean see *Syringa velutina*
   Littleleaf see *Syringa microphylla*
   Preston see *Syringa* × *prestoniae*
Lily Magnolia, Purple see *Magnolia liliiflora* **'Nigra'**
Lily-of-the-Valley Shrub see *Pieris japonica*
Ling see *Calluna vulgaris*
Lithodora see *Lithospermum*

LITHOSPERMUM syn. *Lithodora* (U.S.)
BORAGINACEAE

diffusum syn. *L. prostratum* to 30 cm. (1 ft) ⊙†△✳
France, Spain. Introduced 1825. A prostrate evergreen shrub which forms a wide spreading mass, usually associated with rock gardens but very good also for ground cover or banks. It requires a light well drained lime free soil and should be planted in full sun. In addition to the main flowering season, of May and June, intermittent flowering occurs at other times. A light trimming after flowering will keep the plants tidy. May be increased by summer cuttings which should be potted off and kept in a cold frame over the first winter.

'Grace Ward', the largest flowered form, produces sheets of the most lovely gentian blue flowers. Compact habit. **273**
'Heavenly Blue', the form most often seen in gardens and well named. A very fine plant. A.G.M. 1925. Z.6–7.

Little Favourite see *Berberis thunbergii* **'Atropurpurea Nana'**
Littleleaf Lilac see *Syringa microphylla*
Locust,
   Black see *Robinia pseudoacacia*
   Honey see *Gleditsia triacanthos*

LONICERA CAPRIFOLIACEAE **Honeysuckle**

The honeysuckles may for garden purposes be divided into two types, the climbers, the most popular section, and the bush honeysuckles which are not so often grown. All enjoy a good loamy soil, with cool conditions at the root and while they appreciate full sun will put up with some shade. Climbing forms frequently layer themselves, nature's way of increase but all can be rooted from cuttings of young growth in summer under mist.

× *americana* (*L. caprifolium* × *L. etrusca*) ⊙▼✳

A very fine climbing plant, a hybrid between *L. caprifolium* and *L. etrusca*, whose origin seems wrapped in mystery. In cultivation in 1730 it has frequently been confused with at least one of its parents. It has large fragrant yellow and red flowers which are produced throughout summer. Because neither parent is native to

---

Abbreviations and symbols used in the text

▼ Deciduous   † Lime hater
△ Evergreen   ◍ Shade
✳ Flowers   ◐ Semi shade
● Fruit   ⊙ Sun
🝔 Foliage

A.G.M.   Award of Garden Merit, Royal Horticultural Society
F.C.C.   First Class Certificate, Royal Horticultural Society

Z1–10   The Z numbers represent the climatic zones used in the United States and provide a useful hardiness rating elsewhere. Thus Z1 is for those plants surviving coldest conditions and Z10 is the other extreme

The illustration numbers are in **bold type**.

America, the name apparently arose through some misconception. A.G.M. 1955. **274**

etrusca **Cream Honeysuckle** ⊙ ▼/△❋
A very vigorous, deciduous, climber which may remain semi-evergreen in mild winters. A native of the Mediterranean region and introduced to cultivation about 1750. The fragrant cream flowers deepen to yellow but are only freely produced on well established plants in sheltered gardens. Z.7.

    'Superba', a more vigorous form with larger panicles.

fragrantissima **Winter Honeysuckle** ⊙ △/▼❋●
1·85–2·45 m. (6–8 ft)
China. Introduced by Fortune 1845. A partially evergreen shrub which would not receive much attention in spring but is valuable because of its charming fragrant white flowers in winter, from December to March. A few sprays brought indoors are a delight as the buds open in succession. Commences growth very early; the young leaves mingle with the flowers. Z.5.

japonica *c.* 6 m. (20 ft) ⊙ ◐ △❋➤
Japan, Korea, Manchuria, China. Introduced 1806. An evergreen climber of vigorous growth, with white or purple tinged fragrant flowers from June onwards.

    'Aureo-reticulata', Yellow-net Honeysuckle, a delightfully effective plant in summer when the neat green leaves are noticeably reticulated in gold. Frequently used for furnishing hanging baskets in summer, for ground cover and for indoor decoration by floral artists. A.G.M. 1969.

    'Halliana', considered by some authorities to be the typical form and the one most frequently seen in British gardens. The pure white flowers yellowing with age, are freely produced from June to October and are deliciously fragrant. A very beautiful fast growing plant which may be used for covering banks and benefits from a thinning out of growths in spring. In the mid-eastern U.S. it has naturalised and become a destructive nuisance. A.G.M. 1969. Z.4. **275**

maackii 3·05–4·55 m. (10–15 ft) ⊙ ▼❋●
Manchuria, China. Introduced 1880. A deciduous shrub of some size, with spreading branches arranged in a flat formation and very attractive bark. White, fragrant flowers appear in June and turn yellow with age; they are followed by dark red fruits which are attractive from September onwards. **276, 277**

periclymenum **Woodbine** ⊙ ◐ ▼❋●
to 6 m. (20 ft)
Western Asia, Europe including British Isles. A vigorous deciduous trailer or climber, the much loved common woodbine, so familiar in Europe in the wild scrambling over hedges or in woodland and in gardens, particularly cottage gardens. The yellowish white flowers, purplish on the outside are borne freely on terminal clusters, and are free with their scent particularly in the dew of the morning and the cool of the evening. These flowers are followed by clusters of translucent red fruits. There are many varieties of this indispensable plant. In America it is seldom grown by nurserymen. Z.4.

    'Belgica', sometimes known as the **Early Dutch Honeysuckle** with larger somewhat redder flowers than the type and of more bushy habit. Probably originated on the continent of Europe.

    'Serotina', Late Dutch Honeysuckle, a long flowering but not a late-flowering plant as 'Serotina' would indicate, and evidently not the plant originally so named. Cannot be reliable distinguished from the above form. **278**

× *purpusii* (*L. fragrantissima* × *L. standishii*) ⊙ ▼❋
1·85 m. (6 ft)
A deciduous shrub, a hybrid which like its parents flowers in winter. A medium sized shrub generally around 1·85 m. with beautifully scented, creamy flowers, regarded by some as an improvement on its parents. **279**

sempervirens **Trumpet Honeysuckle** ⊙ ◐ △❋
East and south U.S. Introduced 1656. A fairly vigorous climbing shrub, which remains evergreen in sheltered gardens. This beautiful plant, has scentless bright flowers through the summer, orange scarlet and yellow within. Thriving best in the milder temperate areas it succeeds when planted against a sheltered wall in less favoured districts. Much hardier for English gardens than has previously been believed. America's hardiest honeysuckle. Z.3. **280**

× *tellmanniana* (*L. sempervirens* × ◐ ▼❋
L. tragophylla) **Tellman Honeysuckle**
A beautiful hybrid between a species from China and one from U.S. A deciduous climbing shrub, quite hardy. Likes good soil and prefers to have its lower limbs and roots in the shade. The rich coppery yellow flowers, tinged bronzy red in the bud and at the tips, are produced in June and July and are unscented. A.G.M. 1969. Z.5.

tragophylla ◐/◑ ▼❋●
West China. Introduced 1900. A deciduous climbing shrub which appreciates some shade. It is the largest flowered of the climbing honeysuckles and one of the most beautiful. The scentless bright yellow flowers, in June and July, are followed by red fruits, the flowers are not scented but are very showy. A.G.M. 1928. **281**

M

MAGNOLIA MAGNOLIACEAE
A genus of evergreen or deciduous trees and shrubs which provide some of the most spectacular effects obtainable in British gardens. In the main the tree magnolias are outside the scope of this book being

suitable for only large gardens. There are many others which are quite suitable and worthy of the extra soil preparation required to grow them with success. A soil rich in humus is most suitable, more so if abundant moisture is available. To this end good lime free loam should be added to poor soils, plus at least one quarter by bulk of leaf mould or peat. Cultivation at least two spade blades deep will help to ensure drainages. Sunny sheltered positions if available should be utilized and spring planting will ensure better chance of success than moving in the autumn. Avoid planting too deeply also. Pruning as a rule is not required, but when needed should be done before leaf fall. Some can be grown from seed, while others may have to be grafted onto seedling stocks. Layering is often used also to raise new plants and, in some cases, plants such as *M. liliiflora* 'Nigra', are propagated by cuttings.

cylindrica to 9·1 m. (30 ft) in the wild ⊙†▼✳
China. Discovered 1925. A small deciduous tree or large shrub as yet not common in gardens, where it is hardy, it commences flowering when only 90 cm.–1·2 m. (3–4 ft) high. It is an attractive plant for gardens where the soil is lime free. The specific name refers to the cylindrical fruits. Z.8. **282**

kobus var. **stellata** see **M. stellata** and **M. × loebneri**

liliiflora syn. *M. discolor* up to 3 m. (10 ft) ⊙†▼✳
'Nigra' syn. *M. × soulangiana* 'Nigra', **Purple Lily Magnolia**, Japan. Introduced by Veitch 1861. A deciduous bush of more compact form than the type and most certainly one of the best magnolias for the small garden. The erect, tulip like flowers, in May and June, are deep dark purple outside, creamy white stained purple inside, and can often be seen after the main flowering period of the summer is over. Some authorities consider that the specific name *quinquepeta* has precedence over *liliiflora* and this cultivar should therefore be named *M. quinquepeta* 'Nigra'. A.G.M. 1969. Z.6. **283**

× loebneri (*M. kobus* × *M. stellata*) ⊙▼✳
A deciduous hybrid which originated in Germany prior to 1910 from a deliberate cross by Max Löbner. Somewhat variable, but in general a shrub which produces flowers in profusion even when small. The white fragrant flowers have twelve strap shaped petals, and appear in April. Will grow on most soils including chalk. Some authorities now recognize that *M. stellata* is a variety of *M. kobus* and consequently the parentage of × *loebneri* being *M. kobus* × *M. kobus* var. *stellata* the cultivars should be referred to *M. kobus*. Thus 'Leonard Messel' would be named *M. kobus* 'Leonard Messel'.

'Leonard Messel', originated at Nymans, Sussex, England, believed to be a chance cross between *M. kobus* and *M. stellata* 'Rosea'. A very fine tall shrub with pale lilac pink flowers which are deeper in bud. F.C.C. 1969. **284**

quinquepeta see under **M. liliiflora**

sinensis to 6 m. (20 ft) ⊙◐▼✳●
West China. Introduced by Wilson 1908. A large deciduous shrub of rather spreading habit, too spreading in fact for very small gardens. The white saucer like nodding flowers appear with the leaves in June and contrast strongly with the central red staminal cone. The fruits are also pendulous, pink with seeds which become scarlet. A beautiful magnolia which thrives on most soils, including chalk. F.C.C. 1931, A.G.M. 1969. Z.8. **285**

× soulangiana (*M. denudata* × *M. liliiflora*) ⊙◐†▼✳
This deciduous hybrid is so frequently seen even in quite small suburban gardens, that its popularity is beyond question. Usually a large shrub with several wide spreading stems. Its tulip like flowers appear from April to June, the first before the leaves, but as the flowering is over a long period the later ones appear amongst the leaves. The large flowers are white inside and stained purple on the outside, but some variation in size and staining occurs. This magnolia is fairly tolerant of most soils with the exception of chalk. Some authorities now recognize that the first specific name given to *M. denudata* was *heptapeta* and similarly *M. liliiflora* becomes *M. quinquepeta*: the parentage for this hybrid would then be *M. heptapeta* × *M. quinquepeta*. A.G.M. 1932. **286**

'Lennei', is a popular variety, which originated in Italy sometime before 1850. It produces very large goblet like flowers which open in late April, and carrying on throughout May, usually succeed in escaping frost damage. White within and a beautiful shade of rosy purple outside, a good many flowers are frequently produced through late summer. This is a very vigorous form which if planted in good soil and in a sheltered position may outgrow its position if not carefully pruned. F.C.C. 1863, A.G.M. 1969. **287**
'Picture', a variety of more recent introduction which originated in Japan. It has the great merit of flowering while still young, is a vigorous erect grower

---

Abbreviations and symbols used in the text

▼ Deciduous	† Lime hater
△ Evergreen	◐ Shade
✳ Flowers	◑ Semi shade
● Fruit	⊙ Sun
❧ Foliage	

A.G.M. Award of Garden Merit, Royal Horticultural Society
F.C.C. First Class Certificate, Royal Horticultural Society

Z1–10 The Z numbers represent the climatic zones used in the United States and provide a useful hardiness rating elsewhere. Thus Z1 is for those plants surviving coldest conditions and Z10 is the other extreme

The illustration numbers are in **bold type**.

and has already proved to be a good garden plant. The long erect flowers are stained purplish red on the outside of the petals and are white within. **288**

'Rubra' see *M.* × *soulangiana* **'Rustica Rubra'**

'Rustica Rubra', syn. **'Rubra'**, is very similar to 'Lennei' in growth and habit but with shorter, broader flowers which are more rose coloured. It may be a seedling from, or a sport of, that variety. Being a vigorous grower and a very reliable garden plant it is well worth planting. A.G.M. 1969. **289**

stellata **Star Magnolia** 1·8–4·55 m. (6–15 ft) ◖▼✳
Japan. Introduced in Britain 1877, in U.S. 1862. A compact much branched deciduous shrub, of slim growth, particularly when young, which may in the course of time reach 4·55 m. in favoured gardens but seldom in my experience exceeds 3·05 m. (10 ft). Possibly the most desirable of all magnolias for the small garden, especially as it will commence flowering when little over 30 cm. (1 ft) high. The slightly scented flowers are white with strap shaped petals, which spread first then reflex, and are produced with great freedom during March and April. Unfortunately the delicate flowers, opening so early, can get damaged unless the plant is carefully sited, especially from the early morning sun. However, the loss of early flowers is usually soon replaced by blooms in succession. This species appreciates the addition of leaf mould or peat to the soil when the site is being prepared. Some authorities now consider this plant to be a variety of *M. kobus* F.C.C. 1878. A.G.M. 1923. Z.5. **290**

> **'Water Lily'**, a form raised in the U.S. which has large flowers with more numerous petals.

wilsonii to 7·5 m. (25 ft) ◖▼✳
West China. Introduced by Wilson 1908. A deciduous shrub with spreading branches, generally regarded as one of the finest of Wilson's introductions. The cup-shaped pendulous flowers, which appear in May and June, are white with a conspicuous ring of crimson stamens and are best viewed from below. This can be contrived by planting on a slope. Regarded by some as more suitable for small gardens than *M. sinensis* which is larger in leaf and flower and more spreading in habit. *M. wilsonii* is more likely to succeed if a little shade can be provided. F.C.C. 1971. **291**

Magnolia,
   Purple-lily see *Magnolia liliiflora* **'Nigra'**
   Star see *Magnolia stellata*

MAHONIA BERBERIDACEAE △
A genus of evergreen shrubs related to *Berberis* and at one time included in that genus but differing so much from them that in this case at least the gardener will not feel at odds with the botanist.

aquifolium **Holly Mahonia,** ☉◖✳🐦●
Oregon Holly Grape 1·2 m. (4 ft)

West North America. Introduced 1823. An evergreen shrub usually 60–90 cm. (2 or 3 ft) high, which is a very valuable garden plant being exceptionally hardy. Few plants are more useful than the Oregon Grape for underplanting deciduous trees where it will sucker and spread. The golden yellow flowers borne in terminal clusters flower in succession from March to May and are followed by masses of blue-blackberries which are covered with a purple bloom and so are quite decorative. The leaves assume bronze and purple tints during the winter months when they are valuable for cutting for house decoration. Some forms have shiny leaves, these being preferable to dull-leaved forms. A.G.M. 1930. Z.5.

bealei 1·85 m. (6 ft) ✳🐦
China. Introduced 1845. A medium sized winter flowering shrub closely related to and until recently much confused with *M. japonica*. The flower spikes of *M. bealei* are shorter, more upright and have a shuttlecock appearance. The flowers are yellow and appear during February and March. This species is not often seen in English gardens being inferior as a flowering shrub to *M. japonica*, but in the U.S. it is the more popular of the two because of its superior hardiness. Z.6.

japonica 1·85–2·1 m. (6–7 ft) ◖✳🐦
China. Cultivated in Japan a long time. A beautiful species referred to under *M. bealei*, which has long been popular in England, but not so much in U.S. Lustrous green pinnate leaves and long hanging racemes of lemon yellow flowers which pervade the air around them with their exquisite Lily-of-the-Valley scent, and are produced between November and March. A few sprays in a room may not be spectacular in appearance but will add much to the atmosphere. If allowed to develop will in time become a large shrub, quite a spectacle where room is available. Where it is not, pruning in spring after flowering can keep it quite small and compact, and well within the compass of a small garden. Worth growing as an architectural plant, in a tub especially in a slightly shaded area. A.G.M. 1962. **292**

× *media* ✳🐦
This name is used for hybrids between *M. japonica* and *M. lomariifolia*, inclusive of second generation seedlings and back crosses.

> **'Charity'**, a superb evergreen shrub the original plant left unpruned has attained a height of 4·35 m. (14 ft) in the Savill Garden, Windsor Great Park, England. Its value is great as a winter flowering shrub, the flowers appearing from November to January. The racemes of deep yellow, lightly fragrant flowers are produced in a succession so that only those fully developed may get damaged by frost. The plant, itself is quite hardy and amenable to pruning if room is not available for what is quite a large shrub. The growths removed when pruning may be used for propagation. Leaves removed with the basal bud intact will root in pots under mist during the summer. F.C.C. 1962, A.G.M. 1969. **293**

'Faith', a seedling raised from 'Charity' is more closely allied to *M. lomariifolia* in foliage and habit, but with flowers of a softer yellow. Hardy in England, flowers somewhat earlier.

'Hope', also raised from 'Charity' in the Savill Garden, Windsor Great Park, has densely set flowers of soft yellow. A beautiful plant which appears to be more difficult to propagate. F.C.C. 1966. Z.8.

MALUS ROSACEAE ▼

'Golden Hornet' 3·65 m. (12 ft) ✳●

A small tree which, during April and May, produces white flowers followed in due course by a large crop of deep yellow crab apple fruits. These last on the tree until quite late in the year giving a brilliant display. This is one of the most decorative of plants grown for their fruits. F.C.C. 1961, A.G.M. 1969. **294**

× robusta (*M. baccata* × *M. prunifolia*) ✳●
Cherry Crab Apple (U.S.)

A variable large group of hybrids, between *M. baccata*, the Siberian Crab Apple and *M. prunifolia*, and which have become popularly, although incorrectly, known as Siberian Crab. Cultivated since about 1815. The white or pale pink flowers are succeeded by round, cherry like red fruit or on the form known as Yellow Siberian, yellow fruits. The fruits persist on the trees until February. A.G.M. 1958.

sieboldii Toringo Crab Apple ✳
2·75–3·05 m. (9–10 ft)

Korea, Japan. Introduced 1856. A small tree, sometimes more like a shrub, of graceful habit, with pale pink flowers which are of deeper colour in bud and appear in April. The small fruits are of pea size and reddish brown in colour. **295**

Maple see *Acer*
Maple,
    Brazil Flowering see *Abutilon megapotamicum*
    Coral Bark see *Acer palmatum*
    Flowering see *Abutilon*
    Grape-leaved Flowering see *Abutilon vitifolium*
    Japanese see *Acer palmatum*
    Sycamore see *Acer pseudoplatanus*
Matilija Poppy see *Romneya coulteri*
Mayflower Rhododendron see *Rhododendron racemosum*
Mediterranean Heath see *Erica erigena*

MENZIESIA ERICACEAE †▼

Small deciduous shrubs which grow slowly and require lime free soil. Seldom seen in gardens, where they require similar conditions to rhododendrons. The species mentioned and pictured is a delightful plant for a small garden, deserving to be better known.

ciliicalyx 60–90 cm. (2–3 ft) ✳

Japan. Introduced about 1914. A small shrub with nodding flowers in May, produced in clusters at the ends of the previous years growth. The corolla colours from cream at base to a delicate purple at tips. A pretty plant. **296**

    'Purpurea', a variant with larger purplish pink flowers, a charmer which is quite hardy and flowers freely in an open well lighted site.

Mespilus, Snowy see *Amelanchier*
Mexican Orange Blossom see *Choisya ternata*
Mezereon see *Daphne mezereum*
Mock
    Orange see *Philadelphus*
    Orange, Evergreen see *Carpenteria californica*
    Orange, Sweet see *Philadelphus coronarius*

MOLTKIA BORAGINACEAE

suffruticosa 45 cm. (1½ ft) △✳

Italy. Introduced into commerce 1888. A low semi-evergreen shrub, related to *Lithospermum*, which is essentially a plant for a sunny place in a rock garden or raised bed where drainage is good. The blue flowers are tinged with purple after being pink in bud and are borne in branched pendulous clusters. Worth growing for the glorious colour of its flowers. **297**

Morning Glory, Bush see *Convolvulus cneorum*
Morocco Broom see *Cytisus battandieri*
Mount Etna Broom see *Genista aetnensis*
Mountain
    Ash, Japanese see *Sorbus matsumurana*
    Ash, Vilmorin see *Sorbus vilmorinii*
    Laurel see *Kalmia latifolia*
Moutan Paeony see *Paeonia suffruticosa*
Mrs Wilson's Rose see *Rosa helenae*

Abbreviations and symbols used in the text

▼ Deciduous	† Lime hater
△ Evergreen	▥ Shade
✳ Flowers	◖ Semi shade
● Fruit	☉ Sun
☙ Foliage	

A.G.M. Award of Garden Merit, Royal Horticultural Society
F.C.C. First Class Certificate, Royal Horticultural Society

Z1–10 The Z numbers represent the climatic zones used in the United States and provide a useful hardiness rating elsewhere. Thus Z1 is for those plants surviving coldest conditions and Z10 is the other extreme

The illustration numbers are in **bold type**.

Myrtle see *Myrtus*
Myrtle, Common see *Myrtus communis*

Nightshade see *Solanum*
Nightshade, Jasmine see *Solanum jasminoides*
Norway Spruce see *Picea abies*
Nut, European Bladder see *Staphylea pinnata*
Nutmeg, Flowering see *Leycesteria formosa*

MYRTUS MYRTACEAE **Myrtle**　　　　　△

communis **Common Myrtle**　　　　　✳▰
3·05–3·65 m. (10–12 ft)
South and east Europe, west Asia. Cultivated in Britain since the 16th century. The common myrtle is an evergreen, leafy shrub, hardy in warm gardens particularly in maritime areas. In colder and more northerly gardens it is frequently found in cool greenhouses, often propagated in England from a sprig from a bride's bouquet. It will also grow well on a sheltered wall and in hot dry country near the sea. The white flowers are freely produced in July and August. They are fragrant as are the leaves when bruised. Cuttings are easily rooted in gentle heat or under mist. There are several varieties of myrtle available. Z.8–9. **298**

NYSSA NYSSACEAE

sylvatica **Tupelo, Black Gum,**　　†⊙◐▼▰
Pepperidge
Eastern North America. Introduced 1750. An upright small to medium sized tree except in very sheltered gardens. In its native home it grows in swamps but in cultivation it is much more successful in good soil with no lime. The Tupelo is particularly handsome in the autumn when its dark glossy green leaves change into a wonderful range of yellow, orange and red shades before falling. Tupelo is an American Indian word. F.C.C. 1968, A.G.M. 1969.

N

NANDINA BERBERIDACEAE

domestica **Sacred Bamboo** 1·85 m. (6 ft)　⊙△▰
Japan, central China, India. An erect evergreen shrub, bamboo-like in appearance. A monotypic genus related to *Berberis*. It produces erect panicles of white flowers, on unbranched stems, but its decorative value resides in its foliage and long-lasting bright red or purple berries.

　　To succeed in most gardens it requires a sheltered site in full sun and well drained soil in warm temperate areas. In such a situation its large, compound leaves colour attractively in spring and again in autumn with red and purple shades. The Sacred Bamboo is a decorative foliage plant, at one time much grown under glass in pots and for this purpose the plants were imported from Japan. Can be increased from cuttings in a heated propagating frame, but these are of slow growth and require growing in pots or containers for some time before planting. May also be grown from seeds which likewise are slow to germinate. Z.7.

NEILLIA ROSACEAE

longiracemosa 1·5–1·85 m. (5–6 ft)　⊙▼✳
West China. Discovered 1890. Introduced by Wilson 1904. An attractive deciduous shrub of elegant habit. The erect downy stems bear terminal racemes of rosy pink tubular flowers in May and June. An easily grown shrub which appreciates good soil and a sunny position, but dislikes dry conditions in summer. Little pruning required unless overcrowded when old flowering growths can be cut away. Semi-ripe cuttings can be rooted in a frame in late summer.

O

OLEARIA COMPOSITAE **Daisy Bushes,**　⊙△
Tree Daisies
A large genus of evergreen shrubs, few of which are reliably hardy in the British Isles or U.S. They are from New Zealand and Australia. They like a sunny position and well drained soil, succeeding also on chalk.

× *haastii* (*O. avicenniifolia* × *O. moschata*)　✳▰
to 2·75 m. (9 ft)
New Zealand. Introduced 1858. Probably the best known daisy bush succeeding in temperate climes, particularly around the coast. Very popular in subtropical U.S. A densely branched rounded shrub with small leaves, green above, grey below it is ideally suited for hedging and providing shelter in seaside gardens. It also succeeds in town or city gardens, seemingly impervious to grime or fumes. As a rule pruning is unnecessary, but can be carried out in April where required. The white daisy like flowers are produced in masses during July and August and have a sweet hawthorn like fragrance. Can be propagated from summer cuttings under mist. F.C.C. 1873. A.G.M. 1928.

mollis　　　　　　　　　　　　　　✳▰
New Zealand. A small shrub which I only became acquainted with in 1970. Rounded and compact in habit it is worth a place in small gardens for its silvery-grey foliage. White flowers in May, the wavy edged leaves providing an attractive foil. Some plants under this name may actually be hybrids. **299**

× *scilloniensis* (*O. lyrata* × *O. phlogopappa*)　✳▰
2·6 m. (8½ ft)
A neat, rounded grey-leaved hybrid shrub which originated at Tresco in the Isles of Scilly. The white flowers

swamp the plants in May and are exceedingly effective at that time.

Although reputed to be likely to succumb in a severe winter, the plant illustrated has survived for some years at the Royal Horticultural Society's Garden, Wisley, on a well drained site. **300**

Oleaster see *Elaeagnus*
Orange, Mock see *Philadelphus*
Orange Ball Tree see *Buddleia globosa*
Orange-peel Clematis see *Clematis orientalis*
Oregon Holly Grape see *Mahonia aquifolium*
Oriental Arbor-vitae see *Thuya orientalis*

OSMANTHUS OLEACEAE △

delavayi syn. *Siphonosmanthus delavayi* ⊙ ◑ ✳ ➘
2·45–2·05 m. (8–10 ft)
China (Yunnan). Introduced by Abbé Delavay 1890. A beautiful evergreen shrub which grows slowly taking several years to reach its ultimate height. Densely bushy and well furnished with small glossy green leaves. The white, fragrant, jasmine-like flowers are produced freely in April. Reasonably hardy, it will grow in any reasonably good soil either in sun preferably or partial shade but requires some shelter in exposed gardens. Pruning is not required unless encroachment is taking place when careful use of the secateurs or shears after flowering will be required. Cuttings of young growth will root under mist in July. Has been well described as one of China's gems. A parent of × *Osmarea*. A.G.M. 1923, F.C.C. 1931. Z.7. **301**

heterophyllus 1·85–2·75 m. (6–9 ft) ⊙ ◑ ✳ ➘
Japan. Introduced 1856. An evergreen shrub with handsome holly like foliage, which will make a useful hedge, especially in milder localities where it will grow faster and attain a height considerably greater than stated. The small white flowers are produced in autumn and are usually brought to notice by their fragrance. F.C.C. 1859.

'Variegatus', a form which seems to be slow growing and a very neat shrub on which the leaves are bordered with creamy white. Z.6. **302**

× *OSMAREA* OLEACEAE △
(*Osmanthus delavayi* × *Phillyrea decora*)

'Burkwoodii' 2·1–2·45 m. (7–8 ft) ✳ ➘
A useful evergreen hardy shrub, with neat leaves of glossy olive green, which will grow up to 2·1–2·45 m. and make a delightful hedge. The small fragrant white flowers are produced in April and May. A bi-generic hybrid between *Osmanthus delavayi* and *Phillyrea decora* which was raised by Burkwood and Skipwith, England about 1930. Pruning is not generally required but when grown as a hedge this should be trimmed after flowering. Z.6. A.G.M. 1950.

Oval-leaf Privet see *Ligustrum ovalifolium*

OXYDENDRUM ERICACEAE

arboreum **Sorrel Tree** to 18·3 m. (60 ft) ⊙ ◑ † ✳ ➘
Eastern North America. Introduced 1752. A deciduous tree which may grow to 18·3 m. (60 ft) in the U.S., but seldom attains this height in the U.K. where it is more likely to be a shrub or tree of up to 3·05 m. (10 ft). The small white flowers are produced in arching racemes from the tips of the shoots in July and August. Does well in the same conditions as rhododendrons. When exposed to sun, makes a lovely display in the autumn of brilliant dark red foliage. Can be grown from seed. A.G.M. 1947. **303**

P

PAEONIA RANUNCULACEAE ⊙ ▼
This is a genus which in the main is composed of herbaceous plants, but in this book we are concerned only with the Tree Paeonies which are fairly hardy shrubs. Few, if any shrubs produce flowers with the spectacular beauty of *Paeonia suffruticosa* and its various clones in brilliant colours and with petals of crinkly satin appearance. Such splendours have their price and in some gardens where growth commences rather early this is paid for in the form of protection at night from spring frosts. The young growths are easily damaged and should be protected by a screen of hessian, burlap or other suitable material erected on a tripod formed from stakes. This should be removed during the day and replaced at night until the young growths have become hardened. Tree Paeonies appreciate good well drained soil, well enriched with organic material to prevent drying out in summer and, being gross feeders, benefit from an annual mulch with farmyard manure in late

---

Abbreviations and symbols used in the text

▼	Deciduous	†	Lime hater
△	Evergreen	◑	Shade
✳	Flowers	◐	Semi shade
●	Fruit	⊙	Sun
➘	Foliage		

A.G.M.   Award of Garden Merit, Royal Horticultural Society
F.C.C.   First Class Certificate, Royal Horticultural Society

Z1–10   The Z numbers represent the climatic zones used in the United States and provide a useful hardiness rating elsewhere. Thus Z1 is for those plants surviving coldest conditions and Z10 is the other extreme

The illustration numbers are in **bold type**.

---

spring. When suited, large plants will result, so that if isolated as specimens the effect can be more spectacular than if planted in the middle of other shrubs. Protection from early morning sun in conjunction with a sheltered site will generally pay a good dividend. Named cultivars are generally, grafted and should be planted deep enough to cover the union with a few inches of soil. Pruning is not required, any dead or damaged wood can be removed in spring. Species can be grown from seeds if available, otherwise by layering before the growing season commences in spring.

delavayi 1·85 m. (6 ft)
West China, discovered 1884. Introduced to cultivation about 1908. A deciduous suckering shrub worth growing as a specimen for its large deeply cut fern like leaves which are often tinted red and decidedly decorative. The deep maroon-crimson flowers with golden anthers are somewhat pendulous and most likely to be appreciated when the plant has become established and attained some height. Does well on chalky or limey soils and, not starting into growth early, is unlikely to suffer damage from late frost. The large black seeded fruits are surrounded by persistent sepals which are also decorative because of their conspicuous colouring. A very handsome shrub. **304**

× *lemoinei* (*P. lutea* × *P. suffruticosa*)
A cross between *P. lutea* and *P. suffruticosa* which has produced cultivars with very large flowers and colour combinations meriting the description gorgeous. They thrive on chalky soils, especially if provided with a diet of well decayed farmyard manure which, unfortunately, is not available to everybody.

'Argosy', a very fine and free flowering clone. Light yellow with a red blotch at base. **305**

lutea
ludlowii, 1·5 m. (5 ft). South-east Tibet. A splendid plant which was originally collected by Kingdon Ward and subsequently by Ludlow and Sheriff. In May and June it has large golden yellow single flowers which are bowl shaped. Sturdy, straight branches arise from the ground furnished with fan like leaves which expand as the flowers open. A superb plant, which can be raised from seed. A.G.M. 1963.

suffruticosa Moutan Paeony 1·5 m. (5 ft)
North China. A stiff branched deciduous shrub, somewhat gaunt in appearance in winter when leafless, but handsome when in full leaf. The pithy stems die back part of their length after flowering. This shrub, the Moutan Paeony, has been cultivated for centuries by the Chinese and Japanese and is quite hardy in temperate climates. A number of clones, generally grafted plants, are listed by specialist nurserymen under oriental names and vary in colour from white through pink to red and crimson.

'Godaishu', has large, semi-double to double flowers, white with a yellow splash at the base of each petal. **306**

Paeony,
  Moutan see *Paeonia suffruticosa*
  Tree see **Paeonia**
Panicle Hydrangea see *Hydrangea paniculata*
Paper Bush see *Edgworthia chrysantha*
Pearlbush see *Exocorda*
Pearlbush, Common see *Exocorda racemosa*
Pencil Cedar see *Juniperus virginiana*
Penzance Brier see *Rosa 'Anne of Geierstein'*
Pepper, Sweet see *Clethra alnifolia*
Periwinkle,
  Greater see *Vinca major*
  Lesser see *Vinca minor*

PERNETTYA ERICACEAE

mucronata Chilean Pernettya
60 cm.–1·5 m. (2–5 ft)
Chile and Argentina. Introduced 1828. A hardy evergreen shrub which spreads freely by suckers and in time forms a thicket of wiry stems. The small, numerous white bell shaped flowers, produced in May and June, although attractive in themselves are surpassed by the large marble like berries which follow and commence to colour in September, ranging, according to variety, from pure white through pink and red to purple. These remain on the plants right through the winter until the following spring, so that without doubt it must be classed as one of the best ornamental fruited shrubs. Although not altogether dioecious, with male and female flowers on separate plants, it is best to plant in small groups of three or five which include one of a known male form in order to ensure a good crop of fruits. Pernettyas like sunny open positions in peaty moist soil, unlikely to dry out during summer. To this end, plenty of humus forming material should be added, leaf mould, peat or compost. Propagation may be by seeds which can be sown in peaty soil in a cold frame in spring or by division in autumn. Cuttings may also be rooted under mist in summer when particular varieties or a proven male form is required. Pruning is not required. An attractive plant for winter decoration. A.G.M. 1929. Z.7. **307**
Several clones have been selected.

'Atrococcinea', a form with fruits of large size and ruby red in colour. **308**
'Bell's Seedling', bisexual form with large, dark red berries. A.G.M. 1969.
'Coccinea', fruit bright red.
'Davies's Hybrids', a selected strain of large berried forms available in a wide range of beautiful colours. A.G.M. 1969.
'Pink Pearl', medium sized lilac pink berries. **309**
'White Pearl', medium to large, shining white, berries. **310**

Pernettya, Chilean see *Pernettya mucronata*

PEROVSKIA LABIATAE

atriplicifolia 90 cm. (3 ft)

West Himalaya to Tibet. In cultivation 1904. A deciduous semi-woody shrub with grey green leaves and whitish stems. The beautiful lavender blue flowers are borne in panicles terminating the current years growth and make a considerable contribution to the garden scene in July and August. It succeeds best in deep, well drained soil in a sunny position and does not object to chalk or lime. The stems partially die back in winter and should be cut back to the basal buds in March. Young growths taken off in June can be rooted under mist or in a propagating frame. A.G.M. 1935.

> **'Blue Spire'**, superior to type with larger panicles of lavender blue flowers and more deeply cut leaves. Well worth growing especially by those who like grey effects and the sage like fragrance. A.G.M. 1969. **311**

PHILADELPHUS PHILADELPHACEAE
Mock Orange

A genus of deciduous shrubs popularly known as Mock Orange presumably because of the flowers resemblance to that of the orange blossom, along with a suggestive fragrance; also mistakenly as 'Syringa', the botanic name for the lilacs. Easily grown shrubs in most soils, thriving also on chalk or lime, but requiring good drainage. They will grow in partially shaded situations but flower more abundantly in sun. There is a wide range suitable for gardens of all sizes from the large to small. Pruning should be carried out immediately after flowering, removing stems which have borne flowers back to young growths to succeed them. By judicious annual pruning many varieties can be kept to a reasonable size and will produce flowers of better quality. Cuttings of young growths are easily rooted under mist during summer while hard wooded cuttings will root in a sheltered border outside if inserted in October.

'Beauclerk' 1·5–1·85 m. (5–6 ft)

One of the best hybrids, producing in June large milky white flowers which have a purple flush at the centre and are strongly scented. F.C.C. 1951, A.G.M. 1955.

coronarius **Sweet Mock Orange** to 3·65 m. (12 ft)

Possibly south east Europe, south west Asia. In cultivation 16th century. The most commonly cultivated species in gardens where room is available. The yellowish white flowers are heavily scented, too heavily for some, so that planting some distance from the house may be necessary. Some inferior forms have lost their fragrance. Z.4.

> **'Aureus'**, a dense form round about 90 cm. (3 ft) high, golden leaved in spring when it is very effective. Later in the season the leaves become greenish. Flowers are of little significance.
>
> **'Variegatus'**, another small shrub very suitable for a small garden, growing slowly, upright to 1·2 m. (4 ft). In cultivation since 1770, the broad irregular margin of creamy white is very effective. **312**

'Enchantment' 1·5 m. (5 ft)

A small to medium shrub with arching growths thickly set with double, sweet scented white flowers in June and July. A variety which benefits from annual pruning.

× *lemoinei* (*P. coronarius* × *P. microphyllus*) 1·85 m. (6 ft)

A deciduous shrub about 1·85 m. in height, a hybrid raised by M. Lemoine of Nancy, France about 1883. The very fragrant white flowers are produced freely in June. This is the original hybrid of which there are many named clones. Z.5. **313**

'Manteau d'Hermine' 75 cm (2½ ft)

A popular small, compact shrub with a profuse display of double, creamy white fragrant flowers in June. A.G.M. 1969.

'Silver Showers' 1·05 m. (3½ ft)

A valuable shrub for small gardens. The deeply cup shaped flowers are produced in great profusion in June and July and are sweetly scented.

'Sybille' 90 cm–1·5 m. (3–5 ft)

A fine shrub whose arching branches produce single white flowers with pronounced purple staining at the base, in June and July. Orange scented. A.G.M. 1955.

'Virginal' 1·05 m. (3½ ft)

A strong erect shrub with large richly fragrant double flowers produced in clusters in June and July. One of the most popular cultivars and still regarded by many as the best double flowered form. F.C.C. 1911, A.G.M. 1926.

PHILLYREA OLEACEAE △

decora **Lance-leaf Phillyrea**
1·85–2·75 m. (6–9 ft)

West Asia. Introduced 1866. An evergreen shrub wider than its height and with attractive, narrow dark shiny leaves. The small white flowers, produced in April and

---

Abbreviations and symbols used in the text

▼ Deciduous   † Lime hater
△ Evergreen   ◍ Shade
✳ Flowers   ◑ Semi shade
● Fruit   ☉ Sun
🍂 Foliage

A.G.M.   Award of Garden Merit, Royal Horticultural Society

F.C.C.   First Class Certificate, Royal Horticultural Society

Z1–10   The Z numbers represent the climatic zones used in the United States and provide a useful hardiness rating elsewhere. Thus Z1 is for those plants surviving coldest conditions and Z10 is the other extreme

The illustration numbers are in **bold type**.

May, are fragrant and are succeeded by purple black fruits. A very hardy easily grown plant, seldom seen in gardens but worth planting as a background or foil to other shrubs. Can be pruned in spring if it is desired to restrict its size but where there is room this is not essential. Can be propagated from seed or by cuttings of young growth in July, under mist. A parent of × *Osmarea*. F.C.C. 1888. Z.9. **314**

Phillyrea, Lance-leaf see *Phillyrea decora*

PHLOMIS LABIATAE ⊙△

chrysophylla 75 cm. (2½ ft)
Lebanon. An evergreen small shrub with felted, soft pale gold sage like leaves and rounded cushion like in habit. The flowers of golden yellow are produced in June and July in axillary whorls, but its main value is as a beautiful foliage shrub worthy of a sheltered corner which it requires in cold areas.

fruticosa **Jerusalem Sage** 1·2 m. (4 ft)
Southern Europe. In cultivation 1596. A small evergreen shrub of spreading growth and with glaucous leaves, which are hairy, felted and sage like in appearance. The bright yellow tubular flowers are produced in June and July in whorls and are quite attractive in summer. A useful plant on sunny banks which are well drained and will make itself at home on poor soils. It sometimes gets damaged in severe winters, especially where growing on good soil, but is easily produced from cuttings of young wood during summer. If pruned back lightly after flowering it will preserve a tidy habit. A.G.M. 1929. Z.9. **315**

PHYGELIUS SCROPHULARIACEAE ⊙▼

capensis **Cape Figwort, Cape Fuchsia** ❋
to 1·85 m. (6 ft)
South Africa. Introduced about 1850. A small shrub in sheltered gardens, but which in colder areas can be grown as a semi-herbaceous plant. The nodding funnel-shaped flowers are carried elegantly in loose sprays and are scarlet with a yellow throat. It is easily increased from cuttings under mist during summer. A.G.M. 1969.
‘**Coccineus**’, a form with deeper coloured flowers, and the plant usually offered by nurserymen.

PICEA PINACEAE **Spruce** △❧

abies **Norway Spruce**
‘**Gregoryana**’, a very popular dwarf conifer which has been in cultivation since 1862. Its sea green leaves are very striking.
‘**Nidiformis**’, a comparatively dwarf, dense, flat-topped spreading bush which after many years can attain 1·2 m. (4 ft) in height and twice as much across.

Originating in Germany around 1907, this very popular dwarf conifer is most attractive when covered with the bright green fresh tips of the new season’s growth. Z.2 **316**

glauca
albertiana ‘**Conica**’, a very popular cultivar, originally found near Alberta, in 1904. Very distinctive in its cone shape, of bright green leaves, growing to about 2 m. (6 ft) in height. However, in my experience it is prone to suffer from Red Spider, which rapidly defoliates the plant. A.G.M. 1969.

mariana
‘**Nana**’, a very slow-growing bush, making it suitable for rock gardens. It has distinctive grey-green leaves and has been in cultivation since 1884.

pungens **Colorado Spruce**
‘**Procumbens**’, a dwarf spreading conifer with branches extending close to the ground in all directions. The glaucous blue leaves are effective at all times but particularly so in winter and when sprawling over a large rock in the rock garden. Occasionally it attempts to resume an upright form, such terminal reversions should be removed. In cultivation since 1910. Z.2. **317**

PIERIS ERICACEAE ⊙†△
Evergreen shrubs of dense habit which thrive in similar conditions to rhododendrons. They have gained considerably in popularity since the advent of forms with young spring growths of bright scarlet. These growths are liable to be caught by late frosts and should be protected by planting under an overhead canopy of shrubs or trees. Shelter from northern winds and the early morning sun in the east is also desirable. Pruning is not required but regular flowering is helped by the removal of the old flowers to prevent seed formation. Plants can be raised from seed sown in peaty soil in a frame or by layers put down during spring or summer.

‘**Forest Flame**’ (*P. formosa forrestii* ‘Wakehurst’
× *P. japonica*)
A beautiful shrub, with the bright red young foliage of ‘Wakehurst’ and which changes to pink, white then green. A hardy shrub, raised and introduced about 1957. It produces flowers in large drooping panicles.

formosa
***forrestii*, Chinese Pieris**, to 2·45 m. (8 ft), south west China, north east Burma. Introduced by Forrest about 1910. A shrub with handsome foliage and large creamy white flowers in April and May. The flowers are borne in drooping panicles which, when enhanced by the brilliant scarlet of the young growths, combine to produce one of the most beautiful of all shrubs, especially in the spring. F.C.C. 1930, A.G.M. 1944. Z.7. **318**
‘**Wakehurst**’, a fine and broader-leaved form. The young leaves are a brilliant red.

japonica **Lily-of-the-Valley Shrub** ✳☙
1·85–2·45 m. (6–8 ft)
Japan. In cultivation 1870. An evergreen shrub with attractive foliage, coppery coloured when young. Hardier than *P. formosa* and with creamy white pendulous flowers in long branching panicles. F.C.C. 1882, A.G.M. 1924. Z.5. **319**

'**Blush**', a form with flowers rose pink in bud becoming pale blush pink on opening. **320**
'**Variegata**', a form with narrower leaves, prettily variegated yellowish white, the young growths tinged pink. An attractive slow growing plant, for small gardens where soil is suitable and some shade available. A.G.M. 1969. **321**

Pieris, Chinese see *Pieris formosa* '**Forestii**'

PILEOSTEGIA HYDRANGEACEAE   △

viburnoides   to 5·5 m. (18 ft)   ✳
India, Taiwan, south China. Introduced Wilson 1908. A growing evergreen climbing shrub which is self clinging and will clothe a tree trunk or wall in any aspect, given fertile soil. The creamy white flowers in crowded terminal panicles are attractive and useful in that they are produced in late summer and autumn. Z.7. **322**

Pine,
  Arolla see *Pinus cembra*
  Scots see *Pinus sylvestris*
  Swiss Stone see *Pinus cembra*
  Umbrella see *Sciadopitys verticillata*

PINUS PINACEAE   △☙

cembra **Arolla Pine, Swiss Stone Pine**
to over 6·1 m. (20 ft)
Mountains of central Europe and north Asia. In cultivation 1746. The Arolla Pine is a dense tree of columnar habit and slow growth which is very handsome as a small tree. It is unlikely to outgrow a garden of reasonable size. A tree I would like to see planted more frequently.

sylvestris **Scots** or **Scotch Pine**
'**Beuvronensis**', a Scots Pine in miniature, a small compact shrub, broadly rounded in habit. The short, densely packed growths are clothed with blue grey needles. In cultivation since 1891 this superb plant is most suitable for the rock garden and will attain a height, after many years, of 1·2 m. (4 ft) and a little more across. Such specimens are not very plentiful. A.G.M. 1969.
'**Watereri**', syn. '**Pumila**', a slow growing bush of medium size which will after many years become a picturesque small tree of rounded shape. Found in Surrey, England, by Mr Anthony Waterer about 1865; the original tree in Knap Hill Nursery, England is about 7·5 m. (25 ft) in height so plants are likely to outgrow a normal rock garden. They are, however, particularly suitable for siting amongst heathers. Blue grey foliage. A.G.M. 1969. **323**

PITTOSPORUM PITTOSPORACEAE   ⊙△

tenuifolium **Kohutu**   to 9·1 m. (30 ft)   ☙
New Zealand. An evergreen small tree or shrub which will only attain the height given in sheltered gardens in warm areas. In other gardens it is more likely to reach 3·05 m. (10 ft). The pale green undulate leaves are very charming set as they are on black twigs. Used largely as a hedging plant in mild climates and much prized for cutting for floral arrangements. The honey scented, chocolate coloured flowers are not conspicuous enough to have garden value.

'**Garnettii**', a neat form with variegated white leaves which have a pink tint. Z.8. **324**

PLAGIANTHUS MALVACEAE   ⊙▼

betulinus   to 9·15 m. (30 ft)   ✳☙
New Zealand, South Island. Introduced about 1870. A graceful small tree, suitable for gardens in the warmer temperate areas. In other areas it requires a sheltered position, preferably near a wall where 3·75 m. (12 ft) or so may be attained. The white flowers, borne in May, are produced in dense panicles and although not very conspicuous have some attraction. Z.9. **325**

Pleioblastus viridistriatus see *Arundinaria viridistriata*
Plume
  Cedar see *Cryptomeria japonica* '**Elegans**'
  Cryptomeria see *Cryptomeria japonica* '**Elegans**'
Poppy Bush, Californian see *Dendromecon rigida*
Poppy,
  Bush see *Dendromecon rigida*

Abbreviations and symbols used in the text

▼	Deciduous	†	Lime hater
△	Evergreen	⦾	Shade
✳	Flowers	◖	Semi shade
•	Fruit	⊙	Sun
☙	Foliage		

A.G.M.   Award of Garden Merit, Royal Horticultural Society
F.C.C.   First Class Certificate, Royal Horticultural Society

Z1–10   The Z numbers represent the climatic zones used in the United States and provide a useful hardiness rating elsewhere. Thus Z1 is for those plants surviving coldest conditions and Z10 is the other extreme

The illustration numbers are in **bold type**.

Matilija see *Romneya coulteri*
Tree see *Romneya*
Portugal
Heath see *Erica lusitanica*
Laurel see *Prunus lusitanica*
Portuguese Broom, White see *Cytisus multiflorus*

POTENTILLA ROSACEAE **Cinquefoil** ⊙ ◑ ▼

The shrubby potentillas are deciduous shrubs of great value in gardens large or small, flowering from mid-summer to late autumn. Easy to grow on well drained soil, they will tolerate a little shade but flower most freely in full sun. Pruning consists generally of cutting out a few of the older stems to ground level in March while retaining the best of the younger growth. In small gardens it may be necessary to extend this to keep the plants in their alloted space. Most varieties, particularly the shorter growers, are ideal for ground cover.

arbuscula syn. *P. fruticosa arbuscula*
60 cm. (2 ft)
Himalaya. A dwarf shrub related to *P. fruticosa* but with leaves of sage green and with shaggy branches. The large deep yellow flowers are abundantly produced throughout the late summer and autumn. A.G.M. 1969. **326**

> 'Beesii', has silvery foliage which serves as a background for its small golden flowers, a delightful dwarf for the smallest garden. A.G.M. 1956.
>
> 'Goldfinger', a recent introduction from Europe, welcome because of its continuous production of bright yellow flowers even into the dull days of October. **327**

'Elizabeth' *(P. arbuscula × P. fruticosa mandshurica)*
90 cm.–1·1 m. (3–3½ ft)
A long flowering and excellent hybrid. Appearing from the spring to autumn the flowers are deep canary yellow. A.G.M. 1969.

fruticosa 90 cm.–1·2 m. (3–4 ft)
Temperate northern hemisphere; Asia, America, Europe. A dense deciduous shrub found over a vast area in the temperate regions so that considerable variations occur.

> *arbuscula* see *P. arbuscula*
>
> *grandiflora*, a strong and upright shrub, with sage green leaves, and large canary yellow flowers in clusters.
>
> 'Jackman's Variety', a seedling from *P. fruticosa grandiflora* of extra good form and large brilliant yellow flowers. It makes a good 1·2 m. (4 ft) hedge which can be clipped in March and will flower from June to September. A.G.M. 1969. **328**
>
> 'Katherine Dykes', a bushy shrub producing primrose yellow saucer shaped flowers from May to October. Will make a nice informal hedge up to 1·5 m. (5 ft) high. A.G.M. 1969.
>
> *mandshurica*, a dense, dwarf spreader 30 cm. (1 ft) high, producing white flowers from May to October

over dense grey leaves. A charmer for small gardens. In cultivation 1911. A.G.M. 1969.

> *parvifolia*, a popular variety, semi-erect up to 90 cm. (3 ft). The golden yellow flowers are abundantly produced in early summer easing off later until September. Found in central Asia. A.G.M. 1969. **329**
>
> 'Primrose Beauty', a bushy shrub about 60 cm. (2 ft) high with greyish green foliage. The primrose yellow flowers have dark, rich yellow centres, and are produced from June to October, A.G.M. 1969. **330**
>
> 'Red Cross', a deciduous dwarf spreading shrub which I assume will eventually attain a height of 60 cm. (2 ft) and spread at least 30 cm. (1 ft) wider, so will be very suitable for small gardens. This new plant was discovered in the garden of Dr D. A. Barker, Hertfordshire, England in 1973 and is possibly a seedling from *P. fruticosa* 'Sunset'. Named after the ambulance service, whose emblem is known throughout the world, this fine cultivar seems destined, because of its remarkable colour, to bring joy into many gardens, large and small during the next decade. The scarlet vermilion flowers have a yellow reverse and are 2·5 cm. (an inch) across. Freely produced in terminal clusters over nearly half the season from June to November and are remarkable for colour stability, even when fully exposed to sunlight, at least in England. Foliage also seems to be retained for a longer period than other cultivars.
>
> 'Tangerine', a dwarf spreading shrub up to 60 cm. (2 ft) with soft coppery red flowers in autumn when grown in partial shade. Bright yellow if growing in a sunny position, from June to September. **331**
>
> 'Veitchii', a small shrub about 90 cm (3 ft) from Hupeh, China, and introduced 1902. The arching branches bear grey leaves, which are glaucous underneath, and pure white flowers. A.G.M. 1969.

Preston Lilac see *Syringa × prestoniae*
Primrose Rose see *Rosa primula*
Privet see *Ligustrum*
Privet,
Chinese see *Ligustrum sinense*
Golden see *Ligustrum ovalifolium* 'Aureum'

PRUNUS ROSACEAE ⊙

glandulosa **Chinese Bush Cherry,** ▼ ✳ �
Dwarf Flowering Almond 90 cm. (3 ft)
Central and northern China. Cultivated for many years in Japan. In cultivation 1835. A deciduous small shrub of graceful habit with slender willowy growths wreathed with small flowers. These may be pink or white. The Chinese Bush Cherry prefers a warm sunny position and can be pruned hard after flowering. It is quite delightful in its autumn dress also. Z.6. **332**

> 'Albiplena', a beautiful small shrub which is pendulous with the weight of its double white flowers. An excellent shrub for forcing and may also be cut for

house decoration. If all the well budded sprays are cut for this purpose further pruning will not be necessary. Cultivated since 1852.

'Sinensis', double bright pink form in cultivation since 1774, and very popular in gardens during the Victorian and Edwardian eras. Like the plant mentioned above is also excellent for forcing and for cutting.

laurocerasus **Common** or **Cherry Laurel** †△✳●
(U.K.), English Laurel (U.S.) to 5·5 m. (18 ft)
East Europe, Asia Minor. Introduced 1576 U.S., 1629 U.K. This shrub is so well known in U.K. as to hardly warrant a description, though not quite so popular in U.S. One of the most extensively planted evergreens for screening and shelter belts, and hedges also. When left unpruned it produces candles of white flowers in axillary and terminal racemes, followed by cherry like fruits, which are red at first, eventually turning black. Z.7.

'Otto Luyken', is a very distinct and attractive form, generally 90 cm. (3 ft) high and twice as much across, a shrub which has been planted extensively for ground cover in recent years. The small pointed leaves are dark green and the upright spikes of white flowers are produced at every joint. A lesser, second flowering frequently takes place in autumn. **333**

'Zabeliana', another excellent ground cover plant with long narrow, willow shaped leaves on a very prostrate plant.

lusitanica **Portugal Laurel** to 6·1 m. (20 ft) △✳🦴
Spain, Portugal. Introduced 1648. An evergreen shrub sometimes attaining small tree size. Hardier, but slower growing than *P. laurocerasus* it has smaller dark green glossy, shallowly serrate leaves, shorter than the racemes, with reddish petioles, whereas, the Common Laurel has leaves which are entire and longer than the racemes. The small white flowers are hawthorn scented and are followed by bright red to dark purple fruits. Grows quite happily on chalk or lime and is useful as a hedge or as a specimen. Z.7.

'Variegata', a form with leaves margined with white, sometimes tinged pink in winter. Makes quite an attractive specimen bush, of slower growth than *P. lusitanica*. **334**

mume **Japanese Apricot** 6·1 m. (20 ft) ▼✳
China, Korea. Extensively cultivated Japan. Introduced 1844. The Japanese Apricot is a deciduous small tree with single flowers, pink in colour and almond scented. Requires a sheltered, warm position.

'Beni-shi-don', a fine form with strongly fragrant double flowers, produced from late March to early April. They are a rich deep pink, darker in bud, which pales slightly with age. Succeeds best on a warm wall.

'Brightness', a bright pink form of the Japanese Apricot which, when grown on a sheltered wall, will produce flowers in March or early April. Useful for cutting. **335**

'Peggy Clarke', deep rose, double flowers with very long stamens.

subhirtella **Spring** or **Rosebud Cherry** ▼✳
to 6·1 m. (20 ft)

'Autumnalis', the **Autumn Cherry**, from Japan. In cultivation 1900. A deciduous small tree which has become fairly popular because of its habit of flowering during the worst months of the year, between November and March. The clusters of semi-double white flowers are produced spasmodically, especially in milder periods. A few small branches cut even in bud will open indoors and being fragrant are most welcome. A.G.M. 1924, F.C.C. 1966.

tenella **Dwarf Russian Almond** 90 cm. (3 ft) ▼✳
'Fire Hill', a small shrub, erect branching, wreathed with rosy red flowers which make a brilliant display in spring. Easily accommodated in a small garden, especially if pruned hard after flowering. Propagated by root cuttings or rooted suckers. A.G.M. 1969. Z.2. **336**

Purple

Broom see *Cytisus purpureus*
Lily Magnolia see *Magnolia liliiflora* **'Nigra'**
Purple-leaf Sage see *Salvia officinalis* **'Purpurascens'**
Purple-leaved Filbert see *Corylus maxima* **'Purpurea'**
Purslane, Tree see *Atriplex halimus*
Pussy Willow, Rose-gold see *Salix gracillstyla*
Pygmy, Crimson see *Berberis thunbergii* **'Atropurpurea Nana'**

PYRACANTHA ROSACEAE **Firethorn** △

Highly valuable evergreen shrubs, probably most valued for their sumptuous crops of brightly coloured fruits in autumn, the display of hawthorn like flowers in early summer affording extra pleasure. Most popularly used for planting against walls, even on those facing

---

Abbreviations and symbols used in the text

▼	Deciduous	†	Lime hater
△	Evergreen	◖	Shade
✳	Flowers	◐	Semi shade
●	Fruit	☉	Sun
🦴	Foliage		

A.G.M. Award of Garden Merit, Royal Horticultural Society
F.C.C. First Class Certificate, Royal Horticultural Society

Z1–10 The Z numbers represent the climatic zones used in the United States and provide a useful hardiness rating elsewhere. Thus Z1 is for those plants surviving coldest conditions and Z10 is the other extreme

The illustration numbers are in **bold type**.

north, where they thrive and succeed in any reasonable soil. In such a situation pruning after flowering is advisable, removing growths which are not required to fill the allotted space but leaving the fruits.

The firethorns could well be utilized much more for planting in the open where they will make good hedges or screens and being well armed with fierce thorns are vandal proof. Young plants can be raised from seed or from cuttings which can be rooted under mist during summer. The plants are then better started off in pots, or the more modern equivalent containers, as they do not transplant well from open ground.

atalantioides syn. *P. gibbsii* ✳◫

Gibb's Firethorn

'**Aurea**', an excellent wall plant, particularly on a north facing or sunless wall. The rich yellow fruits are freely produced but are somewhat smaller than other red forms. A.G.M. 1969. Z.6. **337**

coccinea to 6·1 m. (20 ft) ✳●

'**Lalandei**', raised in France about 1874. One of the best known and most popular firethorns, a strong erect grower producing masses of white flowers in May and June which are succeeded by masses of brilliant orange red fruits in the autumn and winter. Grows less than the height given if free standing and not against a wall. A.G.M. 1925. Z.5. **338**

crenulata rogersiana see *P. rogersiana*
gibbsii see *P. atalantoides*

'**Mohave**' ✳●

A new cultivar from the U.S., where it was raised in the United States National Arboretum. An impressive plant when covered with its heavy crop of bright red fruits. Resistant to scab. **339**

rogersiana syn. *P. crenulata rogersiana* ✳●

'**Flava**', a large evergreen shrub, very free flowering in June and masses of bright orange yellow berries follow in the autumn. F.C.C. 1919, A.G.M. 1969. **340**

Q

Quince, Japanese Flowering see *Chaenomeles japonica*

R

RAPHIOLEPIS ROSACEAE ⊙△

× ***delacourii*** *(R. indica × R. umbellata)* ✳
1·2–1·5 m. (4–5 ft)
Raised in France towards the end of the 19th century. A slow growing evergreen shrub, suitable for the base of a warm wall in a warm, sunny position where the soil is well drained but fertile. A charming plant which is somewhat variable in the production of its rose pink flowers at different times during the spring and summer. These are borne in erect terminal panicles. It should be grown in a pot or container until placed in its permanent home as it transplants badly. **341**

Red Bearberry see *Artostaphylos uva-ursi*
Red-barked Dogwood see *Cornus alba*
Red-berried Elder see *Sambucus racemosa*
Redbud see *Cercis siliquastrum*
Redleaf Rose see *Rosa rubrifolia*
Redvein Enkianthus see *Enkianthus campanulatus*
Redwood see *Sequoia sempervirens*

RHODODENDRON ERICACEAE †

So far as I know, the genus *Rhododendron* is the largest involved in the embellishment of our gardens, especially as it also includes the plants generally known as azaleas. A very diverse group, deciduous and evergreen, and varying in size from dwarfs only inches high through all sizes of shrubs to trees around 12 m. (40 ft) in height. Valued in the main as flowering plants, many are spectacular in their autumn colours, particularly the deciduous kinds, and some are notable for their handsome foliage.

In spite of this diversity all members of the genus have a common meeting place in the soil. All prefer a soil where free lime is absent, and most fail if this requirement is not forthcoming. There is little doubt that these shrubs thrive best on a peaty soil but any good soil can be made suitable if enriched with leaf mould, bracken, well rotted manure or peat. These materials should be well dug in, remembering that although rhododendrons generally root near the surface, they require a good drainage and need moisture above and below. Breaking up the subsoil and incorporating organic matter is one of the best ways of ensuring both.

A semi-shaded position with some shelter, an open woodland garden is ideal, particularly oak woodland for species and the large leaved rhododendrons. What are generally termed the Hardy Hybrids such as the well known 'Mrs G. W. Leak' are much better in open sites, where the young wood ripens better and more flowers result. The dwarf small flowered types whether species or hybrids are most effective if mass planted in an open site where they are not shaded. Those which flower very early in spring are best planted so that they are not exposed to the morning sun, otherwise the flowers so eagerly awaited will be lost and disappointment result.

Pruning of rhododendrons is not often necessary although, in the course of time, some of the hardy hybrids can get too large or too straggly. Hard, seemingly drastic, pruning in spring must then be undertaken with the resultant loss of blooms for a couple of seasons. Some prefer to do this over a season or two. I have found the drastic method best in the long run. Some of the deciduous azaleas break near the base naturally and older wood can be removed to that point. Species in general do not like pruning and should be given sufficient space, when planting, to attain full size.

The dwarf evergreen azaleas can generally be moved, if you have the space, to a more roomy site, whatever treatment is given, but care should be taken to prevent the plants getting dry if dry weather follows. Removal of dead flowers is of great benefit, preventing the formation of seed heads and encouraging young growths for the next crop of flowers. Mulching with leaf mould, peat or bracken annually, if possible, is of great benefit to these plants.

Propagation of the hardy hybrids is usually done by layering where only a few plants are required or by grafting on seedlings of *R. ponticum*. Small leaved rhododendrons can be propagated under mist in summer while species can be raised from seed, especially where it is desired to raise new forms by cross-pollination, an interesting but long term project.

The species rhododendron are further subdivided into groups known as series, the best known of which is probably the Azalea series, the hybrids and varieties of which are usually known as 'azaleas'. The series name is given below after the specific name.

augustinii Triflorum series to 4·55 m. (15 ft)
Hupeh, Szechwan, China. A large, small leaved shrub which will take many years to attain the height stated except in sheltered woodland gardens. There are many variations of flower colour, from lavender blue to purple blue and my own personal favourite of light blue with a green throat and light stamens. A good deal of selection has been done to produce good forms but even individual plants vary from year to year, colour depending on temperature. This rhododendron grows fairly quickly when young and flowers freely on quite small plants in April and May. These can be propagated by cuttings. This is one of the finest rhododendrons, especially in its better forms and many hybrids of value in gardens have been bred from it. The name commemorates Augustine Henry. A.G.M. 1924. Z.7. **342**

calendulaceum Azalea series
Flame Azalea
Eastern North America. Cultivated U.S. 1800, introduced England 1806. A deciduous shrub of medium to large size, one of the most vividly coloured of all the wild azaleas. The funnel shaped flowers produce a remarkable range of orange red and red to yellow. It also provides a wonderful display of orange and crimson leaves before they fall in autumn. Z.5. **343, 344**

dauricum Dauricum series
North Asia east to Korea. In cultivation 1780. A semi-evergreen shrub of considerable charm and medium size flowering between January and March, especially in periods of mild weather. The widely tubular flowers of rosy purple are very conspicuous so early in the season.

'**Midwinter**', a clone with phlox-purple flowers, very beautiful, usually evergreen. F.C.C. 1969. Z.4. **345**

griersonianum Griersonianum series
Yunnan, China, North Burma. Discovered and introduced by Forrest in 1917. A medium sized shrub most arresting when in flower and worth a little protection when young as it is then somewhat tender. Too tender for very cold exposed gardens. The broadly bell-shaped flowers of flaming geranium scarlet are unlike any other rhododendron. Has been much used by breeders so that its hybrid progeny are now numerous. F.C.C. 1924. Z.8. **346**

japonicum syn. *R. molle* Azalea series
to 3·05 m. (10 ft)
Japan. Introduced 1861. A tall deciduous shrub of medium size whose flowers usually appear before the leaves. The fragrant flowers are funnel shaped, orange or salmon red with a large orange basal blotch. This is the plant formerly known as *R. molle* or *Azalea mollis* and it is the dominant parent of many hybrids which do so much in May to beautify our gardens. The foliage also gives rich autumn tints in the autumn. Z.5. **347**

kaempferi Azalea series
to 3·05 m. (10 ft)
Japan. Introduced by Professor Sargent 1892. A hardy deciduous or semi-evergreen, loosely branched shrub of medium size. The funnel shaped flowers, in small clusters, vary in shades of colour from biscuit to orange red and rosy scarlet and flower in May and June. One of the parents of many of the Kurume azaleas. A very beautiful plant. A.G.M. 1969. Z.4.**348**

kiusianum Azalea series **Kyushu Azalea**
to 90 cm. (3 ft)
Japan. A dwarf evergreen or semi-evergreen shrub of dense spreading habit with small oval leaves. The flowers, flat-faced, with hardly a tube, are usually lilac purple sometimes variable, salmon red to crimson or purple. This is considered one of the species from which the Kurume Azaleas, originally introduced by Wilson, were developed. Z.6–7. **349**

Abbreviations and symbols used in the text

▼	Deciduous	†	Lime hater
△	Evergreen	◍	Shade
✳	Flowers	◑	Semi shade
●	Fruit	☉	Sun
☙	Foliage		

A.G.M.   Award of Garden Merit, Royal Horticultural Society
F.C.C.   First Class Certificate, Royal Horticultural Society

Z1–10   The Z numbers represent the climatic zones used in the United States and provide a useful hardiness rating elsewhere. Thus Z1 is for those plants surviving coldest conditions and Z10 is the other extreme

The illustration numbers are in **bold type**.

leucaspis Boothii series to 60 cm. (2 ft)
Burma, Tibet frontier. Introduced by Kingdon Ward 1925. A bushy low shrub with long hairy leaves. The flowers in clusters of two or three are saucer shaped and milky white, contrasting strongly with the dark brown stamens. Flowering in February and March it is always liable to frost damage so must have a sheltered site and protection from morning sun. Beautiful flowers. F.C.C. 1944. Z.7. **350**

lutescens Triflorum series
to 3·05 m. (10 ft)
Szechwan, Yunnan. Discovered by the Abbé David, introduced by Wilson 1904. An evergreen shrub with nice bronzy red young foliage on the new growth. Flowering early, sometimes in March it requires some shelter. A beautiful but variable species in which it is better to choose a good form, such as the Exbury one with clear lemon yellow flowers. F.C.C. 1938, A.G.M. 1969. Z.7. **351**

luteum Azalea series 3·05 m. (10 ft)
Caucasus, eastern Europe. Introduced 1793. This is the common, well known yellow azalea, renowned for its fragrance and for its leaf colour in autumn. A very effective woodland plant in both seasons, flowering and before leaf fall. In gardens where it is established and happy it naturalizes freely and self sown seedlings abound. The yellow flowers appear before the leaves in May densely viscid on the outside, with a strong rich fragrance which pervades the air for a considerable distance. A parent of Ghent Azaleas. A.G.M. 1930. Z.6. **352**

molle see **R. japonicum**

obtusum Azalea series **Kirishima Azalea**
90 cm (3 ft)
North west Japan. Introduced from China by Fortune 1844. A dwarf evergreen, sometimes semi-evergreen, spreading and densely branched shrub which sometimes is almost prostrate. In May clusters of one to three funnel shaped flowers, usually of red or crimson, cover the plant. Has been cultivated for a long time in China as well as Japan and is a parent of many of the Kurume azaleas. Z.6.

'**Amoenum**', **Hatsu-giri Azalea**, a somewhat taller, more spreading shrub, the flowers are usually hose-in-hose, brilliant rosy purple. This is the hardiest form, and was introduced from Japanese gardens in 1845. A.G.M. 1965. **353**

pemakoense Uniflorum series
6 in. (2 ft)
Province of Pemako, east Tibet. Discovered by Kingdon Ward 1930. A lovely, very dwarf and very floriferous suckering shrub. Small leaves and comparatively large flowers for the size of the plant. These are funnel shaped, pale lilac pink or purple in March and April. The plant is hardy but flower buds are liable to get damaged in a hard winter before they open. Valuable as a

rock garden shrub and worth a little protection. A.G.M. 1969. Z.7. **354**

racemosum Scabrifolium series
Mayflower Rhododendron to 1·85 m. (6 ft)
Yunnan, Szechwan. Introduced by Abbé David about 1889, when it was grown in the Jardin des Plantes in Paris. This is an invaluable shrub for the garden, although somewhat variable. Normally a small to medium sized shrub of dense habit with leathery leaves. The funnel shaped flowers vary from pale to bright pink to deep rose, very numerous from axillary buds, so that they form racemes along the branches in March and April. This rhododendron can be kept low by pruning after flowering using it as a ground cover plant. The form grown in gardens as 'Forrest's Dwarf', with red branchlets and bright pink flowers and supposedly a dwarf form does not, I understand, invariably retain the dwarf habit. F.C.C. 1892, A.G.M. 1930. Z.5. **355**

reticulatum Azalea series
to 4·55 m. (15 ft)
Japan. Introduced 1865. A very variable deciduous shrub of medium to large size. The leaves are conspicuously reticulate underneath, purplish in the young stages, changing colour in autumn to vinous or blackish purple. The flowers, which appear in April and May, before the leaves, are usually solitary or in pairs, are funnel shaped and bright purple. Z.5. **356**

vaseyi Azalea series to 4·55 m. (15 ft)
South-eastern U.S. A medium to large deciduous shrub with narrow oval leaves which frequently turn fiery red in autumn. The wide funnel shaped flowers appear before the leaves, and are somewhat variable in colour, pale pink, rose pink or white with orange-red spots. The best forms are most beautiful when in flower, a beauty so delicate that words are inadequate. A.G.M. 1927. Z.4. **357**

viscosum Azalea series **Swamp Honeysuckle**
or **Azalea** to 4·55 m. (15 ft)
Eastern North America. Introduced 1734. A medium sized deciduous shrub generally a good deal less in height than stated. The so called Swamp honeysuckle is a valuable plant because of its late flowering season, June and July, and for its wonderful spicy fragrance. The narrow funnel shaped flowers, white sometimes stained pink, which appear after the viscous or sticky leaves. A.G.M. 1937. Z.3. **358**

williamsianum Thomsonii series
to 1·2 m. (4 ft)
Szechwan, China. Discovered and introduced by Wilson 1908. A small spreading shrub generally as great in width as in height. It has some value as a foliage plant, with its attractive young bronze growths and small bright green rounded leaves. The 56 cm. (2¼ in.) bell shaped flowers, shell pink in colour make a delicate effect. Should be planted in a sheltered place where frost will not damage the young growths or with some other

protection afforded. Has been used for breeding some fine plants. Z.7. **359**

yakushimanum Ponticum series   ◑△❋➥
1·2 m. (4 ft)
The island of Yakushima, Japan. Introduced 1934. A most distinctive shrub of compact rounded appearance as wide as or wider than it is high. The young growths are like silvery spears emerging from the dark leathery leaves, which are densely brown, woolly underneath. The bell shaped flowers are in a compact truss, deep rose pink in bud, when partially open delicate pink, when fully open white. It is only found on the rain drenched, windswept mountain peaks of its native island. Much use is already being made of this species for breeding, but so far I have seen no new plants which excel the Exbury form which received the F.C.C. F.C.C. 1947, A.G.M. 1969. Z.5. **360**

HYBRIDS   ◉◑❋
'Avalanche' (R. calophytum × R. Loderi)
3·65 m. (12 ft)
Raised Rothschild, England 1933. A large shrub with bold leaves and bold trusses of very large funnel shaped flowers. Pure white, flushed pink in bud and with a small basal blotch of magenta rose the flowers are fragrant and contrast nicely with the conspicuous red pedicels. Flowers early. F.C.C. 1938.

'Bluebird' (R. augustinii × R. intricatum)   △
90 cm (3 ft)
Raised Aberconway, Wales 1930. A small leaved shrub of neat dwarf habit ideal for a small garden or front of a border. Small compact clusters of lovely violet blue flowers are borne early. A.G.M. 1969. **361**

'Blue Diamond' (R. augustinii × R. 'Intrifast')   △
90 cm. (3 ft) or more
Raised Crosfield, England 1935. A small compact shrub, slow grower with terminal clusters of showy violet blue flowers. Suitable for small garden or edge of woodland border. F.C.C. 1939, A.G.M. 1969. **362**

'Blue Tit' (R. augustinii × R. impeditum)   △
to 90 cm. (3 ft)
Raised Williams, England 1933. A dense shrub which produces small funnel shaped flowers in clusters at the tips of the branches. A lovely shade of lavender blue which deepens with maturity. A fine shrub for rock or small garden.

'Byron' Rustica azalea   ▼
Raised by Uuylsteke, 1888. Double white flowers, outer petals with slight tinges of carmine rose. Double flowers, a lovely plant. **363**

'Cecile' Knap Hill azalea   ▼
Raised Rothschild, England 1947. A large flowered cultivar, with deep salmon pink buds which open to salmon pink with a yellow flare. A.G.M. 1969. **364**

'Choremia' (R. arboreum × R. haematodes)   △
1·5 m. (5 ft)
Raised Aberconway, Wales 1933. A medium sized shrub resembling R. haematodes in habit and also in its waxen, crimson scarlet trumpet shaped flowers. Lasts in flower for a long time and is frost-resistant. F.C.C. 1948. **365**

'Christopher Wren' syn. R. 'Goldball'   ▼
Mollis azalea
Large orange yellow flowers flushed flame with deep orange brown spotting. **366**

'Cilpinense' (R. ciliatum × R. moupinense)   △
90 cm. (3 ft)
Raised Aberconway, Wales 1927. A lovely free flowering hybrid with shallow bell shaped flowers in loose clusters. These open in March and are white, flushed pink, buds pink. Should be shaded from early morning sun during frosty weather. F.C.C. 1938, A.G.M. 1969 **367**

'Coccinea Speciosa' Ghent azalea   ▼
Raised Seneclause before 1846. Brilliant orange red flowers, one of the best known of all the old azaleas and still one of the best. A.G.M. 1969. **368**

'Crest' Hawk rhododendron group   △
(R. 'Lady Bessborough' × R. wardii)
Raised Rothschild, England 1953. One of the magnificent Exbury hybrids. Large clusters of yellow flowers slightly darker around the throat. F.C.C. 1953. **369**

'Elizabeth' (R. forrestii repens × R. griersonianum) △
1·2 m. (4 ft)
Raised Aberconway, Wales 1939. A small spreading shrub, one of the most well known and best of the Bodnant hybrids for the ordinary garden. The trumpet shaped flowers are borne in trusses, generally of five or six, deep red and flowering in April. F.C.C. 1943, A.G.M. 1969. **370**

Abbreviations and symbols used in the text

▼	Deciduous	†	Lime hater
△	Evergreen	◑	Shade
❋	Flowers	◑	Semi shade
●	Fruit	◉	Sun
➥	Foliage		

A.G.M.   Award of Garden Merit, Royal Horticultural Society
F.C.C.   First Class Certificate, Royal Horticultural Society

Z1–10   The Z numbers represent the climatic zones used in the United States and provide a useful hardiness rating elsewhere. Thus Z1 is for those plants surviving coldest conditions and Z10 is the other extreme

The illustration numbers are in **bold type**.

RHODODENDRON

'Frome' Knap Hill azalea ▼
Parentage unknown. Raised R.H.S. Wisley, England 1958. A deciduous shrub with saffron yellow flowers, overlaid. Fine red in throat with waved and frilled margins.

'Goldball' see *R.* **'Christopher Wren'**

'Golden Oriole' Knap Hill azalea ▼
Raised Knap Hill Nursery, England 1939. A striking plant, the young leaves suffused bronze, blending with the deep golden yellow flowers which have an orange blotch. **371**

'Grosclaude' *(R. eriogynum × R. haematodes)* △
Raised Rothschild, England 1941. A neat compact plant which produces lax trusses of ten to twelve flowers in each truss, a beautiful red and with frilled edges. **372**

'Hinodegiri' Kurume azalea △
Introduced by Wilson from Japan. One of the popular forms with bright crimson flowers A.G.M. 1969. **373**

'Hinomayo' Kurume azalea △
Obtained from Emperor's garden in Tokyo about 1910 by C. B. van Nes and Sons. A form of *R. obtusum* from Japan, one of the best known and deservedly popular of the Kurumes. A lovely soft pink with speckled throat. Lovely also as a pot plant for indoor decoration. Cannot be surpassed for mass effect. A.G.M. 1954. **374**

'Homebush' Knap Hill azalea ▼
Raised Knap Hill Nursery, England 1925. One of the most attractive azaleas with semi-double flowers in tight rounded heads of fourteen to sixteen flowers. These are of an open funnel shape, rose madder shaded pale rose. A.G.M. 1969. **375**

'Hope Findlay' *(R. 'Elizabeth' var. 'Jenny' ×* △
(R. Loderi × R. 'Earl of Athlone'))
Raised Savill Garden, Windsor, England. A medium sized shrub named for the raiser well known in Britain as a distinguished horticulturist and Keeper of the Savill Garden, Windsor Great Park. This new cultivar with its large scarlet campanulate flowers would appear to be a plant of the future and already rated highly as a possible improvement on the popular *R.* 'Elizabeth'. **376**

'Lady Chamberlain' *(R. cinnabarinum roylei ×* △
R. 'Royal Flush' orange form)
Raised Rothschild, England 1930. A tall stiffly branched shrub, best in woodland, with neat glaucous leaves. The long narrowly bell shaped pendulous flowers are borne with great freedom. They are mandarin red shading to rose and orange and are particularly lovely when seen against the sun. There are many different forms, some very beautiful, of this rhododendron raised at Exbury, England. F.C.C. 1931. **377**

'Lady Rosebery' *(R. cinnabarinum roylei ×* △
R. 'Royal Flush' pink form)

Raised Rothschild, England 1930. A plant very similar to 'Lady Chamberlain' except in colour which is crimson outside, rosy red within. F.C.C. 1932.

'Louise Gable' Gable azalea *(R. indicum ×* △
(R. kaempferi × R. poukhanense))
Named by Gable 1930. Violet-red, semi-double flowers. Has been described as the best azalea raised by Joseph B. Gable, at Stewartstown, Pa., U.S. **378**

'Malvaticum' △
Raised Koster, Boskoop, Holland about 1910. An evergreen azalea with large mauve flowers with darker streaks and purple speckles. **379**

'Margaret Findlay' 1·85 m. (6 ft) △
Parentage *R. griersonianum × R. wardii*
A lovely hybrid raised by the late Sir James Horlick in 1933 and introduced in 1942. Named after the wife of Mr T. Hope Findlay, an outstanding expert on rhododendrons. The flowers are almost white with a deep red stain deepening to port wine in the throat. **380**

'Martha Hitchcock' Glenn Dale azalea △
(R. mucronatum × R. 'Shinnyo-no-tsuki')
Raised United States Bureau of Plant Introduction 1948. Single-flowered 3 in. blossoms, 1–3 in a cluster, white margined with magenta. Young plants frequently produce purple flowers. **381**

'Mary Helen', Glenn Dale azalea △
(R. 'Katgetsu' × (R. mucronatum × R. Vittata Fortunei))
Raised United States Bureau of Plant Introduction 1948. White with chartreuse green blotch, anthers are conspicuously brown. **382**

'Merlin' Glenn Dale azalea *(R. 'Modele' ×* △
R. poukhanense)
Raised United States Bureau of Plant Introduction 1949. A cultivar with abundant rosy lavender flowers. **383**

'Meteor' see *R.* **'Rasho-mon'**

'Mother's Day' Kurume azalea △
('Hinodegiri' hybrid)
Raised van Hecke. Very free flowering. Rosy-red flowers. A.G.M. 1969. **384**

'Mrs G. W. Leak' *(R. 'Chevalier Felix de* △
Sauvage' × *R. 'Coombe Royal')*
Raised Koster and Sons, Holland 1916. An old established Dutch hybrid which has long been a favourite. The widely funnel-shaped flowers are light rosy pink with a conspicuous splash of dark brown and crimson spotting. A.G.M. 1969. **385**

'Orange Beauty' Kaempferi hybrid azalea ▼
(R. 'Hinodegiri' × R. kaempferi)
Raised van Nes and Sons about 1920. A very striking

plant, the bright salmon orange flowers are freely produced. F.C.C. 1958, A.G.M. 1969. **386**

'Palestrina' syn. 'Wilhelmina Vuyk' Vuyk azalea △ (*R*. 'J. C. van Tol' × *R. kaempferi* hybrid)
Raised Vuyk van Nes, Holland 1926. A very distinct and attractive azalea. The beautiful white flowers are enhanced by a faint ray of green. A good garden plant. F.C.C. 1967, A.G.M. 1969. **387**

'Pearl Bradford' Glenn Dale azalea △ (*R. indicum* × *R*. 'Joh-ga')
Raised United States Bureau of Plant Introduction 1948. Deep rose pink flowers – blotched with very distinct tyrian rose.

'Praecox' (*R. ciliatum* × *R. dauricum*) △
Raised Davies, Lancashire, England about 1855. A very popular, small compact grower which flowers very early in February and March. The rosy purple flowers are purplish crimson in bud and are produced in clusters of two or three at the tips of the growth. The leaves are aromatic when crushed; many drop in hard winters so the plant becomes partially deciduous. One of the heralds of spring especially in mild spells of weather. A hedge of this fine plant is one of the famous features of the Royal Botanic Garden, Edinburgh, Scotland. A.G.M. 1926. **388**

'Queen Elizabeth II' (*R*. 'Crest' × *R*. 'Idealist') △
Raised Windsor Great Park, England. The bell shaped, large yellow flowers are produced freely on a vigorous plant 3·05 m. (10 ft) in height and as much across. F.C.C. 1974. **389**

'Rasho-mon' Kurume azalea △
Introduced by Wilson from Japan. Bright salmon red with darker anthers. Sometimes known as 'Meteor'. **390**

'Red Rum' (*R. barclayi* × *R. forrestii repens*) △
Raised Windsor Great Park, England. A promising new hybrid for the small garden, possibly up to 90 cm. (3 ft) in height and of greater width. **391**

'Roman Pottery' (*R. dichroanthum* × △
R. griersonianum)
An attractive rhododendron as seen growing in the Savill Garden, Windsor Great Park, England. Exhibited by Crosfield 1934. The pale orange flowers have coppery lobes. **392**

'Rosebud' Gable azalea (*R*. 'Caroline Gable' × △
R. 'Louise Gable')
Raised U.S. A late flowering azalea of spreading habit with distinctive deep rose pink hose-in-hose, double flowers. Appears to be becoming popular as a pot plant. **393**

'Seven Stars' (*R*. Loderi 'Sir Joseph Hooker' × △
R. yakushimanum)
Raised, Windsor Great Park, England. A remarkable

free flowering hybrid, the original plant in the Savill Garden being some 1·85 m. (6 ft) in height but twice as much across. It flowers very freely as a young plant so can easily be accommodated in an average garden by careful pruning. The bell shaped flowers are white flushed pink and have reddish buds. **394**

'Tay' Knap Hill azalea ▼
Parentage unknown. Raised R.H.S., Wisley, England 1959. A deciduous azalea with compact trusses of funnel-shaped flowers, chinese yellow with an orange blotch in the throat and frilled and waved margins. **395**

'Temple Belle' (*R. orbiculare* × *R. williamsianum*) △
Raised Royal Botanic Garden, Kew, England 1916. A shrub of great charm with rounded leaves attractively glaucous underneath. Usually semi-dwarf, but has been known to reach 3 m. (10 ft). The bell shaped flowers are produced in a loose cluster of soft pink flowers. **396**

'Tessa' (*R. moupinense* × *R*. 'Praecox') △
Raised Stevenson, England 1935. A small shrub up to 90 cm. (3 ft). Flowering in March or early April, the soft pink flowers with a touch of purple are produced freely in loose flat umbels. A.G.M. 1969. **397**

'Thames' Knap Hill azalea ▼
Raised R.H.S., Wisley, England 1956. Flowers of neyron rose with darker veins, the throat blotched apricot. The petals have frilled margins. **398**

'Trewithen Orange' (*R. concatenans* × △
R. 'Full House')
Raised, Johnstone, Cornwall, England. A remarkable and lovely hybrid bearing deep orange brown flowers with a faint rosy tint in loose pendant trusses. F.C.C. 1950. **399**

'Unique' (*R. campylocarpum* hybrid) △
Raised Slocock, Woking, England. A plant of dense, leafy habit with creamy white flowers, slightly tinged

---

Abbreviations and symbols used in the text

▼	Deciduous	†	Lime hater
△	Evergreen	◍	Shade
✳	Flowers	◑	Semi shade
•	Fruit	⊙	Sun
❧	Foliage		

A.G.M.   Award of Garden Merit, Royal Horticultural Society
F.C.C.   First Class Certificate, Royal Horticultural Society

Z1–10   The Z numbers represent the climatic zones used in the United States and provide a useful hardiness rating elsewhere. Thus Z1 is for those plants surviving coldest conditions and Z10 is the other extreme

The illustration numbers are in **bold type**.

with pink and faint crimson spots within the funnel shaped flower. The dense flower clusters are dome-shaped. **400**

'Venapens' (*R. forrestii repens* × *R. venator*) △
Raised Ramsden, England 1940. A very free flowering, little known hybrid with crimson tubular flowers on a compact plant. **401**

'Vuyks' Rosyred' Vuyk azalea △
Raised Vuyk van Nes, Holland 1954. Flowers of deep satiny rose red with a flash of darker colour. **402**

'Vuyks' Scarlet' Vuyk azalea △
Raied Vuyk van Nes, Holland 1954. Flowers bright deep red with wavy shiny petals. A.G.M. 1969.

'Wilhelmina Vuyk' see *R.* **'Palestrina'**

Rhododendron, Mayflower see *Rhododendron racemosum*

RHUS ANACARDIACEAE

cotinus see *Cotinus coggygria*

typhina **Stag's-Horn Sumach** 3·05 m. (10 ft) ▼●
Eastern North America. In cultivation 1629. The Stag's-horn Sumach is a deciduous small tree or shrub of rather gaunt appearance in the winter months. The thick, pithy branches exude a yellowish thick juice if cut, which may cause slight irritation to some people, and when young are coated with short, dense reddish hairs. The large green clusters of male flowers and the smaller clusters of female are borne on separate plants during the summer, and the female bears dense panicles of fruits, most decoratively covered with crimson hairs, in autumn and early winter. The large pinnate leaves turn to rich shades of orange and yellow, red and purple in the autumn. Suckers are sometimes produced providing a ready means of increase if required, otherwise these can be chopped away with a spade. This is a plant which succeeds in town gardens where good specimens can be frequently seen. Pruning is not necessary, but larger more sumptuous leaves are produced by hard pruning in February. Thinning the subsequent growths will provide an exotic or sub-tropical effect which can be most spectacular. A.G.M. 1969.

'Laciniata', a female form which does not grow so large. It has deeply cut leaves which are particularly striking in their orange and yellow autumn colours. Handsomely fern-like in appearance and easily grown in any good garden soil. A sunny position will result in better autumn colours. A.G.M. 1969.

RIBES GROSSULARIACEAE

sanguineum **Flowering** or ⊙◐▼✳
Winter Currant 1·85–2·1 m. (6–7 ft)
Western North America. Introduced 1826. A deciduous shrub well known as the Flowering Currant, very popular and hardy. Easily grown in any good garden soil in full sun or even in partial shade, this popular bush flowers freely every spring, during March and April, particularly if old branches are removed after flowering to ensure production of new growths, for these bear the finest flowers. Can be used for hedges, which are very effective when in bloom, if clipped immediately after flowering. The quite pungent currant odour of this plant, especially after rain, is not universally approved. Those who relish it or don't object to it can extend their enjoyment by bringing in a few branches in February or March to flower indoors, a form of pruning which avoids wastage. All the forms of *R. sanguineum* are easily increased by cuttings of ripened wood in autumn in sandy soil in a sheltered border. There are several forms of which the following are a small selection. Z.5.

'Album', a form with white flowers.
'Atrorubens', a clone with deep crimson flowers sometimes known as 'Atrosanguinea'. **403**
'Brocklebankii', a small slow growing shrub worth planting in semi-shade for the effect, particularly in spring, of its golden yellow foliage. Flowers pink.
'King Edward VII', a more compact plant which can be planted in small gardens, especially if pruned hard after flowering. Deep crimson flowers. A.G.M. 1969.
'Pulborough Scarlet', a form with deep magenta red flowers, very freely produced. A.G.M. 1969.
'Splendens', the rosy red flowers are freely produced in long racemes. A.G.M. 1928.

speciosum **Fuchsia flowered Gooseberry** ▼✳
1·85–2·75 m. (6–9 ft)
California. Introduced 1828. An attractive deciduous spring shrub which will retain some of its leaves in mild winters and is reasonably hardy. In cold areas it succeeds against a sunny wall, where it appears at its best, and this holds even in milder areas. The rich red flowers, appearing in April and May and lasting even longer, are pendulous, hanging from the gooseberry like, spiny growths in profuse rows and very reminiscent of a fuchsia. Cuttings of this species do not root as readily as *R. sanguineum* and should be tried in July under mist. A few plants can be produced by layering in the spring. Z.8.

ROBINIA LEGUMINOSAE

hispida **Rose Acacia** 1·85–2·45 m. (6–8 ft) ⊙▼✳
South east United States. Introduced 1743. The Rose Acacia is a suckering shrub with attractive pinnate leaves and a somewhat irregular gaunt habit. The short racemes of large deep rose flowers are very lovely and are freely produced especially when planted against a warm wall. The wood is very brittle so that a sheltered position as free from wind as possible should be chosen. Frequently grown as a small tree grafted onto *R. pseudoacacia*, but can be increased from rooted suckers. Z.5. **404**

pseudoacacia **Common** or **False Acacia,** ⊙ ▼ ❧
Black Locust 4·55 m. (15 ft)

'**Frisia**', is an outstanding richly yellow-leaved form of the False Acacia. It is a medium sized deciduous tree which can be planted in small gardens as it responds to annual pruning to keep it to shrub like dimensions. Pruning fairly hard in early April annually results in young growths of 1·5–1·85 m. (5–6 ft). When either grown naturally or pruned, the rich golden yellow foliage is most striking creating a brilliant splash of colour until autumn, then displaying more subtle colourings of soft yellow and apricot. Worth giving a sheltered position in colder parts, succeeding best on light well drained soils. A.G.M. 1969. **405**

Rock Rose see *Cistus*
Rockspray see *Cotoneaster horizontalis*
Rod, Withe see *Viburnum cassinoides*

ROMNEYA PAPAVERACEAE **Tree Poppy**

coulteri **Matilija Poppy** ⊙ ▼ ✳
1·5–1·85 m. (5–6 ft)
California and Mexico. Discovered by Dr Coulter 1844. A beautiful deciduous, sub-shrubby plant which has very glaucous stems and leaves that enhance the satiny flowers. The white poppy like flowers with a centre of golden stamens can reach 22 cm. (9 in.) across, and are delightfully fragrant. It is not always an easy plant to establish and requires a sunny sheltered site and well drained light soil. When well suited it spreads by underground suckers. Propagation is most readily effected by root cuttings of the thick fleshy roots. Cut into 6 cm. (2 in.) lengths, place in pots just covered with light sandy soil and put in a frame with gentle heat. The young plants should be grown on in pots or containers until planted permanently as this plant resents root disturbance. A.G.M. 1929. Z.9.

trichocalyx ⊙ ▼ ✳
Is very close to the above plant, but is less likely to sucker and has more slender stems with bristly buds which are rounded not beaked. There are hybrids between the two plants which are probably stronger growers. Covering with peat or bracken in early winter until the plants have become well established is a worthwhile exercise. The previous year's growth should be cut back in spring nearly to ground level.

ROSA ROSACEAE **Rose** ⊙ ▼
Many thousands, nay millions, of words have been devoted to the rose, to its history and to its cultivation. Numerous gardens have been made and planted solely for roses and even more have roses in conjunction with other shrubs and plants. In a modest way I have tried to make a contribution to both these phases which illustrate the popularity of this large and very distinct genus of plants belonging to the great family of Rosaceae.

In a general book on shrubs, only a small number can be mentioned to help those who wish to make a selection for their gardens. I have included some of my own particular favourites as a base to work from.

You will find a few wild roses or closely related derivations, prickly they may be but I still find the simple charm of the single rose fascinating. Allied to this in some degree is fragrance, in flower in most but of foliage also, who can but appreciate and treasure the delicious fragrance of the Sweet Briar, *Rosa rubiginosa* which I have not included as a garden plant, but might well be planted in an out of the way corner for its fragrance alone. I have however, included *Rosa primula*, mainly because of its fragrance, although it is also an attractive plant in flower and foliage, but is less rumbustious than the sweet briar and far less subject to black spot.

I would not be without a few of the old garden roses. Perhaps more could have been included but for reasons of space. Some schools of thought are not favourably disposed to modern roses. Many modern roses, shrub roses or those grown as shrubs bring much added colour into our gardens by extending the season and thereby giving much pleasure to many.

I have always admired and enjoyed the rugosa roses, not only because they are easily cultivated and generally useful, but because they have a sumptuous air of well-being brought about by the healthy foliage, aided and abetted by the opulence of their fruits, hips or heps. All shrubs have their particular merits in suitable situations and I frequently think a rugosa hedge would without much trouble provide a more admirable feature in many areas than the subject used, provided always there is room, since narrow spaces are unsuitable.

To handle disease and other health problems, many chemicals are available. Systemic insecticides are now available which will curb the infestation with aphis that often occurs on early growth. A systemic fungicide is also available now which in some areas at least has given good results in the control of mildew. Simazine

---

Abbreviations and symbols used in the text

▼ Deciduous   † Lime hater
△ Evergreen   ◑ Shade
✳ Flowers   ◐ Semi shade
• Fruit   ⊙ Sun
❧ Foliage

A.G.M.   Award of Garden Merit, Royal Horticultural Society
F.C.C.   First Class Certificate, Royal Horticultural Society

Z1–10   The Z numbers represent the climatic zones used in the United States and provide a useful hardiness rating elsewhere. Thus Z1 is for those plants surviving coldest conditions and Z10 is the other extreme

The illustration numbers are in **bold type**.

(England) and Casoron (U.S.) are very efficient weed-killers, especially when applied early in the season and the soil is moist. Care has, as always, to be taken to comply with instructions on the container, and if ground cover plants are used this may not be possible.

californica **California Rose** 2·45 m. (8 ft)

U.S. A vigorous shrub with single deep pink flowers produced in clusters. A variable species with delicate foliage and which has proved of value to breeders of roses.

> **'Plena'**, more frequently grown and will make a splendid plant. The semi-double pink flowers are freely produced and have a pleasing perfume, the whole effect being of pink cascades of flowers around mid-summer. A splendid shrub where space can be afforded. Z.5. **406**

caudata to 3·65 m. (12 ft)

West Hupeh, China. Introduced by Wilson 1907. A vigorous and beautiful deciduous shrub, seldom seen in gardens but thriving at the display garden of the Royal National Rose Society, England. The bright pinkish red single flowers are produced in June, a few at a time in corymbs. Quite beautiful but they are excelled in decorative value by the orange red fruits, distinctive in shape with a long narrow neck and persisting until November. Z.5.

chinensis **China rose** 2·45 m. (8 ft)

> *mutabilis*, syn. *R*. 'Tipo Ideale'. Origin unknown. Introduced before 1896. Single flowers of soft yellow changing to coppery pink and crimson. A slender growing shrub which may reach the height stated in favoured gardens but generally only half. An unusual shrub with very narrow pointed buds, the flowers flame coloured, changing daily and finishing up coppery crimson. Keeps flowering for a long time, commencing in June and going on to December in a warm corner. The copper foliage provides a good foil. Thrives in good soil and prefers some shelter. **407**

davidii 2·75 m. (9 ft)

East Tibet, west China. Introduced by Wilson 1903. A tall shrub of loose spreading habit. The single mallow pink flowers are produced in large corymbs of many flowers in late July after most other species are over. A most handsome plant in autumn when laden with pendulous clusters of small bottle shaped hips. **408**

ecae **Mrs Aitchison's Rose** 1·5 m. (5 ft)

Afghanistan. Introduced by Dr Aitchison in 1880 and named after his wife by using her initials E.C.A. A small deciduous shrub, with slender upright growths of dainty appearance. The chestnut brown branches carry reddish twigs enhanced by reddish thorns and small dark green leaves. The small flowers are deep buttercup yellow, the most startling yellow in the rose family and are followed by small spherical red hips. Requires a well drained soil in a sunny position and in cold gardens benefits from having a wall at its back. Z.7.

farreri 1·85 m. (6 ft)

> *persetosa*, **Threepenny-bit Rose.** Raised in England. Small single soft pink flowers. A seedling selected from a batch of seedlings of *R. farreri* by the late E. A. Bowles because of the deeper colour of the flowers and the excessive crop of hair like thorns which occur all up the stems. Because of the size and form of its flowers is often called the Threepenny-bit Rose. The arching branches make a spreading bush, with dainty foliage that colours in autumn and combines with the small orange hips to make a distinctive shrub. *Rosa farreri* itself does not appear to be in cultivation. **409**

helenae **Mrs Wilson's Rose** 4·55 m. (15 ft)

Hupeh and Szechwan, China. Introduced Wilson 1907. A large deciduous scrambling shrub, growing as wide as high where space permits. Ideal for clambering over an old decrepit tree or hedge where its strong hooked prickles aid its progress. The single creamy white flowers which are borne in umbels are fragrant and quite spectacular during June and July, especially when seen against the background of an old yew. Although the flowers are erect, the decorative hips droop in gracefully distinctive bunches in autumn and last for a considerable time. This fine species is named after Helen Wilson, wife of the introducer, who discovered it in 1900. Z.5. **410**

kordesii 1·85 m. (6 ft)

Raised Kordes, Germany 1952. Previously known as *R.* × *kordesii* this is in effect a new species which arose in cultivation as a result of spontaneous chromosome doubling in the cultivar 'Max Graf'. Worth growing as a pillar rose, or on a fence, being healthy, hardy and disease resistant. Semi-double pink flowers. Has been much used as a parent, many of the perpetual flowering climbers having been produced from it in conjunction with other roses. Z.5. **411**

macrantha syn. *R.* 'Macrantha'
1·5 × 3·05 m. (5 × 10 ft)

Origin uncertain. A rambling shrub, ideal for banks or threading its way through an old hedge or small tree. The large single pink flowers, which fade to nearly white and have conspicuous stamens, are deliciously scented. The origin of this plant has not yet been determined, a fact somewhat confused because the same name of *R. macrantha* has also, in the past, been given to another rose of hybrid origin. **412**

× *micrugosa* (*R. roxburghii* × *R. rugosa*)

> **'Alba'**, single white flowers. 1·5 m. (5 ft). A second generation of the original *R. roxburghii* × *R. rugosa* raised by Dr Hurst at Cambridge, England. An erect shrub with light green leaves and fragrant flowers produced in successive crops. **413**

multibracteata 1·85–2·45 m. (6–8 ft)

West Szechwan, China. Introduced by Wilson 1908. A deciduous shrub of graceful habit and moderately vigorous. The bright pink single small flowers are produced in small clusters, sometimes single over a long period until late summer and enshrouded with grey green bracts which have a distinctive effect. The finely divided foliage is fan like and attractive, indeed this is an attractive shrub when healthy and particularly so in autumn when carrying a heavy crop of rounded red hips which have glandular bristles. Z.6. **414**

× *penzanceana* syn. *R.* 'Lady Penzance' ❋➷
1·85 m. (6 ft)
Raised in England. Parentage *R. eglanteria* × *R. foetida bicolor*. A fairly vigorous shrub with arching growth with dark somewhat aromatic foliage. Single flowers, coppery salmon with yellow centre. Susceptible to black spot due no doubt to the infusion of Austrian Copper (*R. foetida bicolor*) blood. **415**

primula Primrose Rose ❋➷
2·45 × 2·45 m. (8 × 8 ft)
Turkestan to North China. Discovered by Meyer, an American collector. A medium sized deciduous shrub with arching stems furnished with delicate, incense scented foliage and scarlet thorns. The creamy yellow single flowers are produced early in the season, in May and are slightly scented. Succeeds on chalky or limey soils and is worth planting for its distinctive leaf scent which is especially noticeable on warm summer evenings or after a summer rain shower. Plants are sometimes supplied raised from seed, some of which are inferior forms with almost white flowers.

rubrifolia Redleaf Rose ❋➷●
2·15 × 2·15 m. (7 × 7 ft)
Mountains of central and southern Europe. A deciduous, very hardy shrub of erect habit with reddish violet stems which are almost thornless. Allied to *R. canina* it is easily distinguished by its glaucous purple leaves. The small clear pink or deep red flowers are borne few to a cluster, so are rather inconspicuous, and are followed by brownish red hips which are freely produced and quite effective in autumn. A very effective plant in colour schemes where it can be most decorative and is also useful for cutting for house decoration. Self sown seedlings are frequently produced which seem to be quite true to type. A.G.M. 1969. Z.2.

virginiana Virginia Rose 1·5 m. (5 ft) ❋➷●
Eastern North America. A shrub with lovely shining leaves which in the autumn become vivid orange red. The bright cerise pink to magenta flowers of June and July are followed by clusters of glittering red rounded hips which last for a long time. Grows well on light soils where it suckers freely. Z.3. **416**

HYBRIDS

'Alfred de Dalmas' syn. *R.* 'Mousseline' Moss ❋
1·2 m. (4 ft)
Introduced, France 1855. Known also as 'Mousseline', the name here used is the one preferred in the International Check List of Roses, Modern Roses 7. This is a nice compact bush with few thorns, flower-

ing freely from June to October. The creamy pink blooms are large, cup-shaped and well filled with petals and possess a delicate perfume. **417**

'Aloha' to 3·05 m. (10 ft) ❋
Raised in U.S. by Boerner, introduced 1949. A climber, but can also be grown as a free-standing shrub by fairly hard pruning of the leading growths. The double hybrid tea type blooms are deep coral pink fading towards the edges and are scented. Many of its good qualities are inherited from 'New Dawn' one of its parents.

'Altissimo' up to 3·65 m. (12 ft) ❋
Raised by Delbard-Chabert, France and introduced 1966. A climbing rose with beautiful single flowers of velvety-red which when fully open reveal bright golden stamens. A modern repeat flowering cultivar, with healthy green foliage and a little scent. By shortening the main stems, when pruning, back to 4 or 5 ft this rose can be grown as a free flowering shrub, right through into the autumn. C.M.

'Andersonii' Shrub 1·85 m. (6 ft) ❋
Known before 1912. Believed to be a hybrid of *R. canina*, it is a worthwhile off-shoot of that species, with considerably larger and more brilliant, rich rose pink flowers, which have a rich fragrance. Grows into a wide arching bush with good hips. **418**

'Anne of Geierstein', Penzance Briar ❋➷●
1·85–2·45 m. (6–8 ft)
Raised by Lord Penzance, England. A tall, vigorous shrub raised from *R. eglanteria*, the Sweet Briar. Suitable for an informal hedge. Aromatic foliage but less so than the parent. Carries a crop of hips in autumn. **419**

'Autumn Fire' see *Rosa* 'Herbstfeuer'

'Belinda' Hybrid musk 1·5 m. (5 ft) ❋
Probably raised by Pemberton and introduced by Bentall, England, 1936. A vigorous shrub with large erect

---

Abbreviations and symbols used in the text

▼	Deciduous	†	Lime hater
△	Evergreen	⑪	Shade
❋	Flowers	⑪	Semi shade
●	Fruit	⊙	Sun
➷	Foliage		

A.G.M. Award of Garden Merit, Royal Horticultural Society
F.C.C. First Class Certificate, Royal Horticultural Society

Z1–10 The Z numbers represent the climatic zones used in the United States and provide a useful hardiness rating elsewhere. Thus Z1 is for those plants surviving coldest conditions and Z10 is the other extreme

The illustration numbers are in **bold type**.

clusters of soft pink flowers. Useful as an informal hedge or pillar flowering over a long season. Slightly fragrant. **420**

'Canary Bird' 2·1 × 2·1 m. (7 × 7 ft)   ✳
A vigorous shrub rose, nowadays generally considered to be a hybrid, possibly *R. xanthina* crossed with *R. hugonis* or vice versa. A fairly large shrub with arching brown stems and fern like leaves. The single flowers are bright canary yellow and cover the branches in May and June. This is usually one of the first roses in bloom but does not recur later in the season. Subject to 'die back', in some gardens, this has never been my experience, indeed I regard it when growing well as one of the most spectacular shrub roses, especially on well drained soils. A.G.M. 1969.

'Celestial' syn. *R.* 'Celeste' to 1·85 m. (6 ft)   ✳⬥
A vigorous deciduous shrub, as much through as high with the characteristic grey-green tinged blue foliage of the Alba roses. It appears to be of Dutch origin at the end of the eighteenth century. The large fragrant semi-double flowers of soft blush pink open from the most exquisite of buds of a deeper shade of pink. One of the finest of the old garden shrub roses eulogized by many writers and extolled by lovers of the older roses. Does not require much pruning, older flowering wood can be thinned out when flowering has finished, and weak growths removed at the same time or during winter.

'Complicata' 1·5–2·45 m. (5–8 ft)   ✳
A fairly vigorous deciduous shrub sometimes placed among the Gallica group of roses but its origin seems never to have been discovered and is not recorded in any of the old rose books. Planted in the open it grows into a spreading shrub about 1·5 m. in height, but will clamber into a tree or hedge to a greater elevation. One of the most beautiful and indeed spectacular shrubs when in full bloom. The large, subtly fragrant, single, bright clear pink flowers have a white centre unsurpassed by any single rose – like an enlarged, deeper coloured dog rose. It is frequently seen in European gardens and should be in every garden where there is room. Succeeds on most soils, particularly where soil is light and easily rooted from hard wood cuttings. Bears a crop of quite decorative but unspectacular hips. F.C.C. 1958, A.G.M. 1969.

'Fountain' Modern Shrub 1·5–1·85 m. (5–6 ft)   ✳
Parentage not stated. Raised by M. Tantau, Germany, 1972. A vigorous upright grower breaking freely from the base and flowering over a long season. The rich and velvety blood red blooms are moderately full and are fragrant. They are sometimes borne singly, at other times in clusters. The dark green semi-glossy foliage is red when young. Seems to require a sheltered site, basal growths suffering damage from wind. **421**

'Frau Dagmar Hartopp' (Fru Dagmar   ✳⬥●
Hastrup)
Hybrid Rugosa 1·5 × 1·5 m. (5 × 5 ft)

Raised Hastrup *c.* 1914. Seedling from *R. rugosa*. A shrub spreading in conjunction with its height. Compact in habit it can be kept of moderate size by hard pruning every year. The lovely, clear shell pink single flowers have golden stamens, bloom profusely, and are followed by large tomato red hips often borne with the later flowers. Typical rugosa foliage, fresh apple green, makes this a most satisfactory plant useful for low hedges which can be clipped to a formal pattern in winter. A.G.M. 1958. **422**

'Fritz Nobis' 1·5–1·85 m. (5–6 ft)   ✳●
Parentage *R.* 'Joanna Hill' × *R. eglanteria* 'Magnifica'. Raised and introduced by Kordes, Germany in 1940 this vigorous shrub produces a fine crop of long pointed salmon pink buds which open up into large creamy pink semi-double flowers. Summer flowering only and deliciously clove scented, they are followed by dullish red round hips which last well into the winter. A most attractive modern shrub rose. A.G.M. 1969.

'Frühlingsgold' Modern Shrub   ✳
2·45 × 2·45 m. (8 × 8 ft)
Raised by W. Kordes, Germany 1937. (*R.* 'Joanna Hill' × *R. spinosissima hispida*). Without any doubt this rose can hold its own with any other flowering shrub in early summer. Vigorous in growth, the branches arching outwards are festooned along their length with the large almost single creamy-yellow very fragrant flowers in late spring to early summer. Thriving in any reasonable soil this is the shrub rose par excellence for flowering in large enough gardens. F.C.C. 1955, A.G.M. 1965. **423**

'Goldbonnet' Modern Shrub 1·5 m. (5 ft)   ✳
((*R.* 'Anne Elizabeth' × *R.* 'Allgold') × *R.* 'Golden Showers'). Raised by Harkness, Hitchin, England, 1973. A vigorous upright growing shrub which produces its yellow flowers with great freedom over a long season. Handsome dark green, semi-glossy foliage. **424**

'Golden Chersonese' 1·85–2·75 m. (6–9 ft)   ✳
Parentage *R. ecae* × *R.* 'Canary Bird'. An attractive deciduous shrub, raised in 1963 by Allen, England, with upright stems and small fernlike leaves. The fragrant buttercup yellow flowers although larger are less intense in colour than *R. ecae*, and are very freely produced in late May. Thrives best in a slightly sheltered position, the tips of the young growths suffer damage in an exposed site. Worth trying as a hedge.

'Golden Showers' to 3·05 m. (10 ft)   ✳
Raised in U.S. by Dr Lammerts and introduced in 1956. A good large-flowered climber with semi-double flowers freely produced in clusters. Deep golden yellow in bud, becoming clear yellow when fully open changing to creamy yellow before fading. Pleasantly fragrant and flowering continuously over a long season. Makes a fine shrub by pruning fairly hard.

'Golden Wings' Modern Shrub   ✳●
1·85 × 1·85 m. (6 × 6 ft)

(R. 'Soeur Therese' × (R. *spinosissima altaica* × R. 'Ormiston Roy')). Raised R. Shepherd, U.S. 1956. A vigorous, very hardy recurrent flowering shrub. Although attaining the dimensions stated can, by more severe pruning, be restricted and so made more suitable for the smaller gardens. The large single flowers have some resemblance to 'Mermaid', the lovely yellow petals contrasting with reddish amber stamens. A somewhat open habit generally and is seldom without its slightly fragrant flowers. The hardy *Geranium* 'Johnson's Blue' provides a wonderful foil for it and makes a lovely garden picture. A.G.M. 1973. **425**

'Handel' ✳

Raised by McGredy IV, Northern Ireland. Introduced 1965. A fine vigorous cultivar with fine dark green foliage which provide a foil for the neat classical shaped buds and half open flowers of creamy white flushed and heavily edged pink. A most distinctive and attractive combination, produced over the season and especially fine in autumn. A climber which makes an excellent shrub if pruned to shape by shortening the leading growths.

'Herbstfeuer' syn. R. 'Autumn Fire' ✳●

Modern Shrub 1·85 m. (6 ft)

Parentage not stated. Raised Kordes, Germany 1961. A large arching shrub with dark red blooms which have dark velvety shadings but are apt to blue in hot weather. Produces some late flowers in September while the early crop is succeeded by very large hips. These become orange in late autumn and are quite spectacular. **426**

'Joseph's Coat' to 3·05 m. (10 ft) ✳

Raised in U.S. by Armstrong & Swim. Introduced 1964. A rose which although classified as a climber can by dint of fairly hard pruning become an excellent free flowering shrub, particularly so in the autumn. The slightly-fragrant semi-double flowers, produced in large trusses are bright yellow, flushed with orange and cherry red.

'Lady Penzance' see R. × *penzanceana*
'Macrantha' see R. *macrantha*

'Marguerite Hilling' syn. R. 'Pink Nevada' ✳

2·45 × 2·45 m. (8 × 8 ft)

A sport from 'Nevada' discovered by Sleet, of Sunningdale Nurseries, England and Mrs Steen, New Zealand and introduced by Hilling, England 1959. Identical with its parent except in the colour of its flowers which are a pleasing light pink with deeper shades. A.G.M. 1974.

'Max Graf' Hybrid Rugosa ✳🍃

60 cm. × 1·85 m. (2 × 6 ft)

(R. *rugosa* × R. *wichuraiana*) Raised Bowditch, Conn., U.S. An invaluable hardy rose for covering banks, or for ground cover, growing into a dense mat covered with bright green leaves. The white centred, pink flowers are sweet scented and are borne in clusters for a considerable period around midsummer. **427**

'Mousseline' see R. 'Alfred de Dalmas'

'Mozart' Hybrid Musk 90 cm. (3 ft) ✳

(R. 'Robin Hood' × R. 'Rote Phariser') Raised P. Lambert, Germany 1937. A small shrub with a strong resemblance to R. 'Ballerina' but with deeper pink flowers borne in clusters and edged deeper red. Keeps flowering profusely throughout the season. **428**

'Nevada' 2·45 × 2·45 m. (8 × 8 ft) ✳

Supposed to be a hybrid between R. 'La Giralda' and R. *moyesii* possibly the tetraploid form of the latter, R. *moyesii fargesii* was used. Raised by Pedro Dot, Spain and introduced 1927. Although doubts have been expressed regarding the published parentage of this rose as being authentic, surely none can exist about its value as a shrub. When in bloom, the long spraying branches are covered with masses of creamy white semi-double or single flowers to such an extent that the foliage is obscured. This, the June and July flush, is succeeded by others of a minor nature. Being sterile few hips are set. This most spectacular of shrubs provides its own ground cover, the lower branches spraying over close to the soil. Little fragrance. Requires prevention treatment against black spot in some areas. F.C.C. 1954, A.G.M. 1969.

'New Dawn' ✳

A sport from Dr W. Van Fleet, introduced by Dreer, U.S. 1930. A well known rambler with most abundant growth but which, if the main growths are curtailed by pruning, will grow into a spreading shrub. Its pale blush, silvery pink flowers are freely produced and have a delightful perfume.

'Penelope' 1·5 × 1·85 m. (5 × 6 ft) ✳●

Parentage R. 'Ophelia' × R. 'William Allen Richardson' or R. 'Trier'. A vigorous shrub rose, possibly the most popular of the Pemberton Musks, being raised by Pemberton, England and introduced 1924. Bushy in habit, it bears its creamy white and pink flowers freely in

---

Abbreviations and symbols used in the text

▼	Deciduous	†	Lime hater
△	Evergreen	◧	Shade
✳	Flowers	◖	Semi shade
●	Fruit	⊙	Sun
🍃	Foliage		

A.G.M.   Award of Garden Merit, Royal Horticultural Society

F.C.C.   First Class Certificate, Royal Horticultural Society

Z1–10   The Z numbers represent the climatic zones used in the United States and provide a useful hardiness rating elsewhere. Thus Z1 is for those plants surviving coldest conditions and Z10 is the other extreme

The illustration numbers are in **bold type**.

large sprays and produces magnificent trusses in the autumn. The flowers are richly fragrant and produce hips which change slowly from green to pink, a pleasant change from the brighter colours of other fruits. Can be grown as a bedding rose in smaller gardens by fairly hard spring pruning or can be used as an informal hedge.

'Pink Nevada' see *R.* **'Marguerite Hilling'**

'Raubritter' Modern Shrub ✳
90 cm. × 1·5 m. (3 × 5 ft)
(*R. macrantha* 'Daisy Hill' × *R.* 'Solarium'). Raised W. Kordes, Germany 1936. A very pretty trailing shrub for hanging over low walls or sprawling over a bank. The semi-double pale pink flowers are borne in clusters and are incurved, reminiscent of the old Bourbons. A sharp refreshing scent accompanies the blooms which are produced during July and August. Of great charm. **429**

'Roseraie de L'Hay' 2·15 × 2·15 m. (7 × 7 ft) ✳➤
Introduced by Cochet-Cochet, France 1901. A superb shrub rose for those who appreciate the rich crimson purple colouring of its flowers, backed by clear apple green foliage. The richly scented flowers are seldom followed by hips. This is a recurrent flowering shrub very suitable for a hedge in a large garden where it will provide a very fine feature. A.G.M. 1969.

rugosa scabrosa see *R.* **'Scabrosa'**

'Scabrosa' syn. *R. rugosa scabrosa* ✳➤●
1·5–1·85 m. (5–6 ft)
A deciduous shrub of considerable vigour which, although known prior to 1939 has not had its early history recorded. It is thought to have arisen in the Harkness Nursery at Hitchin, England either as a sport or selection from that fine clone *R. rugosa rubra*. A handsome shrub with large luxuriant leaves, a fine background for the large single purplish crimson flowers, with typical cream stamens. Flowering in June, there is some recurrent bloom eventually swamped by the large hips. These are broadly flask shaped orange red and very decorative. Worth planting either as a shrub or as a hedge in large gardens where there is sufficient space.

'Scarlet Fire' see *R.* **'Scharlachglut'**

'Scharlachglut' syn. *R.* 'Scarlet Fire' ✳●
Modern Shrub 2·45 m. (8 ft)
(*R.* 'Poinsettia' × *R.* 'Alika'.) Raised by Kordes, Germany 1952. A very vigorous large arching shrub, which can be grown on a pillar or wall also. The large single, blazing scarlet crimson, flowers are borne freely and provide a display spectacular in its brilliance over a long period but without any later repeat. However, the large pear-shaped hips continue to show, becoming orange scarlet and lasting through most of the winter. A.G.M. 1969. **430**

'Schneezwerg' syn. *R.* 'Snow Dwarf' ✳➤●
Hybrid Rugosa 1·5 × 1·5 m. (5 ft × 5 ft)

(*R. rugosa* × unknown.) Raised by P. Lambert, Germany 1912. A very pleasing shrub with good foliage of rugosa type with smaller leaves than other rugosas. The pure white semi-double flowers have great charm and are followed with small scarlet hips which mingle with the later flowers. Makes a very good hedge which can be trimmed during winter with shears. **431**

'Snow Dwarf' see *R.* **'Schneezwerg'**
'Tipo Ideale' see *R. chinensis mutablis*

Rose,
    California see *Rosa californica*
    China see *Rosa chinensis*
    Common Sun see *Helianthemum*
      nummularium
    Guelder see *Viburnum opulus*
    Mrs Wilson's see *Rosa helenae*
    Primrose see *Rosa primula*
    Redleaf see *Rosa rubrifolia*
    Rock see *Cistus*
    Sun see *Helianthemum*
    Threepenny-bit see *Rosa farreri persetosa*
    Virginia see *Rosa virginiana*
Rose
    Acacia see *Robina hispida*
    Daphne see *Daphne cneorum*
    of Sharon (U.K.) see *Hypericum calycinum*
    of Sharon (U.S.) see *Hibiscus syriacus*
Rose-gold Pussy Willow see *Salix gracilistyla*
Rosebud Cherry see *Prunus subhirtella*

RUBUS ROSACEAE **Bramble**

cockburnianus syn. *R. giraldianus* ⊙◑▼
2·45–3·05 m. (8–10 ft)
North and central China. Introduced by Wilson 1907. A vigorous deciduous shrub with attractive pinnate leaves which have a fern-like appearance, grown for its winter splendour. The terminal panicles of small purple flowers have little value and are followed by black fruits. It is in the winter when the 'whitewashed bramble' comes into its own. The biennial stems, much branched and pendulous at the tips are covered with a vivid white, waxy covering which remains decorative throughout the winter months. Easily grown in any reasonable soil, in the open or in partial shade. Young plants can be raised from seed or by pegging the tips of the plants into the soil in late July. Pruning consists of removing the two year old stems which have flowered in early spring. Z.5. **432**

giraldianus see *R. cockburnianus*

Tridel (*R. deliciosus* × *R. trilobus*) ⊙▼✳
2·75 m. (9 ft)
Raised Ingram, England 1950. A vigorous, deciduous shrub, a hybrid which is of great beauty in the spring. The erect growths are thornless and, in May, produce large white single flowers with a central boss of golden

stamens all along the arching branches. Can be pruned if overreaching its space or getting overcrowded. Cuttings can be rooted under mist. A.G.M. 1962.

    'Benenden', a fine clone, and the form most often grown. A.G.M. 1962, F.C.C. 1963. **433**

Rue see *Ruta graveolens*

RUTA RUTACEAE

***graveolens* Rue** 60 cm. (2 ft)   ⊙△➧
Southern Europe. Cultivated in Britain in 1652. A small erect evergreen shrub, popularly known as rue. Usually grown as a herb, it has for long been noted for its medicinal properties. It is well worth growing for its glaucous foliage which provides a contrast to the yellow flowers and as it keeps on blooming for a considerable time. Thriving in any well drained soil, without any objection to lime, rue appreciates a sunny position.

    'Jackman's Blue', popular because of its striking opalescent blue foliage and compact bushy habit. The shape can be retained by an annual clip over of the previous year's growth in April. Excellent for edging or ground cover and more effective if the flowers are removed. A.G.M. 1969. **434**

    'Variegata', striking as a small specimen plant the blue leaflets are variegated with creamy white. **435**

Running-Myrtle see *Vinca minor*

S

Sage,
    Common see *Salvia officinalis*
    Garden see *Salvia officinalis*
    Jerusalem see *Phlomis fruticosa*
    Purple-leaf see *Salvia officinalis*
        'Purpurascens'
Sacred Bamboo see *Nandina domestica*

SALIX SALICACEAE **Willow**

The willows constitute a large, variable, mainly deciduous genus, from large trees to tiny earth hugging shrubs. Several are desirable and useful in small gardens or can be rendered so by pruning. The following are a small selection.

aegyptiaca syn. *S. medemii* 6·1 m. (20 ft)   ▼❋
Southern Russia, Asia. In cultivation 1820. A handsome large deciduous shrub which may in good soil and with adequate moisture attain the stature of a small tree. Furnished with densely pubescent grey twigs this beautiful willow provides an early spring effect in February and March when covered with its large male catkins. These are conspicuously bright yellow and most

noticeable when planted against a background of dark evergreens. As *S. medemii*. A.G.M. 1969. Z.5.

***alba* White Willow**   ▼❋
    'Chermesina', syn. 'Britzensis', the **Scarlet Willow**, is most conspicuous in winter, particularly in winter sunshine when the brilliant orange scarlet branches are effective, especially when reflected in nearby water. To get this effect annual or biennial pruning in March or early April is required. Z.2.
    'Sericea', is a less vigorous form of the White Willow which is most effective particularly as a background plant because of the brilliance of its silvery leaves. By pruning every second year it can be kept to shrub size. A.G.M. 1969.
    'Vitellina', Golden Willow, a male form, smaller than the type. Hard pruning in March each or alternate years produces strong young growths of egg-yolk yellow which justify the common name. A.G.M. 1969.

apoda   ▼❋
Caucasus. In cultivation before 1939. An attractive dwarf willow whose prostrate stems hug the ground and are furnished with glossy green leaves. The upright male catkins appear in spring all along the branches before the leaves. Silvery, furry they gradually elongate and become greatly enhanced with bright yellow anthers. A fine plant for the rock garden or in an old stone sink or trough. A.G.M. 1969 to the male form.

× ***balfourii*** (*S. caprea* × *S. lanata*)   ▼❋
2·45 m. (8 ft)
A deciduous hybrid shrub, said to have been originally found in Scotland. A useful shrub, intermediate in character between its parents, the young woolly leaves becoming green later in the year. The catkins of the male plant appear before the leaves in April and are conspicuously yellow and silky with very small red bracts. A fine shrub especially where moisture is available. Z.4.

Abbreviations and symbols used in the text

▼	Deciduous	†	Lime hater
△	Evergreen	◍	Shade
❋	Flowers	◐	Semi shade
●	Fruit	⊙	Sun
➧	Foliage		

A.G.M.   Award of Garden Merit, Royal Horticultural Society
F.C.C.   First Class Certificate, Royal Horticultural Society

Z1–10   The Z numbers represent the climatic zones used in the United States and provide a useful hardiness rating elsewhere. Thus Z1 is for those plants surviving coldest conditions and Z10 is the other extreme

The illustration numbers are in **bold type**.

bockii 90 cm.–2·75 m. (3–9 ft)
West China. Introduced by Wilson 1908–9. A small shrub of spreading habit which flowers on the growths of the current year, between August and October, the only willow in general cultivation to do so. A quietly attractive plant. Z.5. **436**

daphnoides **Violet Willow**
North Europe, central Asia, Himalayas. In cultivation 1829. An erect deciduous tree which however can be kept to large shrub proportions. A very pleasing willow for winter effect if pruned hard in March in alternate years. The long, purple violet growths have an overlay of white bloom which is most attractive. A striking crop of silky catkins is produced before the leaves on male plants, useful for decoration at a time when flowers may be rather scarce. A.G.M. 1969. Z.4.

fargesii 1·85–2·45 m. (6–8 ft)
Central China. Introduced by Wilson 1911. A medium sized open shrub with smooth shoots which are brownish green when young and become dark shining brown by the second year. A handsome plant during the winter months when its buds which are large and conspicuous become red. The catkins appear with or after the leaves and are erect and very slender. Has been much confused with a closely related willow, *S. moupinensis*. Z.6.

gracilistyla **Rose-gold Pussy Willow**
1·5–1·85 m. (5–6 ft)
China, Japan, Korea, Manchuria. Introduced *c*. 1895. A spreading shrub with silky downy leaves but which is most effective when the catkins are produced on the naked growths early in the year, from February to April. The males are grey, suffused red, becoming yellow as they age. A.G.M. 1969. Z.5.

'Kurome' see ***S. melanostachys***

irrorata 2·45–3·05 m. (8–10 ft)
South-west United States. Introduced 1898. A strong-growing shrub of medium size with long growths green when young, becoming purple and coated with a very white bloom which is particularly noticeable during the winter months. The catkins appear on growths in advance of the leaves, the males with brick red anthers which become yellow. Makes a beautiful association with the scarlet and gold willows in winter, an effect most readily obtained by severe pruning in March every year. Z.4.

lanata **Woolly Willow**
'Stuartii', a dwarf gnarled form of the Woolly Willow, growing to about 45 cm. (1½ ft) high and with smaller leaves. Outstanding in winter on account of its yellow branches and orange buds. The large, upright yellowish to grey catkins appear in spring while the silvery grey downy leaves are very effective during the summer as a foil to highly coloured plants. Easily accommodated in a small garden, spreading can be controlled by judicious pruning. A.G.M. 1969. **438**

medemii see ***S. aegyptiaca***

melanostachys syn. *S.* '*Kurome*'
1·2–1·5 m. (4–5 ft)
A medium sized deciduous shrub of Japanese origin, known in cultivation in the male form only and probably of mixed parentage. It is sometimes regarded as a form of *S. gracilistyla*, a species from which it differs considerably, particularly in its catkins, which are non-silky and very dark, with blackish scales and brick red anthers which become yellow when open. Appearing before the leaves they are quite unusual not only in the garden but for decoration in the home, with a suitable background.

repens **Creeping Willow**
argentea, is a wide spreading semi-prostrate shrub which, given time, builds up to 1·2 m. (4 ft) in height but considerably more across. The silvery grey leaves are attractive, as are the dainty yellow male catkins which provide bees with valuable pollen. It is sometimes grafted onto the stem of a stronger growing willow, in which form it will make a very pretty weeping tree. Should not be planted on rich soil, as it retains its character much better on a limited diet. Z.4.

sachalinensis
'Sekka', a male clone of Japanese origin becoming a large shrub if left unpruned; when pruned hard produces curiously flattened and twisted stems which floral arrangers find useful and especially for Japanese floral arrangements. Z.4.

'Wehrhahnii'
A small to medium slow growing shrub which comes alive in spring when the purple growths become studded with upright silvery male catkins which later become yellow. Makes a beautiful picture when underplanted with the Grape Hyacinth, *Muscari armeniacum*. A.G.M. 1969. Z.5. **437**

Salt Cedar see ***Tamarix pentandra***

SALVIA LABIATAE

officinalis **Common** or **Garden Sage**
60–90 cm. (2–3 ft)
Southern Europe. In cultivation in Britain 1597. Well known as Common Sage and cultivated as a herb, this sub-evergreen aromatic shrub is valuable for ground cover purposes and for its grey appearance which can be used effectively in garden schemes. Easily rooted from cuttings in a cold frame, low branches frequently layer themselves. Grows best in a sunny position in well drained soil. Any pruning required should be carried out in April.
'Purpurascens', **Purple-leaf Sage**, is even more effective as the stems and foliage are suffused purple. A.G.M. 1969. Z.3.

SAMBUCUS CAPRIFOLIACEAE **Elder**

racemosa **Red-berried Elder** ⊙ ▼ ✳
2·45-3·65 m. (8–12 ft)
Europe, west Asia. In cultivation since 16th century. The Red-berried Elder is a deciduous shrub which produces cone-shaped terminal panicles of yellowish white flowers in April. These are followed by panicles of densely clustered scarlet fruits which ripen in June and July. The elders are easily grown in good soil which retains moisture and the golden form retains its colour better in full sun. Hard wood cuttings can be rooted in autumn in a sheltered border. Z.4.

    'Plumosa Aurea', a very fine foliage plant which has been in cultivation since 1895. The beautifully cut leaves retain their golden colour throughout the summer. Slower growing than the type it can be kept compact by pruning in spring. One of the best shrubs for colour effect. **439**

Santa Barbara Ceanothus see *Ceanothus dentatus*

SANTOLINA COMPOSITAE **Lavender Cotton** ⊙ △

chamaecyparissus 90 cm. (3 ft) ✳ ✍
Southern France, Pyrenees. Cultivated since mid-16th century. The Lavender Cotton is a popular evergreen shrub whose finely divided leaves, aromatic when rubbed or crushed, are covered with a white felt which ensures its very silvery effect in the garden. The colour is more effective when grown in well drained soil which is on the poor side and a sunny position is preferred. Pruning to the base in April each year will ensure non-production of citrus yellow flowers which tend to spoil the foliage effect. Easily propagated from cuttings in a cold frame in late summer. A.G.M. 1969. Z.6–7.

    var. *corsica* **'Nana'**, a dwarf form of above from Corsica and Sardinia. It is a more compact shrub, very suitable for the very small garden or rock garden. A.G.M. 1969.

virens 60 cm. (2 ft) ✳ ✍
An evergreen shrub up to 60 cm. with longer thinner leaves than *S. chamaecyparissus* and of a vivid green which in conjunction with the bright lemon yellow flowers has quite a unique effect. **440**

SAPIUM EUPHORBIACEAE ⊙ △

japonicum
Japan, China, Korea. A small uncommon evergreen shrub, which appears to be hardy. The inconspicuous flowers appear in June and form catkin like, greenish yellow racemes. Its garden value lies in the glorious glowing crimson of its entire leaves in autumn. Z.8. **441**

SARCOCOCCA BUXACEAE **Christmas Box** △

hookerana 60 cm. (2 ft) ✳ ✍
    digyna Western China. Introduced by Wilson 1908. A dwarf evergreen shrub, commonly known as Sweet or Christmas Box, with shiny green leaves of neat pleasing appearance and admirable for ground cover. A plant which appreciates moisture and succeeds best in some shade. The white flowers are small and not startling in appearance, but make up any deficiency in this respect by fragrance, a few twigs brought indoors will scent a room. It bears attractive black berries. Little pruning is required, a few twigs cut for house decoration will suffice. Spreading by suckers it can be increased by chopping off those with roots or it can be rooted from summer cuttings. A.G.M. 1963. Z.6. **442**

SASA GRAMINEAE

veitchii **Kumazasa** 90 cm. (3 ft) ✍
Japan. Introduced 1880. A small, dense bamboo which forms thickets of deep purplish green canes which later become dull purple. Valuable for winter effect when the margins of the green leaves change to pale straw colour and appear to be variegated. Z.8.

Sawara Cypress see *Chamaecyparis pisifera*
Scarlet
    Clematis see *Clematis texensis*
    Willow see *Salix alba* **'Chermesina'**

SCIADOPITYS PINACEAE † △

verticillata **Umbrella Pine** *c.* 37 m. (120 ft) ⊙ ◍ ✍
Japan. Introduced by Lobb 1853, England, 1861 U.S. A hardy evergreen conifer which in nature reaches the height stated, but in gardens it is usually seen as a small tree, sometimes almost shrub like in appearance. Popularly known as the Umbrella Pine because of the arrangement of the needles, which bear a striking

---

Abbreviations and symbols used in the text

▼	Deciduous	†	Lime hater
△	Evergreen	◍	Shade
✳	Flowers	◐	Semi shade
•	Fruit	⊙	Sun
✍	Foliage		

A.G.M. Award of Garden Merit, Royal Horticultural Society
F.C.C. First Class Certificate, Royal Horticultural Society

Z1–10 The Z numbers represent the climatic zones used in the United States and provide a useful hardiness rating elsewhere. Thus Z1 is for those plants surviving coldest conditions and Z10 is the other extreme

The illustration numbers are in **bold type**.

resemblance to the ribs of an umbrella. Slow in growth it is a valuable and very distinct tree, not least because of its attractive cones, which, green at first, become brown in the second year. Thrives on good soil which must be lime free and not lacking in moisture and does not object to a little shade. Z.5. **443**

Scotch
 Broom see *Cytisus scoparius*
 or **Scots Pine** see *Pinus sylvestris*
Sea Buckthorn see *Hippophae rhamnoides*

SENECIO COMPOSITAE

greyi 90 cm.–1·85 m. (3–6 ft)

The plant grown under this name in gardens and sometimes also known as *S. laxifolius* is now I understand considered to be a hybrid between the true *S. greyi* and another species. This is a very popular spreading evergreen, ideal for seaside planting, with silvery grey leaves, very useful for underplanting standard trees or in shrub borders where it will grow 90 cm. high. It can also be grown on a wall or fence where it will attain a greater height, at least 1·85 m. Masses of yellow daisy like flowers are produced in June from silvery buds. These are not to everyone's taste and can be cut off so as not to spoil the foliage effect, but personally I like the silvery bud stage. Easily pleased if in well drained soil and a sunny position this very useful shrub responds to hard pruning in April if your garden is small. The foliage is much appreciated for floral arrangements. Cuttings roots readily in summer under mist. A.G.M. 1936. **444**

laxifolius see under *S. greyi*

Senna, Bladder see *Colutea*

SEQUOIA TAXODIACEAE

sempervirens Redwood

 'Prostrata' A remarkable dwarf form of one of the largest trees, the Redwood, a native of California and Oregon U.S. In cultivation since 1951, it originated as a branch sport at the University Botanic Gardens, Cambridge, England. The spreading branches are furnished with two-ranked leaves of a glaucous green colour. Any vertical shoots which develop should be cut away. **445**

Sharon,
 Rose of (U.K.) see *Hypericum calycinum*
 Rose of (U.S.) see *Hibiscus syriacus*
Shore Juniper see *Juniperus conferta*
Showy
 Deutzia see *Deutzia × magnifica*
 Hebe see *Hebe speciosa*

Shrubby Althea see *Hibiscus syriacus*
Siberian
 Crab Apple see under *Malus × robusta*
 Dogwood see *Cornus alba* 'Sibirica'
Silk-Tassel see *Garrya elliptica*
Silky-leaf Woadwaxen see *Genista pilosa*
Siphonosmanthus delavayi see *Osmanthus delavayi*
Silver, Backhouse see *Chamaecyparis lawsoniana*
Simon's Cotoneaster see *Cotoneaster simonsii*

SKIMMIA RUTACEAE

japonica 90 cm. (3 ft)

Japan. In cultivation 1838. A neat evergreen shrub considerably wider than high, producing dull white flowers in terminal panicles, male and female flowers on different plants, during March to May. Grown for its decorative red fruits which last on the plants throughout the winter months, sometimes to the following summer. To produce these fruits it is necessary to plant both sexes, one male to three females. A very adaptable plant suitable for the front of shrub borders. May be grown from seed in which case the resultant plants are likely to be a mixture, some of either sex. There are many named forms, these can be increased by summer cuttings under mist. F.C.C. 1863, A.G.M. 1969. **446**

 'Foremanii', a female form with larger fruits and of greater vigour than *S. japonica* and which grows better in some shade. A.G.M. 1969.

 'Fragrans', a male form with conical spikes of cream flowers which are fragrant and decorative. Planted with 'Foremanii' a good crop of fruits will be ensured. A.G.M. 1969.

 'Rubella', a male form of compact habit which is decorative throughout winter with red buds in open panicles which bloom being pinkish white with yellow anthers in Spring. A.G.M. 1969. **447**

Slender Deutzia see *Deutzia gracilis*
Smoke Tree see *Cotinus coggygria*
Snow Heath see *Erica herbacea*
Snowball,
 Fragrant see *Viburnum × carlcephalum*
 Japanese see *Viburnum plicatum*
Snowberry see *Symphoricarpos rivularis*
Snowmound see *Spiraea nipponica tosaensis*
Snowy Mespilus see *Amelanchier*

SOLANUM SOLANACEAE **Nightshade**

crispum **Chilean Potato Tree** 6 m. (20 ft)

Chile. Introduced about 1830. A semi-evergreen shrub of vigorous habit which if planted and trained on a wall will reach the height stated. Is seen at its best in temperate climates in the milder areas but can be a most decorative plant elsewhere if given a sheltered corner with a wall behind. The beautiful and fragrant rich purple flowers resemble those of a potato so that it is sometimes known as the Chilean Potato tree. Will grow in any reasonable soil if well drained and thrives on chalk or lime. A.G.M. 1939. Z.8.

'Glasnevin', syn. **'Autumnale'**, an improved form with a longer flowering season. A.G.M. 1969. **448**

jasminoides **Jasmine Night Shade**   △⊙✳

5·5 m. (18 ft)

Brazil. Introduced 1838. A slender semi-evergreen climber which grows in similar situations to *S. crispum* but being more tender requires the shelter of a warm wall. The pale blue flowers are produced in great profusion over a long season. Easily propagated by summer cuttings under mist.

'Album', the pure white form seen in the photograph is the one most often seen growing in gardens. Z.9. **449**

SORBUS ROSACEAE

cashmeriana **Kashmir Mountain Ash**   ▼✳●

to 4·55 m. (15 ft)

Kashmir. A deciduous small mountain ash with fern like leaves and of open habit. The delicate pink flowers in May are followed by loose drooping clusters of white marble like fruits on pink to red stalks, which persist long after the leaves have fallen. A beautiful small tree which can be grown in any garden of reasonable size and is worthy of more attention. F.C.C. 1971. Z.4. **450**

esserteauana 11 m. (34 ft)   ▼●

Western China. Introduced 1907. A small, deciduous mountain ash of open habit. The scarlet fruits are small and borne in dense clusters, colouring later than most species. Rich autumn tints are characteristic.

'Flava', a very fine form with rich lemon-yellow fruits in crowded corymbs. Z.7. **451**

hupehensis to 6·1 m. (20 ft)   ▼●

Central and western China. Introduced Wilson 1910. A small deciduous mountain ash with purplish brown ascending branches, and easily recognized bluish green leaves. The drooping clusters of white fruits sometimes have a pink or reddish tinge and last well into the winter months. One of the most valuable species with leaves a glorious red in autumn. A.G.M. 1969.

obtusa **'Rosea'**, a very charming form with lovely pink fruits. **452**

'Joseph Rock'   ▼●

This remarkable small mountain ash commemorates a famous American plant collector Dr Rock, but its origin still remains a mystery. Regarded by some authorities as a species from China but by others as a hybrid. Erect and compact in habit with leaves which turn brilliant shades of red, purple and coppery orange in autumn providing a strong contrast to the clusters of globular fruits. These are unique in colour, creamy yellow deepening to amber yellow with red stalks. In my experience, unless pro-

tected, birds are rather appreciative of the fruits. A.G.M. 1969, F.C.C. 1973. **453**

matsumurana **Japanese Mountain Ash**

5·5 m. (18 ft)

An excellent and uncommon small tree from Japan adding height to the shrub border. Leaves mid-green; autumn colours magnificent, in yellow, orange scarlet shades. Flowers white, late spring. Berries, often taken by birds when green, brilliant orange. F.C.C. 1973. Z.7. **454, 455**

pinnatifida see *S. thuringiaca*

reducta 60 cm. (2 ft)   ▼●

Burma, western China. Introduced Kingdon Ward 1943. This miniature mountain ash is a most unusual suckering shrub of considerable charm and easily fitted into shrub borders in quite small gardens. The small fruits are white with a rose flush, unfortunately eagerly devoured by birds. The dark shining green leaves assume bronze and scarlet colourings in autumn. Z.7.

scalaris to 9 cm. (30 ft)   ▼●

Western China. Discovered and introduced by Wilson 1904. A small but rather wide spreading mountain ash with neat attractive leaves which assume rich red and purple colours in autumn. The large flattened clusters of white flowers in spring are in due course followed by flattened heads of small bright red fruits at much the same time as changes in leaf colour are taking place. A useful tree where space is available. A.G.M. 1969. Z.6. **456**

× *thuringiaca* syn. *S. pinnatifida*   ▼●

6·1 m. (20 ft)

A small deciduous tree which develops by virtue of its ascending branches into a close compact tree. It is thought to be a natural hybrid between the Whitebeam, *S. aria* and the Rowan, European Mountain Ash (U.S.) *S. aucuparia*. The white flowers are produced in

---

Abbreviations and symbols used in the text

▼ Deciduous	† Lime hater
△ Evergreen	◍ Shade
✳ Flowers	◐ Semi shade
● Fruit	⊙ Sun
⌇ Foliage	

A.G.M.   Award of Garden Merit, Royal Horticultural Society

F.C.C.   First Class Certificate, Royal Horticultural Society

Z1–10   The Z numbers represent the climatic zones used in the United States and provide a useful hardiness rating elsewhere. Thus Z1 is for those plants surviving coldest conditions and Z10 is the other extreme

The illustration numbers are in **bold type**.

corymbs in May and are replaced in autumn by clusters of glossy red fruits. A handsome tree particularly when in fruit and enhanced by fine foliage. Z.6. **457**

vilmorinii **Vilmorin Mountain Ash**   ▼ ♣ ●
to 4·55 m. (15 ft)
Western China. Introduced Abbé Delavay 1889. A less vigorous but charming deciduous tree with slender arching branches which bear clusters of delicate fern like leaves. These become purple and red in autumn. The drooping clusters of fruits are cherry red and gradually fade through pink to white flushed pink, and frequently persist beyond leaf fall decorating the naked branches. A.G.M. 1953. Z.5. **458**

Sorrel Tree see *Oxydendrum arboreum*
Southern Heath see *Erica australis*
Southernwood see *Artemisia abrotanum*
Spanish
  Broom see *Genista hispanica* and *Spartium junceum*
  Broom, White see *Cytisus multiflorus*
  Dagger see *Yucca gloriosa*
  Gorse see *Genista hispanica*
  Heath see *Erica australis* and *Erica lusitanica*

SPARTIUM LEGUMINOSAE

junceum **Spanish Broom**   to 3·05 m. (10 ft)   ▼ ✴
Circum-Mediterranean and the Canary Islands. Supposedly introduced 1548. Has become naturalized in the U.S. A tall somewhat gaunt shrub if allowed to grow naturally with very few leaves but with many erect rush like stems. It thrives on any well drained soil including lime or chalk. The rich glowing yellow pea like flowers are fragrant and freely produced over a long season. A very showy plant, useful for cutting and lasting well in water. It can only be raised from seeds, which are usually abundant and can be sown under glass or in a frame in spring. Seedlings should either be sown direct in small pots or the seedlings transferred to pots or containers when young as transplanting is resented. The Spanish broom can be an asset in a small garden if pruned regularly in April. By doing so when the plant is young it can be kept around 90 cm.–1·2 m. (3–4 ft) each year. Do not prune into old wood. A.G.M. 1923. Z.7. **459**

Spindle Tree see *Euonymus*
Spindle Tree, Common see *Euonymus europaeus*
Spinning Gum see *Eucalyptus perreniana*

SPIRAEA ROSACEAE   ⊙ ▼

An easily grown but rather diverse group of hardy deciduous shrubs which in their flowering period cover quite a long season. They will grow with success on any good garden soil, especially if well supplied with moisture and while better in sun will put up with a little shade. All can be increased by cuttings of young growth in summer under mist or from hard wooded cuttings in autumn outdoors in a sheltered border. Those which sucker can be increased by chopping out rooted suckers with a sharp spade in autumn.

× *arguta* (*S. multiflora* × *S. thunbergii*)   ✴
Bridal Wreath (U.K.), **Garland Wreath** (U.S.)
1·5–1·85 m. (5–6 ft)
Cultivated by 1884. A medium sized shrub and a most prolific producer of snowy white flowers in arching sprays in April and May, set off by the fresh green narrow leaves. Will form a very nice hedge which should be trimmed after flowering. A few old growths removed after flowering is all the pruning required. A fine shrub. A.G.M. 1927. Z.4.

× *bumalda* (*S. albiflora* × *S. japonica*)   ✴
90 cm. (3 ft)
In cultivation before 1890. A dwarf hybrid shrub which produces deep pink flowers in flat terminal panicles on growths of the current year. It flowers non-stop throughout the summer. Z.5. **460**
  'Anthony Waterer', is a selection from above which can be kept around 60 cm. (2 ft) in height by spring pruning. The flat terminal heads are deep carmine. The foliage is frequently variegated cream and pink. Very popular. To avoid inferior plants, grow from cuttings and not seed. A.G.M. 1969.

japonica   ✴
  'Alpina', a delightful small shrub which is only about 45 cm. (1½ ft) high and rather more across so can find a home in the smallest of gardens, even a window box. Very showy with tiny heads of rose pink flowers in July and August. A.G.M. 1969. **461**

nipponica
  tosaensis, 60 cm. (2 ft), Japan, a small shrub sometimes listed as Snowmound, a descriptive name for the floriferous mound like appearance of the plant. In June and July the white flowers cluster the upper side of the branches virtually smothering the leaves. Do not grow from seed. Z.4. **462**

thunbergii   1·2 m. (4 ft)   ✴
China. Introduced from Japan c. 1863. A popular small shrub, generally the first spiraea in flower, pure white flowers smothering the wiry stems. Useful for a low hedge which can be trimmed after flowering. Thin out some old wood after flowering. Z.4. **463**

× *vanhouttei* (*S. cantoniensis* × *S. trilobata*)   ✴ ♣
1·8 m. (6 ft)
Garden origin. In cultivation before 1866. A vigorous shrub with graceful arching brown stems. The white flowers are produced in June, in umbel-like clusters all along the branches and are effectively shown off by the blue green leaves. A very showy shrub which makes an excellent hedge even on poorish soil and colours well in autumn. Clip after flowering. Z.4.

Spring
   Cherry see *Prunus subhirtella*
   Heath see *Erica herbacea*
Spruce see *Picea*
Spruce,
   Colorado see *Picea pungens*
   Norway see *Picea abies*

STACHYURUS STACHYURACEAE ☉ ◐

praecox 2·1–3·05 m. (7–10 ft)   ▼ ✳
Japan. Introduced 1864. A medium to large sized shrub, deciduous and quite hardy. Flowering very early in mild winters, sometimes in February but more usually in March and before the leaves appear, it is worth a little shelter to protect the flowers. Cool soil, moist in summer, with plenty of humus, leaf mould or peat added is the recipe for success in cultivating this rather delightful plant. The racemes are stiffly pendulous, hanging on the reddish leafless branches an inch or so apart, with pale yellow flowers. Cuttings may be rooted under mist in June or July. A.G.M. 1964. Z.6. **464**

Stag's-Horn Sumach see *Rhus typhina*

STAPHYLEA STAPHYLEACEAE **Bladder Nut** ☉ ◐
Bladder nuts require no pruning and can be increased during summer by cuttings under mist.

holocarpa 3·65–4·55 m. (12–15 ft)   ▼ ✳ ➴
Central China. Introduced Wilson 1908. A deciduous shrub which may become a small tree. The trifoliate leaves have oblong lanceolate leaflets. The white flowers appear in April and May and are pinkish in bud and produced in short, drooping panicles. Z.5.

pinnata **European Bladder Nut**   ▼ ✳ ●
3·65–4·55 m. (12–15 ft)
Central and South Europe. Cultivated 1596. A large deciduous shrub of upright vigorous habit with pinnate leaves. A well known Bladder-nut and apt to become naturalized in places. The white flowers are produced in terminal drooping panicles which are followed by bladder like capsules which contain the seeds. A shrub worthy of a place in a large garden because of its interesting fruits in addition to its flowers, which appear in May and June, and foliage. Easily grown in any soil which is reasonably fertile either in the open or in semi-shade. **465**

Star Magnolia see *Magnolia stellata*
Stephan Jasmine see *Jasminua stephanense*

STRANVAESIA ROSACEAE ☉ ◐ △
davidiana 3·65–4·55 m. (12–15 ft)   † ✳ ➴ ●
West China. Introduced by Forrest 1917. A fairly large

evergreen shrub, with erect branches and spreading side shoots. The olive green leathery leaves provide a foil for the white hawthorn like flowers, which are followed by pendant clusters of brilliant crimson fruits. These generally persist until early in the New Year when they are complimented by green and scarlet autumn leaves. Very popular in southern California. Likes a well drained, lime free soil and some shelter and does not require pruning, but is far-reaching and unless restricted, needs room. Can be increased from seeds or summer cuttings under mist. A.G.M. 1964. Z.7. **466**

Sumach, Stag's-horn see *Rhus typhina*
Summer Sweet Bush see *Clethra alnifolia*
Sun Rose see *Helianthemum*
Sun Rose, Common see *Helianthemum*
   nummularium
Swamp
   Azalea see *Rhododendron viscosum*
   Honeysuckle see *Rhododendron*
   viscosum
Sweet,
   Summer see *Clethra alnifolia*
   Winter see *Chimonanthus praecox*
Sweet
   Bay see *Laurus*
   Mock Orange see *Philadelphus coronarius*
   Pepper see *Clethra alnifolia*
Sweetleaf see *Symplocos*
Sweetspire, Holly-leaf see *Itea ilicifolia*
Swiss Stone Pine see *Pinus cembra*
Sycamore and **Sycamore Maple** see *Acer*
   pseudoplatanus

SYMPHORICARPOS CAPRIFOLIACEAE ☉ ◐ ▼
A small genus of deciduous shrubs which are grown mainly for their fruits, the flowers being small and insignificant. Popularly known as Snowberry because of

---

Abbreviations and symbols used in the text

▼	Deciduous	†	Lime hater
△	Evergreen	◍	Shade
✳	Flowers	◐	Semi shade
●	Fruit	☉	Sun
➴	Foliage		

A.G.M.   Award of Garden Merit, Royal Horticultural Society
F.C.C.   First Class Certificate, Royal Horticultural Society

Z1–10   The Z numbers represent the climatic zones used in the United States and provide a useful hardiness rating elsewhere. Thus Z1 is for those plants surviving coldest conditions and Z10 is the other extreme

The illustration numbers are in **bold type**.

the white fruits of some forms, these are useful shrubs in areas where the soil is poor. As they will also grow in shade, under the drip of trees or in sun, can be used for hedges and retain their fruits for a long period, their merits are manifold. Floral arrangers find sprays of fruits invaluable in winter for indoor decorations. The Snowberry will grow nearly anywhere and is not fussy about soil. The forms which sucker can be increased by division during autumn or winter. Plants can be grown from seed and particularly good forms can be increased from cuttings inserted in a cold frame in autumn.

albus laevigatus syn. *S. rivularis* **Snowberry** ●
1·85 m. (6 ft)
Western North America. Introduced 1817. A strong growing deciduous shrub which forms dense thickets of upright stems and suckers profusely in good soil. This is the common Snowberry found so frequently in woodland, where it has been introduced intensively for game cover. Fruits in great profusion, globose and shining like white marbles. F.C.C. 1913, A.G.M. 1931. **467**

× ***doorenbosii*** ●
An attractive group of hybrids raised at The Hague, Holland by S. G. A. Doorenbos, a former Director of the Parks, and one of that country's greatest horticulturists. There are several clones and these are a selection.
   'Magic Berry', a dwarf compact grower with masses of rose pink berries.
   'Mother of Pearl' is the type, a dwarf shrub with branches weighed down with marble-like whitish berries touched with faint pink. A.G.M. 1969.
   'White Hedge', a compact, upright growing shrub which does not sucker freely and has become popular in some countries for hedging. Erect clusters of small pure white marble-like berries which are very effective from October onwards.

rivularis see *S. albus laevigatus*

SYMPLOCOS SYMPLOCACEAE Sweetleaf

paniculata Asiatic Symplocos   ⊙▼✳●
2·1–2·45 m. (7–8 ft)
China, Himalaya, Japan. Introduced 1871. A deciduous shrub of elegant appearance which may attain small tree stature given some time. The small white flowers are fragrant and produced in late May and early June in panicles. It is pretty while in flower but it is the crop of brilliant ultramarine berries which follow in autumn that makes this shrub such a wonderful addition, particularly in a woodland garden. A crop of fruits is most likely after a long hot summer, not a regular occurrence in cooler temperate areas. Planting at least two shrubs in close proximity will help cross-pollination. One of the most spectacular of fruiting shrubs when bare of leaves. F.C.C. 1954. Z.5. **468**

Symplocos, Asiatic see *Symplocos paniculata*

SYRINGA OLEACEAE Lilac   ⊙▼
A genus of deciduous shrubs ranging up to small trees, the lilacs are among the best known of all shrubs. Much of the romance associated with these plants is due to the unique fragrance and without doubt accounts for its great popularity, although the flowers are also very charming. The lilacs are hardy and thrive in any good fertile soil in an open position and are very happy on lime or chalk. They will grow in light shade but flower best in full sun. Rather hungry plants, they appreciate a good mulch of well rotted manure in the spring, or failing that, a few handfuls of hoof and horn or bone meal. A favourite plant for cutting for indoor decoration, cutting for this purpose is a useful way to prune. Pruning is best carried out after flowering unless the plants have got completely out of hand when hard pruning in spring will soon result in plenty of new growths, but flowers will be sacrificed for a couple of seasons. Old flowers should also be removed when flowering is over and it always pays to thin out unproductive growths where old bushes have become overcrowded. Newly planted lilacs should be cut back in spring to prominent buds until they become established, and, in order to get a shapely bush, pinching back strong growths in summer is also desirable.

afghanica   ✳➴
Afghanistan to Tibet. A small deciduous shrub with small dainty pinnate leaves and dark stems. In May the lilac flowers, in slender panicles, are sparsely produced in my experience, but it is worth growing as a foliage plant and useful for decoration when cut.

× ***hyacinthiflora*** *(S. oblata × S. vulgaris)*   ✳
A variable hybrid first raised by Lemoine of France (a double form) in 1876. Several clones have been more recently raised by W.B. Clarke of California, using *S. oblata giraldi* and producing singles usually. Flowering in May. Z.3.
   'Esther Staley' *(S. vulgaris × S. oblata giraldii)*, a floriferous form with single pink flowers opening from red buds. Raised by Clarke 1948. A.G.M. 1969. **469**

× ***josiflexa*** *(S. josikaea × S. reflexa)*   ✳
A race of 20th century hybrids raised by Miss Preston in Ottawa, Canada. Fairly large shrubs bearing loose panicles of fragrant rose pink blooms in May and June. Z.3.
   'Bellicent', generally regarded as the best clone of this hybrid. The strong arching growth produces extremely large panicles of clear rosy pink tubular flowers. F.C.C. 1946, A.G.M. 1969.

microphylla **Littleleaf Lilac**   1·5 m. (5 ft)
North and west China. Introduced 1910. A small shrub which is very distinct because of the small round leaves. The very fragrant flowers are lilac, darker on outside, borne in small panicles in June and sometimes again in autumn on shoots of the current year. A.G.M. 1955. Z.5. **470**
   'Superba', a form which flowers with great freedom. Rosy pink flowers are produced from May until

October. A miniature lilac which is ideal for the small garden. A.G.M. 1969. Z.5.

palibiniana see *S. velutina*

× *prestoniae* (*S. reflexa* × *S. villosa*) ✳
Preston Lilac
A vigorous very hardy race of late flowering lilacs which extend the season by some weeks. First raised by Miss Preston, Ottawa, Canada in 1920 and often called the 'Canadian Hybrids'. The rather scentless flowers are borne in large plume like spikes which are more loosely arranged than the *S. vulgaris* forms. Z.2.

'Elinor', upright panicles of dark purplish red buds which open to reveal pale lavender flowers. May and June. **471**

'Isabella', mallow purple flowers in huge upright panicles. A very vigorous variety named after the raiser, Miss Isabella Preston. **472**

velutina syn. *S. palibiniana* **Korean** or ✳
Manchurian Lilac 1·5 m. (5 ft)
Korea, north China. Introduced 1910. A dense, compact shrub ideal for small gardens. The fragrant lilac pink flowers are borne in numerous elegant panicles even on very young, small plants. Makes a fine informal hedge. Z.3.

vulgaris **Common Lilac** 6·1 m. (20 ft) ✳
Europe. Introduced in 16th century. A large shrub often becoming a small tree, with richly scented lilac flowers, but rather addicted to suckering. The vast range of garden lilacs have originated from this species and it is these better cultivars that are usually given precedence in the garden. Many of them are propagated by grafting onto the common lilac so that suckers from the stock are apt to overwhelm the desired cultivar and must be removed at source. Plants on their own roots from layers or cuttings are for this reason to be preferred. Z.3.

'Charles Joly', double flowers of dark purple red with a good scent and with dark foliage. A variety of upright growth. Raised by Lemoine 1896.

'Glory of Horstenstein', single flowers, rich lilac red becoming dark lilac. Raised by Wilke 1921. **473**

'Katherine Havemeyer', double flowers, deep purple lavender, fading to pale lilac pink and very large, gorgeously scented. Raised by Lemoine 1922. A.G.M. 1969.

'Madame Antoine Buchner', double flowers delicate rose shaded mauve in loose narrow panicles. Lovely scent. A tall open grower. Raised by Lemoine 1909. A.G.M. 1969.

'Marechal Foch', large single flowers, bright carmine rose. Raised by Lemoine 1924.

'Maud Notcutt', single pure white flowers in large panicles carried well above the foliage, lasts well in water when cut. Raised by Notcutt 1956.

'Monique Lemoine', double large white flowers of good shape, late flowering. A compact variety. Raised by Lemoine 1939. **474**

'Mrs Edward Harding', double flowers of claret red tinged pink. A very floriferous variety. Raised by Lemoine 1922. A.G.M. 1969. **475**

'Paul Thirion', double, the carmine buds opening to rosy claret flowers in solid trusses. Late flowering. A strong compact grower. Raised by Lemoine 1915. A.G.M. 1969. **476**

'Primrose', single flowers, small compact panicles of primrose yellow freely produced on a dense bush. Raised by Maarse 1949.

'Souvenir de Louis Spaeth', single flowers, deep wine red, one of the most popular lilacs, strong grower and very sound. Raised by Spaeth 1883. F.C.C. 1894, A.G.M. 1930.

'Vestale', single flowers in broad, closely packed white panicles. A good garden lilac. Raised by Lemoine 1910. A.G.M. 1931. **477**

T

Tamarisk see *Tamarix*
Tamarisk, Hardy see *Tamarix petandra*

TAMARIX TAMARICACEAE **Tamarisk** ☉ †▼
A group of shrubs, some of which may attain the size of small trees, excellent for seaside planting. Easily cultivated plants which when away from maritime conditions thrive best in good soil but do not like lime or chalk. These shrubs have an attractive graceful habit of growth, with a delicate appearance which belies their toughness. Easily propagated from hard wood cuttings of pencil thickness, put out in open ground in late October or November.

pentandra **Hardy Tamarisk, Salt Cedar** ✳
1·85–2·75 m. (6·–9 ft)
South-east Europe and west and central Asia. In cultivation 1883. A large deciduous shrub with long slender

---

Abbreviations and symbols used in the text

▼	Deciduous	†	Lime hater
△	Evergreen	◗	Shade
✳	Flowers	◑	Semi shade
●	Fruit	☉	Sun
➳	Foliage		

A.G.M. Award of Garden Merit, Royal Horticultural Society
F.C.C. First Class Certificate, Royal Horticultural Society

Z1–10 The Z numbers represent the climatic zones used in the United States and provide a useful hardiness rating elsewhere. Thus Z1 is for those plants surviving coldest conditions and Z10 is the other extreme

The illustration numbers are in **bold type**.

plum-rose reddish brown branches and attractive glaucous foliage. The rosy pink flowers smother the terminal part of the current years growth in July and August, the whole plant becoming a feathery mass with a distinctive gingery scent. An excellent late flowering shrub, very effective as an informal hedge. Should be pruned hard in March, back almost to the base of the past year's growth. A.G.M. 1962. Z.2.

> **'Rubra'**, a selected form with flowers deeper in colour, a lovely rosy red. A.G.M. 1969.

tetrandra 3·05 m. (10 ft) ❊

South-east Europe, western Asia. Introduced 1821. A large shrub with smooth dark branches and green deciduous foliage. The light pink flowers open in May and early June, ahead of the leaves and are very freely produced. A very effective shrub especially if mass planted. Should be pruned immediately after flowering, removing two-thirds of the flowering growths. Z.4.

Tartarian Dogwood see *Cornus alba*
Tellman Honeysuckle see *Lonicera*
  × *tellmanniana*
Threepenny-bit Rose see *Rosa farreri persetosa*

THUYA PINACEAE **Arbor-vitae** △

occidentalis **American Arbor-vitae** 🍃

> **'Ericoides'**, a small dense form with juvenile foliage. Dull green in summer becoming light brown in winter. Easily damaged by snow if it is left on too long. In cultivation 1867. **478**
> **'Rheingold'**, a slow growing bush which will become a large shrub in time, usually some 90 cm. (3 ft) but occasionally to about 3·65 m. (12 ft) in height. The mainly adult foliage is deep old gold in summer becoming a rich coppery gold in winter. Associates very well with darker conifers and heathers. One of the finest of conifers for gardens, especially in winter. A.G.M. 1969. **479**

orientalis **Chinese** or **Oriental Arbor-vitae** 🍃

> **'Aurea Nana'**, a dwarf rounded bush of dense habit, with crowded vertically arranged sprays of light yellow green foliage which becomes golden in summer. Slow growing, seldom over 60 cm. (2 ft) high, will eventually after many years attain 1·85 m. (6 ft) or so. In cultivation 1804 this unquestionably ranks top as a garden conifer with me, always neat and compact. A.G.M. 1969. **480**

THYMUS LABIATAE **Thyme**

carnosus syn. *T. nitidus* 23 cm. (9 in.) △❊

Portugal. A small fastigiate shrub which is pleasantly aromatic especially when rubbed against, and which grows readily in light well-drained soil. The pale pink or white flowers are produced very freely in June and July and self sown seedlings are quite common in gardens where it succeeds. I have grown this delightful plant for many years under the name *T. nitidus*, now considered a misnomer, the true *T. nitidus* being a different plant. **481**

Toringo Crab Apple see *Malus sieboldii*
Travellers' Joy see *Clematis vitalba*
Tree
  Daisies see *Olearia*
  Heath see *Erica arborea*
  Paeony see *Paeonia*
  Poppy see *Romneya*
  Purslane see *Atriplex halimus*
Tricuspidaria lanceolata see *Crinodendron*
  hookeranum
Trumpet Honeysuckle see *Lonicera sempervirens*
Tupelo see *Nyssa sylvatica*
Twisted Heath see *Erica cinerea*

U

ULEX LEGUMINOSAE **Gorse, Furze, Whin**

europaeus **Common Gorse** ▼❊

1·2–1·85 m. (4–6 ft)

Western Europe including British Isles. An extremely spiny shrub, commonly known in different parts of the British Isles as Gorse, Furze or Whin. Extremely hardy, it is quite at home even in the coldest most exposed areas and provides a feast of colour particularly in some areas of Scotland, that is only rivalled by the broom, *Cytisus scoparius*. In spite of the beauty of its golden flowers it is not a plant really suitable for garden cultivation, thriving best on poor soils. Z.6.

> **'Plenus'**, this is the double-flowered form and is much superior to the type, being more compact in habit, slow growing and lasting longer in bloom. As it doesn't seed, self sown seedlings do not appear. Flowers most freely in poor dry soil and in full sun. Can be kept quite compact by pruning after flowering. Must be propagated from cuttings which can be rooted in summer under mist and grown on in pots as it does not transplant well. A very useful plant for dry banks. A.G.M. 1929. **482**

ULMUS ULMACEAE **Elm** ▼

× *sarniensis* (*U. angustifolia* × *U. hollandica*) 🍃
Jersey or **Wheatley Elm**

> **'Dicksonii'** syn. 'Aurea', Dickson's Golden Elm, a very slow growing deciduous tree. Useful for colour effect all summer, even in small gardens, where its beautiful bright golden yellow leaves can be used in contrast. A.G.M. 1969. **483**

Umbrella Pine see *Sciadopitys verticillata*

V

Veronica see *Hebe*

VIBURNUM CAPRIFOLIACEAE

A large and important genus of evergreen and deciduous shrubs, some valuable for their flowers others for their fruits. As a general rule they are of easy cultivation in good loamy soil which contains enough organic material to ensure the plants do not suffer from lack of moisture. Where grown for fruits, small groups of three plants are more likely to provide sufficient cross pollination. Propagation of evergreen varieties is generally by cuttings under glass in a propagating frame or under mist and deciduous forms may also be increased in the same way.

alnifolium **Hobble Bush,**
American Wayfaring Tree 1·5–3·01 m. (5–10 ft)
Eastern North America. Introduced 1820. A strong growing deciduous shrub with large leaves, a very distinctive feature, especially when they become claret red in autumn. A suckering shrub which objects to lime. It has large inflorescences of white lacecap, round-topped cymes in May and June, followed by fruits which are red at first and then turn black. Thrives in open woodland and appreciates moisture. Z.3. **484**

× *bodnantense* (*V. farreri* × *V. grandiflorum*) ▼✳
A strong growing deciduous hybrid. Raised at Bodnant, North Wales, about 1935. The densely packed clusters of pink tinted flowers are sweetly fragrant, and produced from October onwards, especially in mild periods. The flowers are relatively undamaged by frost and provide a welcome display in the depths of winter. Z.8.
　'Dawn', the first named selection from above, a vigorous plant with pink flowers from December to February. Fragrant. A.G.M. 1960. **485**
　'Deben', a fine clone, raised by Notcutt, England. Outstanding for the length of its flowering season from October to April, during mild weather. Pink buds opening to white flowers which are strongly scented and freely produced. F.C.C. 1965, A.G.M. 1969. Z.8. **486**

× *burkwoodii* (*V. carlesii* × *V. utile*) △✳
A semi-evergreen to evergreen shrub of medium size raised by Burkwood and Skipwith, England in 1924. The clusters of white flowers, which are pink in bud, are delightfully fragrant and produced from January onwards to May. A.G.M. 1956. Z.5.

× *carlcephalum* (*V. carlesii* × ▼✳
V. macrocephalum)
Fragrant Snowball
A compact, deciduous medium sized shrub. A hybrid which produces, in May, beautiful corymbs of white, pink budded flowers. Frequently provides good autumn colour with its leaves. A.G.M. 1969. Z.65.

carlesii **Fragrant Viburnum** 1·2 m. (4 ft) ▼✳
Korea. Introduced 1902. This small deciduous shrub of rounded habit, one of the most sweetly scented shrubs and slow growing, is suitable for gardens of limited size. The clusters of white, pink budded flowers are freely produced. Sometimes suffers from aphis attack, also from a graft-blight disease. A preventative spray with a systemic insecticide will ensure control of aphis. *V.* × *juddii*, is very similar to *V. carlesii*, but is stronger and less likely to suffer from attack by aphis. F.C.C. 1909, A.G.M. 1923. Z.4.

cassinoides **Withe-Rod** †▼✳➤●
1·85–3·65 m. (6–12 ft)
Eastern North America. Introduced 1761. A shapely deciduous bush with leathery dark green leaves, bronze when young becoming green, changing in autumn to crimson. In June it produces small creamy white flowers which are followed by fruits, red at first, becoming blue and finally black. Does not like lime or chalk. Z.2. **487**

farreri syn. *V. fragrans* **Fragrant Viburnum** ▼✳
2·75–3·01 m. (9–10 ft)
North China. Introduced 1910. A deciduous medium sized shrub, probably still better known as *V. fragrans*, which has become popular because of its winter flowering. The flowers are freely produced, especially in spells of mild weather from November to February, pink in bud, opening white and are sweetly scented. A.G.M. 1923. Z.6.
　candidissimum, a form of above distinct with pure white flowers and much greener leaves when unfolding. **488**

foetens 2·45 m. (8 ft) ◐▼/△✳●
Himalayas, Korea. Introduced c. 1844. A deciduous to semi-evergreen shrub of medium size seldom seen in gardens but a beautiful winter flowering shrub, January to March. The white flowers are fragrant. Not easy to grow, it appreciates good soil which doesn't dry out and some shade. **489**

grandiflorum 1·85–3·01 m. (6–10 ft) ▼ ✳
Himalayas. Introduced 1914. A deciduous shrub, very stiff and erect in habit. Buds carmine red the fragrant flowers which are 5–8 cm. (2 or 3 in.) in diameter, open to deep pink and become blush pink as they age. Produced in dense clusters. A.M. 1937. Z.7.

> **'Snow White'**, 4·55 m. (15 ft). China. Introduced about 1948. This is a very fine distinct form with pure white flowers produced in March and April, later than the type. A very strong upright grower, a valuable addition to winter flowering plants. F.C.C. 1974. **490**

juddii see under ***V. carlesii***

opulus **Guelder Rose, Water Elder,** ▼ ✳•
European Cranberry Bush (U.S.)
1·5–1·85 m. (5–6 ft)
Europe, north and west Asia, north Africa. A vigorous deciduous shrub, the Guelder Rose is a good all rounder, which grows into a shapely bush in most types of soil. The flattened corymbs of white flowers have a lace-cap effect and are scented. Copious clusters of shining red translucent berries follow further glorified by the red autumn leaves. A.G.M. 1969. **491**

> **'Compactum'**, is a similar plant to the above but a more dense and lower, compact form. The similar lace-cap type flowers are followed by a heavy crop of translucent fruits. Ideal for gardens of limited size. A.G.M. 1964. **492**
>
> **'Xanthocarpum'**, another fine form with clear golden yellow fruits which become slightly translucent light orange when ripe. F.C.C. 1966, A.G.M. 1969. **493**

'Park Farm Hybrid' △✳
A strong growing evergreen shrub, similar in some respects to *V.* × *burkwoodii*, but more spreading in habit and with somewhat larger fragrant flowers, produced in April and May. **495**

plicatum syn. *V. tomentosum* 'Sterile' ▼ ✳•
Japanese Snowball

> **'Lanarth'**, has tiered horizontal branches which set off the plate-like flower heads. Must be given room to spread sideways. White flowers in May. Later on the leaves turn bronze before falling. An excellent shrub. A.G.M. 1969. Z.4. **496**
>
> **'Mariesii'**, one of the finest garden shrubs, deciduous with a very flat-tiered style of branching, more so than 'Lanarth' and more suitable for a smaller garden. Sideways spread must be allowed for and encouraged by taking out the central growths. A waterfall effect of white flowers will be the result. A.G.M. 1929. **497**
>
> **'Pink Beauty'**, a selection from the wild form in which the rosy florets become pink as they get older. A suitable form for small gardens.

sargentii to 3·65 m. (12 ft) ▼ ✳•
North-east Asia. Introduced 1892. A large vigorous shrub with maple like leaves, which resemble those of *V. opulus* but are of greater size, as are the bright trans-lucent red fruits. These last well into the winter, enhanced by the rich autumn colours of the leaves before they fall. Z.4. **498**

> **'Flavum'**, a yellow fruited form, more popular in U.S. than the species.

tinus **Laurustinus** to 3 m. (10 ft) ☉ ◑ △ ✳•
Mediterranean region, south-east Europe. Cultivated in Britain since 16th century. A dense evergreen shrub with foliage from ground level, consequently in gardens in warmer temperate areas makes an excellent informal hedge. The masses of dark green glossy leaves carry terminal cymes of white flowers preceded by pink buds right through winter usually from October to April, especially in periods when mild weather prevails, sometimes even commencing as early as August. An excellent winter flowering evergreen except in the coldest areas. A.G.M. 1969. Z.7–8. **499**

> **'Eve Price'**, much more compact in form and with smaller leaves than the type. The carmine buds succeeded by pink-tinged flowers are in some seasons followed by highly decorative metallic blue fruits, which eventually turn black. **494**

tomentosum 'Sterile' see ***V. plicatum***

Viburnum, Fragrant see ***Viburnum carlesii*** and
> ***V. farreri***
Vilmorin Mountain Ash see ***Sorbus***
> ***vilmorinii***
Violet Willow see ***Salix daphnoides***
Virginia Rose see ***Rosa virginiana***
Virgins Bower see ***Clematis***

VINCA APOCYNACEAE ☉ ◑ △

major **Greater Periwinkle** 30–90 cm. (1–3 ft) ✳•
Central and southern Europe; naturalised in parts of U.K. A trailing or clambering evergreen which may mass up to about 90 cm. The ovate, green leaves are up to 7·5 cm. (3 in.) long. The lilac blue flowers are 2·5–5 cm. (1–2 in.) across and may appear from mid-spring to early autumn.

> **'Variegata'**, syn. 'Elegantissima', had its leaves variegated with creamy yellow blotches. Flowers blue.

minor **Lesser Periwinkle,** ✳•
Running-Myrtle (U.S.) to 46 cm. (18 in.)
Europe including Britain; west Asia; naturalised in parts of U.S. A trailing evergreen which may mass or clamber up to about 46 cm., but is usually less. Excellent for ground cover, thriving in sun or shade, the trailing stems are able to root at virtually every joint. The flowers are a light violet blue, about 2·5 cm. (1 in.) across. *V. minor* is seldom without a flower here or there but the main flowering season is from mid-spring to the autumn. There are a number of varieties with single or double flowers in shades of blue, white or plum-purple colours.

> **'Variegata'**, has white variegated leaves and blue flowers, single.

W

Warminster Broem see *Cytisus × praecox*
Water Elder see *Viburnum opulus*
Weeping Forsythia see *Forsythia suspensa*

WEIGELA CAPRIFOLIACEAE ☉◐▼

An Asiatic genus, formerly known and sometimes listed as *Diervilla* an American genus. Popular deciduous shrubs being very showy and easily grown in any good garden soil. They will thrive in the full sun or partial shade. Pruning should be carried out as soon after flowering as possible, removing the old flowering growth back to the young unflowered growths near the base of the plant. Cuttings root readily under mist in summer or fully ripe growths in autumn either in a frame or sheltered border. There are several hardy hybrids of *Weigela* which are important and valuable decorative shrubs for gardens.

'Bristol Ruby' 1·5 m. (5 ft) ✽
A strong-growing shrub with an abundant supply of deep red flowers, especially if well pruned. A.G.M. 1969. Z.5. **500**

'Eve Rathke' ✽
An old cultivar of slow compact growth, easy to accommodate in the smaller garden. The bright red flowers have straw coloured anthers and are produced over a considerable period especially in a slightly shaded situation. Z.5.

florida 1·5–2·75 m. (5–9 ft) ✽�).
Japan, northern China, Korea, Manchuria. Introduced by Fortune 1845. A hardy medium to fairly large sized shrub. Rose pink flowers appear from May to June. Z.5.
  'Foliis Purpureis', a slow growing compact form with dark purplish leaves and deep pink flowers. Z.5.
  'Variegata', a much more attractive plant, compact in form, leaves edged creamy white and attractive pink flowers. One of the most reliable variegated shrubs for small gardens or indeed any garden. A.G.M. 1969. Z.5. **501**

'Looymansii Aurea' ✽�)
A very pleasing shrub in spring in a partially shaded position. The light golden leaves will burn in strong sun, but the colour is greatly heightened by the pink flowers, when in good condition. Z.5. **502**

'Mont Blanc' ✽
This is probably the best white flowered cultivar being vigorous and producing large scented flowers. Z.6.

'Styriaca' ✽
A free flowering shrub of great vigour. The flowers are purplish-pink, rose red in the bud stage on arching growths.

Westonbirt Dogwood see *Cornus alba* 'Sibirica'
Wheatley Elm see *Ulmus × sarniensis*
Whin see *Ulex*
White
  Enkianthus see *Enkianthus perulatus*
  Heather see *Calluna vulgaris* 'Alba'
  Portuguese Broom see *Cytisus multiflorus*
  Spanish Broom see *Cytisus multiflorus*
  Willow see *Salix alba*
Wig Tree see *Cotinus coggygria*
Willmott Blue Leadwort see *Ceratostigma willmottianum*
Willow see *Salix*
Willow,
  Creeping see *Salix repens*
  Rose-gold Pussy see *Salix gracilistyla*
  Scarlet see *Salix alba* 'Chermesina'
  Violet see *Salix daphnoides*
  White see *Salix alba*
  Woolly see *Salix lanata*
Willow-leaf Cotoneaster see *Cotoneaster salicifolius*
Winter
  Currant see *Ribes sanguineum*
  Daphne see *Daphne odora*
  Hazel see *Corylopsis glabrescens*
  Hazel, Buttercup see *Corylopsis pauciflora*
  Hazel, Fragrant see *Corylopsis glabrescens*
  Heath see *Erica herbacea*
  Honeysuckle see *Lonicera fragrantissima*
  Jasmine see *Jasminum nudiflorum*
  Sweet see *Chimonanthus praecox*
Winter's Bark see *Drimys winteri*
Wintergreen Cotoneaster see *Cotoneaster conspicuus*
Wisteria, Chinese see *Wisteria sinensis*

WISTERIA LEGUMINOSAE ☉▼

sinensis **Chinese Wisteria** to 15 m. (50 ft) ✽
China. Introduced 1816 from a garden in Canton. A

Abbreviations and symbols used in the text

▼	Deciduous	†	Lime hater
△	Evergreen	◍	Shade
✽	Flowers	◐	Semi shade
●	Fruit	☉	Sun
🌒	Foliage		

A.G.M. Award of Garden Merit, Royal Horticultural Society
F.C.C. First Class Certificate, Royal Horticultural Society

Z1–10 The Z numbers represent the climatic zones used in the United States and provide a useful hardiness rating elsewhere. Thus Z1 is for those plants surviving coldest conditions and Z10 is the other extreme

The illustration numbers are in **bold type**.

strong growing deciduous climber which, although it can reach a great height can also, by training, be restricted to small tree or large shrub size. Indeed the plant photographed for this book although of very large size is free standing and of great age. The lilac, bluish mauve or violet flowers appear in May and are scented. An annual hard pruning in February to the basal buds on the spurs will require supplementing by summer pruning in August when young growths should be pinched back. Unfussy about soil but preferably one that is fertile is required. Layering is the best method for producing new young plants. Seed raised plants seem reluctant to flower. A.G.M. 1928. Z.5. **503**

Witch Hazel see *Hamamelis*
Witch Hazel, Chinese see *Hamamelis mollis*
Withe Rod see *Viburnum cassinoides*
Woadwaxen,
   Ashy see *Genista cinerea*
   Silky-leaf see *Genista pilosa*
Woodbine see *Lonicera periclymenum*
Woolly Willow see *Salix lanata*
Wreath,
   Bridal see *Spiraea* × *arguta*
   Garland see *Spiraea* × *arguta*

Y & Z

Yellow Azalea see *Rhododendron luteum*
Yellow-net Honeysuckle see *Lonicera japonica*

YUCCA LILIACEAE

This is a genus which in general appearance is quite different to that of any other shrubs. The evergreen plants have rosettes of narrow usually rigid leaves of a sword like appearance and which is highlighted when in summer the stout spikes of creamy white flowers arise. Yuccas prefer light well drained soil and a warm sunny position. Because of their architectural value they are frequently featured in formal surroundings either as single plants or groups where space warrants it. Their effectiveness while in flower is enhanced to a considerable degree if they have a dark background. No pruning other than cutting out old flowering stems is required. Tops can be used for propagation if leaves are removed from the lower part and the stem placed in a pot of sandy soil under glass. Some forms produce 'toes' near the base of the stem which can be removed and placed in pots under glass. Root cuttings can also be used under glass; all forms of propagation are more successful if some heat is available.

filamentosa **Adam's Needle** (U.S.)
to 3·65 m. (12 ft)
South-eastern United States. Introduced 17th century. A very hardy and beautiful plant growing in the warmest temperate areas to 3·65 m. but usually only 1·5 m. (5 ft) in cooler areas. Flowers are creamy white in erect, cone-shaped panicles and are produced on quite young plants

during July and August. Plants grown in U.S. as *Y. filamentosa* are *Y. smalliana*. A.G.M. 1969. Z.4. **504**

flaccida
South-eastern United States. Less rigid in character than *Y. filamentosa* but also flowering in July and August.
   'Ivory', a selected form in which the long spikes of cream coloured flowers stand out at right angles to the stem instead of being pendant. Very free flowering. Short basal side growths or 'toes' are freely produced so clumps are soon formed and these can also be used for increasing the plant. A very distinctive plant. F.C.C. 1968, A.G.M. 1969. Z.4. **505**

gloriosa **Spanish Dagger, Adam's Needle** (U.K.) 1·2–2·45 m. (4–8 ft)
South-eastern United States. A *Yucca* with something of a tree like appearance developing a short trunk, on top of which the leaves spread out, similar to an inverted mop. Flowers July to September. Z.7.
   'Nobilis', a beautiful form of *Y. gloriosa* which has arching grey foliage on short forking trunks. The large spikes of pendulous flowers are cream coloured and tinged red on the reverse side of the petals. **506**

smalliana see under *Y. filamentosa*

ZAUSCHNERIA ONAGRACEAE

californica **Californian Fuchsia**
30–75 cm. (1–2½ ft)
California, U.S. Introduced 1847. A dwarf sub-shrub whose upright or somewhat arching stems are furnished with grey green downy leaves. The Californian Fuchsia is invaluable in the autumn for a hot, dry sunny position where its blaze of red flowers with scarlet tubes are an arresting sight. Truly magnificent as a plant for a dry wall. Can be increased by cuttings which should be overwintered in a cold greenhouse or frame. One of the many fine plants which should have a few cuttings rooted annually, as a precautionary measure in case an exceptionally severe winter results in their loss. Z.9.

ZENOBIA ERICACEAE

pulverulenta 1·2–1·5 m. (4–5 ft)
Eastern United States. A monotypic genus which only thrives in lime free soil and prefers a little shade. Introduced in 1801, this very attractive small shrub is found from North Carolina to Florida. Deciduous or semi-evergreen, it produces its pendent white flowers which strongly resemble a large lily-of-the-valley quite generously in June and July. Scented of aniseed this plant is seldom seen in gardens and deserves to be better known for its quiet beauty. Can be grown from seeds or cuttings of half ripe growths in a heated frame. Pruning is not really required, but old flowers can be removed back to young growths. F.C.C. 1934.